JAPAN POP!

JAPAN POP!

Inside the World of Japanese Popular Culture

Timothy J. Craig, Editor

An East Gate Book

M.E. Sharpe
Armonk, New York
London, England

An East Gate Book

Library of Congress Cataloging-in-Publication Data

Japan pop! : inside the world of Japanese popular culture / edited by Timothy J. Craig
p. cm.
"An East gate book"
Includes bibliographical references and index.
ISBN 0-7656-0560-0 (alk. paper)—ISBN 0-7656-0561-9 (pbk. : alk. paper)
1. popular culture—Japan. 2. Japan—Civilization—1945- I. Craig, Timothy J., 1947-
DS822.5 .J386 2000
952.04—dc21 00-021812

Printed in the United States of America

The paper used in this publication meets the minimum requirements of
American National Standard for Information Sciences
Permanence of Paper for Printed Library Materials,
ANSI Z 39.48-1984.

BM (c) 10 9 8 7 6 5 4 3
BM (p) 10 9 8 7 6 5

Contents

Acknowledgments

Like most books, this one benefited from the help and encouragement of a great number of people. I would first like to express my gratitude to the University of Victoria's Centre for Asia-Pacific Initiatives (CAPI) and to its Director Bill Neilson for the support and resources that allowed me to take on this project. Along the way, much-appreciated assistance was provided by Stella Chan, Tomoko Izawa, Heather MacDonald, and Wendy Farwell.

For inspiration in a variety of forms, a tip of the hat to Fosco Maraini, Fred Schodt, Steve Mindel, John, Curtis, and magic Tango. A special word of appreciation goes to the many publishers and artists in Japan who generously provided permission for the use of photographs, illustrations, and song lyrics, and to Doug Merwin and M. E. Sharpe, for their enthusiasm for a book concept that other publishers tended to view as either too academic or not academic enough. And to my wonderful family—Hiroko, Danny, and Emily—thanks for putting up with the project and for helping me out so much with your ideas and knowledge of Japan pop—I've been lucky to have such a good resource sitting around the dinner table.

Finally, I want to thank all the authors and artists who have contributed their writings and other creations to this volume. Your enchanting and insightful work has provided the real motivation. From my first encounter with it, I knew that I had something special in my hands, and I have since been driven, over a sometimes bumpy road, by a desire to share it with a larger audience. I hope you are happy with the destination.

A Note on Language

In Japan, people's names are usually written with the family name first and the given name last. However, as this book is written not just for Japan specialists but for a more general audience as well, I have listed Japanese names in the usual English order: given name first and family name last.

Japanese words are generally italicized (e.g., *yume*, *namida*). An exception is made for words which are used repeatedly in a chapter; such words are italicized and defined the first time they are used (e.g., *enka*, *anime*), and thereafter printed in roman type (enka, anime). A "long sign" (macron) over a vowel in a Japanese name or word indicates that the sound of the vowel is sustained; thus the difference in pronunciation between *koi* (love) and *kōi* (an act, kind intentions, or goodwill).

In Japanese titles that include "borrowed" English words, I have generally used the standard English spellings of those words rather than phoneticizing them; thus "Diamonds" instead of *Daiamondo* and *Yūkan Club* rather than *Yūkan Kurabu*.

JAPAN POP!

— 1 —

Introduction

Tim Craig

"Where . . . Where am I? I know I must have drowned, but. . . ."

You have **died**. Akanemaru has **ceased** to exist. His body has **decayed** and **dissolved** into the sea. . . . Look around you. . . .

"WHAT?!! What is this?! What am I?!"

You are now a microscopic sea creature. You are nothing more than a miserable little speck. The instant your human form ceased to exist, you were **reborn**.

"But **WHY?!** Why have I changed? What have I done to deserve **this?**"

You didn't do anything wrong. . . . This was simply your **destiny**—to become something **different**, when your life as a human ended. . . .

"**NO!!** I'm a **man!!** And I want to live like one!! . . . **Oh No!** Something **huge** is coming! I'm going to be **swallowed!**"

—From *Phoenix*, by Osamu Tezuka[1]

* * *

Hey you say you were a butterfly
I see you in a peaceful field
Hey you say you were a butterfly
I see you in a beautiful garden
I wanna catch you catch you catch you
Butterfly Boy

—Shōnen Knife

* * *

"Toto, I have a feeling we're not in Kansas anymore."

—Dorothy, in *The Wizard of Oz*

Japan's New Pop Power

Cartoons and comic books, TV dramas and pop music stars, fashion trends and crooning businessmen—until two decades ago such familiar and fun areas of life would have been unlikely entries in the journal of images commonly associated with Japan. For the greater part of this century, Japan presented two very different faces to the outside world. One was the exotic Orient, a land of sword-wielding samurai, kimono-clad geisha, and Zen Buddhism whose fascination and charm lay in its distance—geographic, temporal, and cultural—from our own everyday worlds. The other was Japan the power, first military and later economic, whose impact on our lives was closely felt, formidable, and not always pleasant. In the arena of popular culture, a sphere that is both part of our everyday lives and a source of pleasure, Japan was a very minor player, unless one counts the televisions, stereos, and videocassette recorders that Japan produced so efficiently and that brought us the cultural products of Hollywood, Disney, and our various home countries. Although Japan's own postwar pop culture had in fact been creative, vibrant, and commercially successful domestically, this was a fact that few people outside Japan were aware of. In the international consciousness Japan remained a serious nation and people, accomplished in traditional arts and modern manufacturing, but hardly a wellspring of entertainment and appealing cultural creations that would one day spread beyond Japan's shores.

Today it's a different story. Japan's pop culture has not only continued to evolve and blossom at home, it has also attracted a broad, street-level following overseas, giving Japan a new cultural impact on the world to complement its established economic impact. Japanese animation and comics have built a huge global following, and their Japanese names, *anime* and *manga*, have entered the international lexicon. A new generation of young Americans, Europeans, and Asians have grown up watching not Mickey Mouse and Bugs Bunny but Japanese cartoons, from *Astro Boy*, *Speed Racer*, *Star Blazers*, and *Robotech* to *Doraemon*, *Sailor Moon*, *Dragon Ball*, and *Crayon Shinchan*. Anime fan clubs, "fanzines," and Web sites have sprung up by the hundreds, and hit movies such as *Akira* and *Ghost in the Shell* have helped Japanese animation gross tens of millions of dollars in yearly international box office and video sales. Japan's *manga* (comics) are translated and read eagerly throughout the world, and the influence of manga's fine lines and realistic aesthetic style can be seen in Western fashion and graphic design.[2]

Recent Japanese films have won top awards at the Cannes and Vienna Film Festivals, while Japan's TV dramas and variety shows are in high demand throughout Asia. One Hong Kong shop routinely sells fifty video compact discs of a single Japanese TV drama per day, to customers who want to see the latest episodes as soon as possible.[3] Japanese pop singers perform to packed venues in Hong Kong and mainland China, top "Canto-pop" (Hong Kong pop music) and other Asian recording artists do cover versions of hit Japanese pop songs, and the techno-pop sound of Japanese music tycoon Tetsuya Komuro provides the sound track for major Hollywood movies. Dreams Come True vocalist Miwa Yoshida graces the cover of *Time* magazine, and the all-girl rock group Shōnen Knife has a strong alternative following in the United States. In Taiwan and Hong Kong, teenagers take their fashion cues from the clothes of Japanese "idol" singers and TV stars and from Japanese teen magazines such as *Non-No.* Gossipy stories about Japanese entertainers such as Takuya Kimura and Noriko Sakai fill local newspapers.[4] Among the Nintendo and PlayStation set, which encompasses most of the school-age population in many countries, Japanese video games such as *Street Fighter*, *Tekken*, and *Final Fantasy* rule the roost. *Karaoke* is a household word worldwide, and the parade out of Japan of hit pop culture products like Hello Kitty goods, Tamagotchi virtual pets, and Pokémon toys is unending. Even in South Korea, where anti-Japan sentiment thrives as a result of Japan's 1910–1945 colonial rule of the Korean peninsula, demand for Japan pop is strong among the younger generation. Japanese music, comics, and fashion magazines commonly circulate "underground" despite a decades-long ban on the importation of Japanese cultural products, while popular manga such as *Slam Dunk*, which set off a basketball craze in South Korea, are translated into Korean, with the names and places changed so that they can be imported legally.[5]

In short, Japan pop is ubiquitous, hot, and increasingly influential. Once routinely derided as a one-dimensional power, a heavyweight in the production and export of the "hard" of automobiles, electronics, and other manufactured goods but a nobody in terms of the "soft" of cultural products and influence, Japan now contributes not just to our material lives, but to our everyday cultural lives as well.

Why Japan Pop Is Hot

One sign of the level of interest in Japan's pop culture was a conference on the topic held in Victoria, Canada, by the University of Victoria Centre for Asia-Pacific Initiatives in 1997. Launched with a one-page announcement sent to a few Japan specialists and posted on the Internet, the conference drew a strong international response and evolved into a three-day event featuring over forty presentations by scholars, writers, practitioners, and fans from four continents on Japanese pop music, comics and animation, TV dramas and commercials, movies, stand-up comedy, popular literature, and *sumo* wrestling, as well as issues such as social change, women's roles, and the spread and appeal of Japanese pop culture overseas.[6] In the audience, scholars from Harvard, Stanford, and Tokyo Universities, applying an academic lens to analyze Japanese society through its popular culture, rubbed shoulders with purple-haired, karaoke-singing *otaku* (hard-core aficionados) conversant with the latest pop music groups and manga artists. As diverse a group as one is likely to find at a university conference, all brought valid viewpoints to the subject and shared both a deep enthusiasm for Japan's popular culture and an appreciation of its growing influence.

The Victoria conference received considerable media coverage, and as its organizer, I found myself being asked the same questions over and over: What's so special about Japanese pop culture? Why is it gaining such popularity outside Japan? The chapters of this book provide a fuller answer to that question than I can give here, but in the next few pages I offer some thoughts and insights based on the Victoria conference, the writings presented in this book, and my own dozen years in Japan as a close follower and fan of Japan's pop culture.

Quality and Creativity

Asked why Japan's pop culture products are now so popular internationally, Hidenori Oyama, director of Tōei Animation's International Department, has a simple answer: "It's because they're high quality, that's all."[7] Not all Japan pop is high quality—far from it. Even the most avid fan would readily admit that Japan's pop culture, like that of any nation, has its share of the mediocre, or worse: mindless television shows, cute but off-key pop singers, boring mass-produced manga, and the excessively violent and pornographic. Nevertheless, Oyama's bold statement rings true, for overshadowing the uninspired and the forgettable are numerous examples, in every genre, of artists and works that are outstanding by any standard in their quality and creative genius.

That Japan, long a land of poets and artists as well as warriors and businessmen, should today excel in an area of the arts should come as no surprise to anyone familiar with the nation's rich aesthetic heritage. Japan boasts a long and distinguished record of artistic achievement, and more masters and masterpieces than can be named here, in literature, poetry, theater, film, sculpture, painting, ceramics, gardening, and architecture. The bloodlines of today's popular culture go back in particular to the vibrant bourgeois culture, born of the common people and aimed at the new urban middle class, which developed and flourished during Japan's Edo period (1603–1867). The novels of adventure and eroticism produced during this period by writers like Ibara Saikaku burst with the joy of life, expressing "an unbridled taste for everything pleasurable, amusing, extravagant, sensational."[8] In drama, the popular *bunraku* (puppet) and *kabuki* (popular plays with highly stylized singing and dancing) theaters took their place beside the older and more aristocratic *nō* (classical dance-drama). Chikamatsu Monzaemon, the man considered Japan's greatest playwright, wrote for both bunraku and kabuki, and many of his powerful scripts, which turned simple characters such as shop clerks and prostitutes into tragic figures, remain popular today. This was also the period in which Bashō popularized *haiku* (seventeen-syllable poems), which Japanese of all classes (and many non-Japanese as well) have written and enjoyed since Bashō's time. Still another major art form to emerge from Edo-period mass culture, and perhaps the one best known in the West, is the *ukiyo-e* (pictures of the ephemeral world) woodblock print. The delightful prints of courtesans and kabuki actors, as well as landscapes by masters Utamaro, Hokusai, Hiroshige, and Sharaku influenced the Impressionists and remain popular internationally to this day.[9]

One aspect of Japan pop's quality, then and now, is an extraordinarily high standard of artistic skill and craftsmanship. Examine an *inrō* (medicine box), a sword blade, or a woodblock print from the Edo period (or consider the precision engineering and world-leader quality standards of a Toyota automobile or a Nikon camera), and you will encounter the same level of skill and attention to detail that are found in the drawings of manga artists like Akira Toriyama and Monkey Punch, the *enka* (ballad) singing of Misora Hibari or Takashi Hosokawa, and the beautifully blended music and imagery of Japanese television commercials.

Providing vitality to this artistic skill is a strong strain of innovativeness and creativity which is evident in Japan's more established arts but which bursts forth even more strongly in today's pop world of television, fash-

Figure 1.1 **"The Great Wave at Kanagawa," by Hokusai**

ion, pop music, comedy, video games, and manga, where the weight of tradition is less heavy. One source of this is the cross-fertilization between old and new, native and foreign, one genre and another, which is a hallmark of Japanese culture. Many observers have noted Japan's propensity to "borrow" foreign things—Chinese characters, English words, capitalism, democracy, the transistor, curry—and to tinker with them, merging them with native or other elements so that they become something new and often quite distinct from the original.

Take manga, for instance. Led by Osamu Tezuka, the man known in Japan as the "god of comics," Japanese comic artists have taken a physical form imported from the West, combined it with a centuries-old Japanese tradition of narrative art and illustrated humor, and added important innovations of their own to create what amounts to a totally new genre, one that manga scholar Frederik Schodt calls a "full-fledged expressive medium, on a par with novels and films."[10] Among the features that make manga richer and more interesting than the American comics whose form they borrowed are their length, which allows for more complex storytelling and deeper character development; the "cinematic" drawing style that Tezuka developed, which enables artists to impart greater visual impact and emotional depth to their stories; and the incredible

Figure 1.2 **From Volume 1, "*Reimeihen*" (Dawn), of Osamu Tezuka's *Hi no Tori* ("Phoenix")**

diversity of manga in art styles, subject matter, and target audience. Dozens of manga works enjoy the status of artistic and literary classics, including Tezuka masterpieces such as *Hi no Tori* (Phoenix), a 3,000-page tour de force that spans distant past and far future; leaps between earth and outer space; explodes myths of Japanese history; and dramatically explores the meaning of love, the relationship between mankind and technology, and man's foolish quest for everlasting life. Another is Keiji Nakazawa's *Hadashi no Gen* (Barefoot Gen), a powerful semi-autobiographical portrayal of the atomic bombing of Hiroshima which is shocking in its graphic realism, yet also warm, comical, and ultimately inspirational thanks to the strength, humanity, and indomitable spirit of the war orphans who are its main characters. Yūji Aoki's *Naniwa Kin'yūdo* (Osaka Financiers), the story of a good-hearted man in the ugly business of money lending, is both a primer on finance and a treatment of good and evil reminiscent of Leo Tolstoy's

Figure 1.3 **Ukiyo-e kabuki actor, by Sharaku**

Crime and Punishment, a work that influenced the author.[11] Children's series such as *Doraemon* and *Dragon Ball* are inventive and humorous, and provide dreams and wisdom to young readers the world over. This list could go on and on.[12]

Quality and innovation mark other forms of Japan pop as well. In music, pop and rock groups like Southern All Stars and Shang Shang Typhoon draw upon a variety of instruments, languages, singing styles, and musical traditions to create sounds that are unique, fresh, and universally appealing. In animated film, the works of Hayao Miyazaki and Katsuhiro Otomo are praised by Western critics and fans "for the beauty of their animation and the psychological realism of their characters."[13] Japanese television commercials are imaginative, artistic, and often brilliantly funny. Movies by Jūzō Itami *(Tampopo, The Funeral, A Taxing*

Figure 1.4 **"Lupin and Friends," by Monkey Punch**

Woman) and Masayuki Suo *(Shall We Dance)* have won international acclaim, continuing a tradition established by earlier Japanese directors like Ozu, Mizoguchi, and Kurosawa. Still relatively unknown in the West, though hugely popular throughout Asia, are Japan's recent TV dramas, which incorporate current social issues, high dramatic tension, first-rate comedy, masterful camera work, and beautifully adapted music in ambitious and compelling works unlike any other TV fare found on the planet. The opening title and credit sequences have become an art form in themselves, setting a drama's mood in miniature through beautifully crafted and rhythmic montages of images, miniplots, and music.

Life, Dreams, and Relevance

Quality and innovation go a long way toward explaining the praise and respect that Japan pop's creators receive from critics and connoisseurs. But to understand why Japan pop succeeds as *popular* culture, why it has been so enthusiastically embraced by "ordinary" people, both in Japan and abroad, it is necessary to look into its content, into the themes, values, and messages that it offers to its audiences. Here one walks on slippery ground, as Japan's pop culture, like Japanese society, is not simple and uniform but complex and diverse. Most anything that might be said about Japan pop in general would not be true of some examples and might be flatly contradicted by others. Still, let me point to some characteristics of Japan pop's content which seem to be particularly prominent.

One is that Japan pop wholeheartedly embraces life in all its dimensions, with relatively little in the way of efforts to shield its audience from unpleasant aspects of life or to "raise" people to more noble or politically correct standards. This feature is consistent with a basically optimistic view of human nature, a view Japanese have been brought up on and one that is supported by Japan's native Shinto religion. As the Italian scholar Fosco Maraini writes: "The Japanese, both in work and relaxation, enjoy the mere fact of living to the hilt. . . . No doubts, caused by the memory of some original sin in the backyards of the collective subconscious, trouble their sleep. No need for psychiatrists and couches. The world is good; man is a *kami* [god]; work is good; wealth is good; fruits are good; sex is good; and even war is good, provided you win it."[14] With an outlook like this, the urge to censor or to "elevate" the audience is felt less strongly than in societies that are more ambivalent about man's innate goodness. The world and human nature can be portrayed as they are, not as they should be. This allows Kame-sennin (Turtle Master), the ancient martial arts master and guru to *Dragon Ball*'s young heroes, not only to be incredibly skilled and wise but also to have a dirty mind and to constantly, and comically, plot to catch a glimpse of young ladies in states of undress. It allows Son Gokū, *Dragon Ball*'s naive, raised-in-the-wild, central character, to be drawn naked, without the private parts-covering fig leaf that had to be added for American television. It allows the darker side of life to be portrayed as well. In an episode of *Naniwa Kin'yūdo* titled "If You Don't Have the Cash, Get It at a Massage Parlor," protagonist Haibara encourages the girlfriend of a customer who cannot repay his loan to work as a prostitute to cover her boyfriend's debt. Scenes such as this can be disturbing, not least to Haibara, who is tormented by what he has done. But they are part of life and are neither denied nor hidden, perhaps with the thought that knowledge of the world as it is is not such a bad thing, and may in fact be necessary if one is to cope successfully with life's difficulties, or to endeavor to make the world a better place. Kazuhiko Torishima, editor of Japan's best-selling manga magazine *Shōnen Jump* (Boys' Jump), states: "I feel sorry for U.S. kids, who live in an adult-filtered Disney world."[15]

A second notable characteristic of Japan pop content is a strong strain of idealism, innocence, and what the Japanese call *roman* (from the word "romance"): dreams, daring adventure, striving to achieve great things.[16] On this point there is a rather sharp contrast with current American pop culture, with its heavy doses of cynicism, "attitude," and putting people down.[17] Japan pop's positive, idealistic bent pervades numerous comics, cartoons, TV dramas, and even video games. These frequently have children or teenagers as central characters; are suffused with an atmosphere of romance and innocent wonder; and glorify the imagery of youth and dreams of heroic adventure, passionate love, and eternal struggle and longing. *Shōnen Jump* bases its editorial policy on a survey that asked young readers to name the word that warmed their hearts most, the thing they felt most important, and the thing that made them the happiest. The answers were *yūjō* (friendship), *doryoku* (effort), and *shōri* (victory), and these became the magazine's criteria for selecting stories.[18]

A third feature of Japan's popular culture is its closeness to the ordinary, everyday lives of its audience. American comic artist Brian Stelfreeze has said, "Comics in the United States have become such a caricature. You have to have incredible people doing incredible things, but in Japan it seems like the most popular comics are the comics of normal people doing normal things."[19] Part of the normalcy is that the characters that populate Japan's manga, anime, and TV dramas display plenty of character flaws and weaknesses along with their strengths and good points. Nobita and Serena, the central characters of *Doraemon* and *Sailor Moon*, are lazy, hopeless at sports, poor at school, frustrated in love, and constantly made fun of by their pet cats. They possess positive traits as well—both are occasionally strong, clever, and successful—but their weaker points are perhaps more important, not just as a source of humor but in making them human, and thus easy for their readers and viewers to identify with. Many Japanese artists also identify closely with their audience. On the key to writing a successful children's manga, *Doraemon* creator Hiroshi Fujimoto says, "You can't draw children's comics from the perspective of adults and try to create what you think the children will like. You have to create something you really enjoy, that they also happen to enjoy. You have to be at their eye-level, in other words, with their perspective. I guess that I have a bit of the child in me that refuses to grow up, because I'm extraordinarily lucky in that what I like to draw, they like too."[20] A comparison between *Doraemon* and the popular American cartoon series *The Simpsons* is illustrative. Like *Doraemon*, *The Simpsons* features children as main characters and is clever and entertaining; but with its cerebral humor and frequent pop references, *The Simpsons* has a distinctly adult feel, and is more something to laugh at from a distance than to identify with.

Human Relations, Work, and Spiritual Growth

Another mark of Japan's pop culture is the frequency with which certain themes appear in its stories. Human relations are a pervasive topic, as one would expect from a society that places great importance on the group, harmony, and the smooth management of conflict. The challenges of getting along with classmates, boyfriends, girlfriends, spouses, parents, children, colleagues, and rivals—not only are these central themes in manga after manga, TV drama after TV drama, they are also typically portrayed with a sophistication that does justice to the complexity of human affairs. Issues are many-sided, emotions are mixed, solutions are neither easy nor obvious, and outcomes are often ambiguous—not unlike real life.

Another prominent theme is work, reflecting the positive attitude Japanese hold toward this sphere of life. In countless manga, anime, and TV dramas, work occupies a place that goes far beyond the mere earning of money. Work gives meaning to life, and becoming a good sushi chef, architect, schoolteacher, tofu maker, moneylender, *shōgi* (Japanese chess) player, shoe salesman, beautician, bodyguard, or stand-up comedian is a challenge that many a protagonist takes up with devotion. Balancing career and family is another work-related theme that has become common in recent years, reflecting the weakening of traditional gender, economic, and domestic roles in today's Japan.

"The theme of our comics is growth, boys overcoming problems and getting stronger," says *Shōnen Jump*'s Torishima.[21] The struggle to suc-

Figure 1.5 **Son Gokū and friends ride the *kintoun* in Akira Toriyama's *Dragon Ball***

ceed in the face of adversity is another common motif in Japan pop, and achieving ultimate success is often less important than the strength and wisdom one gains in the process. Particular emphasis is placed on mental or spiritual strength: patience, focus, perseverance, and pureness of intention. The fighting ability of *Dragon Ball*'s Son Gokū is not God-given, but is the outcome of long and rigorous training, both physical and spiritual. Gokū's spiritual purity is also an asset, as it allows him to speed from place to place on the magic *kintoun* cloud, which can only be ridden by the pure of heart. (When the dirty-minded Kame-sennin tries to hop on, he crashes through to the ground.)

Appeal in Asia, Appeal in the West

How do these features of Japanese pop culture explain its international popularity? Aside from its universal appeal—consumers of pop culture everywhere seek quality, humor, dreams, and heroics—Japan pop speaks in special ways to Asia and to the West. For other Asians, Japan's pop culture has a resonance that is derived from ethnic similarity and from shared values, tastes, and traditions. The faces of Japan's pop stars and actors resemble their own. Stories about enduring hardship and overcoming adversity through patience and perseverance echo values widely held in Asia. The hook lines (distinctive musical phrases) and chord structures of Japanese pop music are particularly agreeable to Oriental tastes.[22] References to other Asian cultures and traditions also give Japan pop a familiar feel; Son Gokū's tail and staff, for instance, tip off Chinese readers that he is a modern version of the Monkey King, the popular magician-warrior of Chinese folklore.[23]

An additional resonance comes from similarities connected with the economic and social development that has occurred across Asia in recent decades. Japan, the first Asian nation to carry out a postwar "economic miracle," has served as a model for other Asian nations seeking to raise living standards through industrialization and trade. Economic development produces new social conditions as well: urbanization, consumer cultures, changing family structures and gender roles, and lifestyles and values that are less purely traditional and more influenced by outside information and trends. Because Japan was the first Asian society to experience this kind of economic and social change, it was also the first to reflect new social realities in its popular culture. This gives Japan pop a special relevance for the citizens of Asia's other developed and developing nations, for in it they find portrayed situations and a society that increasingly resemble their own. The widely aired television drama *Oshin*, which traces a woman's rise from a childhood of poverty and suffering to eventual hard-earned success as president of a supermarket chain, has been called "a textbook for economic development" by government officials in Cambodia.[24] Manga about young people struggling to meet the educational expectations of teachers and parents are meaningful to Asian youths under similar pressures to succeed in school and find their place in society. Japan's "trendy dramas," which are very modern romance stories, are especially popular among Asian women, who see romance and contemporary issues dealt with on prime-time television for the first time.[25]

For Western pop culture consumers, on the other hand, much of Japan pop's appeal comes not from its familiarity but from its *difference* from what we are accustomed to in our home cultures. Of Japanese anime, Jeff Yang, co-editor of *Eastern Standard Time: A Guide to Asian Influence on American Culture*, says: "The stories themselves are being woven out of experience and mythology and legend and tradition and fantasy that is 180 degrees out of phase from what we would expect in the West."[26] The same can be said of other forms of Japan pop, and the chance to discover and explore mental universes built up from foundations entirely independent of our own is surely part of its lure. There is also an "opposites attract" sort of complementarity between Japanese and Western pop culture which gives certain aspects of one added value in the other. To the extent that elements that are abundant in Japanese pop culture—complex story and character development; frank portrayals of human nature; dreams and romantic optimism; kids' perspectives; a focus on human relations, work, and mental strength—are scarcer in Western pop culture, Western consumers find that Japan pop enriches their pop culture diet, giving them a fuller range of forms, themes, and viewpoints to enjoy, and perhaps to be influenced by.

An Invitation Inside

Enough *about* Japanese pop culture. What makes this book special is not that it describes and discusses Japanese pop culture—though it does plenty of this as well—but that it takes the reader *inside* Japan's pop culture world to discover for him or herself what is there. Rich in illustrations, manga samples, song lyrics, and the words and thoughts of Japan pop's creators and fans, the writings collected here offer not just the facts but also the flavor of Japan's popular music, its comics and animation, its television and film, and the travels of Japanese pop overseas. Along the way, they open up a window into today's Japan that is far more revealing (to say nothing of far more fun) than the works on Japanese economics, management, culture, society, and traditional arts that crowd bookstore shelves and the pages of academic journals, or the attention-grabbing but misleading bits on Japan one commonly encounters in the newspaper or television media. To understand Japan's complex society and the ways it is changing, to get a sense of what the Japanese people are thinking and what they view as important, to be entertained, even to learn more about ourselves—Are we the same as the Japanese or different?—there may be no better "textbook" than the rich and often-surprising world of Japan's modern pop culture. In inviting the reader into that world, this volume presents not just writings about Japan's pop culture; it presents Japan itself.

Chapters 2 through 5 look at popular music, beginning with E. Taylor Atkins's essay on Japanese jazz. Japanese jazz musicians face a unique challenge: how to be considered authentic and original when jazz, in Japan, is viewed as something that only black Americans can really do well. Atkins explores the strategies Japan's jazz artists have used and the music they have created to cope with this situation, including attempting to create exact replicas of the sounds of American jazz greats; immersing themselves in the social and cultural context (the "hipster scene") in which jazz is produced; asserting the basic affinity of the "colored races"; and incorporating instruments, sounds, and aesthetic principles from traditional music to create a national style of jazz, "which foreigners cannot imitate." Along the way, several important themes are touched upon, including Japan's cultural identity, Japan-U.S. relationships, the nature of jazz and race, and the tension between the universal and the national in popular culture.

Chapter 3 is Christine Yano's tour of the world of *enka,* the popular music genre known as Japan's "national music." Especially popular among the working class (enka bears a striking resemblance to American "country music"), most enka are about tears—lovers parting, broken hearts, longing for home. Yano examines those tears—Who does the crying? Why? For what gain?—and uses lyrics from these sentimental ballads to illustrate traditional Japanese views of man-woman relationships and of love.

James Stanlaw jumps from the traditional to the modern in Chapter 4, providing an overview of Japan's pop music scene and of the changing roles and voices of female singers and songwriters in it. Writing in a colorful style, Stanlaw introduces several important female singers and groups (including Seiko Matsuda, Yuming, Dreams Come True, and Shōnen Knife) and uses quotations and lyrics to give the reader a good feel for their views, personalities, identities, and growing confidence and presence in what was once a male-dominated world. Stanlaw also argues that the use of English provides female songwriters with an expressive freedom which they would lack if they were limited to their native Japanese.

In Chapter 5, Hiro R. Shimatachi explains why karaoke is so much more popular in Japan than in the West: whereas in Japan it is participation and effort that count, Westerners see karaoke as a kind of talent contest, from which the less musically gifted had best abstain. The author argues that karaoke is a positive social development that brings people together; he also offers tips on how non-Japanese business people can sing their way to better relations with their Japanese counterparts.

Comics and animation are the subject of Chapters 6 through 10. Mark MacWilliams begins with a look at one of Osamu Tezuka's major works, the 3,000-page *Budda* (Buddha). Rich in story plots, character sketches, illustrations, and analysis, MacWilliams's essay shows how Tezuka made the story of the Buddha relevant and interesting to a young, modern audience, and provides a good understanding of why this artist is known as the "god" of Japanese comics.

To many people Japan conjures up an image of a serious, formal, and hard-working people whose primary concerns are economic success and keeping a low profile. Eri Izawa turns that image on its head in Chapter 7 by presenting a very different side of the Japanese soul: its affinity for *roman*—the emotional, the heroic, fantastic adventure, intense love, and eternal longing. Izawa shows how such themes pervade the stories, images, music, settings, and characters of Japanese comics, animation, and even video games, vividly demonstrating (for those who didn't know) that Japanese are also very imaginative, sentimental, individualistic, and passionate.

Keiji Nakazawa's *Hadashi no Gen* (Barefoot Gen) is one of the most moving comics ever created, for it is the author's semiautobiographical account of the atomic bombing of Hiroshima, an event which claimed most of the author's family, either in the initial blast or through subsequent radiation sickness. Chapter 8's excerpt from Nakazawa's 2,500-page manga story, which centers on a group of street orphans growing up in survival mode in the aftermath of the nuclear destruction, is both humorous and serious, and offers a good example of the "romantic, passionate Japanese" that Eri Izawa describes in the preceding chapter.

Chapter 9 introduces the reader to the world and characters of *Yūkan Club*, a popular girls' comic. Focusing particularly on the messages this manga sends its young Japanese readers about what makes a person male or female, strong or weak, liked or disliked, Maia Tsurumi's fresh and insightful analysis goes well beyond common stereotypes and does justice to the complexity and subtlety of male-female issues and identities in Japan.

In Chapter 10, William Lee introduces and compares three very popular family-oriented comics/animation series: *Sazae-san*, *Chibi Maruko-chan*, and *Crayon Shin-chan*. Each is from a different time period, and Lee shows how the series portray and reflect changing social and family life conditions in postwar Japan. Early-postwar food shortages, the changing place of women, and a traditional three-generations-under-one-roof family structure are among the topics and features of *Sazae-san*, whose setting roughly corresponds to life in the 1950s and 1960s. With *Chibi-*

Maruko-chan (1970s) and *Crayon Shin-chan* (1990s), the portrayals of family life become less idealistic and nostalgic, and more strained and child-centered, with knowing kids casting a satirical eye on the foibles and pretensions of adults.

In Chapter 11 Hilaria Gössmann leads off the television and film section of the book with a look at how the portrayals of women in Japanese television dramas have evolved: from the old stereotypes of "reliable, strong mother" or "suffering single woman" (common through the 1970s) to increasingly diverse depictions that deal more realistically with family problems (in the 1980s and 1990s). As a case study of the latter, the much-talked-about hit series *Zutto Anata ga Suki Datta* (I've Always Loved You), which portrays a mother's excessive domination of her son, is described in detail. Gössmann also presents a comparison among twelve 1990s television serials, which reflects how male and female roles in marriages are changing in today's Japan.

Chapter 12 examines television from another angle: coverage of the 1959 Imperial marriage of Japan's Crown Prince (today's Emperor) to commoner Michiko Shōda. Jayson Chun shows how the live TV broadcast and other mass-media coverage of this event helped transform the royal couple into egalitarian "pop celebrities." "Managed" by the *Kunaichō* (Imperial Household Agency) and thrust into the relentless glare of media attention, Michiko is the real star, successfully bridging the gap between a traditionally distant, "above-the-clouds" Imperial Family and a populace whose support for the nation's royalty had seriously weakened following World War II.

Otoko wa Tsurai (It's Tough Being a Man) is the world's longest-running film series. In Chapter 13, Mark Schilling provides a tour of the Tora-san series, as it's popularly called, and of the nostalgia, fun, and bittersweet romance that are its trademarks. In one sense all Tora-san movies seem the same, and Schilling provides a perfect description of the series' winning formula. He also shows how Tora-san depicts a changing Japan and addresses deeper issues beneath the surface of slapstick comedy and sentimentalism.

The book's final section follows Japan pop into overseas territory. In Chapter 14, Anne Allison looks at the "transplantability" of Japanese superhero television series to foreign markets, analyzing the appeal and success of two popular programs, *The Mighty Morphin Power Rangers* and *Sailor Moon*, in the United States. Allison highlights differences between these Japanese superheroes and typical Western ones, and describes the changes that are made to the Japanese originals to make them less foreign and more "culturally appropriate" for American kids (and parents). For American viewers, *Sailor Moon* offers a new kind of role model for girls, one that combines fashion and human foibles with strength and self-reliance.

Chapter 15 presents an illustration of *Sailor Moon*'s North American popularity; created originally as part of a school project, "Beauty Fighter Sailor Chemist" is the work of Yuka Kawada, a 15-year-old Japanese-Canadian high school girl who is a fervent manga reader and a talented aspiring artist.

Chapter 16 introduces *Doraemon*, the best-selling comic/animation series in Japanese history and one that is known and loved throughout the world. The title character Doraemon is a bright blue cat with a magic pocket full of high-tech gadgets that can make even the wildest dreams come true. Saya Shiraishi examines the reasons for *Doraemon*'s international popularity, particularly in other Asian countries, focusing on the appeal of core *Doraemon* themes, such as kids' empowerment and technology as friend to man, and the role that the "image alliance" among artists, publishers, television studios, and character merchandising companies plays in the dissemination of Japanese pop culture abroad.

In Chapter 17, Hiroshi Aoyagi looks at Japanese-style "pop idols"—teenage singers and actors—and what it is about them that accounts for their popularity both in Japan and in other Asian countries. Idol characteristics such as the "cute style" and the "life-sized" persona (above average but not outstanding) are introduced, along with the views and words of several idols and fans. Aoyagi also links idols to economic growth, and shows how they contribute to the formation of a common "Asian identity" among young people from different Asian nations.

In putting this volume together, I have tried to do something that is done far too rarely: bridge the gap between the academic and non-academic worlds. Representatives from both worlds attended the University of Victoria Japanese Pop Culture Conference, but communication between the two groups was limited. Although each had much to offer—analytical skills and academic training on one side, familiarity with the currently popular on the other—they spoke different languages; postmodern, deconstruction, and *Nihonjin-ron* were as foreign to the fans as Speed, *purikura* ("print-club" photo booths) and *Kochikame* (a popular manga) were to the scholars. My aim has been to create a book that is of interest to a broad audience—fans as well as scholars, students as well as professors—anyone at all with an interest in Japan and its popular culture. For a few of the chapters this has meant editing material to make it more broadly accessible—explaining phenomena and concepts that nonspecialists may be unfamiliar with and replacing academic terminology with more ordinary phrasing, though never "dumbing down" the content. I hope the result is one that pleases: scholastically sound writings that are interesting, enlightening, and enjoyable. I hope as well that this book may lure readers into venturing more deeply inside the world of Japanese pop culture, to the extent that availability and language allow. It is not only a world that is entertaining and rewarding on its own terms, but also one that can teach us much about Japan and about ourselves.

Notes

1. Osamu Tezuka, *Hi no Tori* (Phoenix), trans. Dadakai. In Frederik L. Schodt, *Manga! Manga! The World of Japanese Comics* (New York: Kodansha International, 1983), pp. 170–171.

2. D. James Romero, "Asia Puts Some Pop Back into Culture," *Los Angeles Times* (June 15, 1997), p. E1.

3. Makoto Sato, "Japan TV Fare Victim of Its Own Success," *Nikkei Weekly* (December 1, 1997), p. 26.

4. Ibid.

5. Michael Baker, "S. Korea Doesn't Find It Easy to Block Japanese Culture," *Christian Science Monitor* (October 29, 1996), p. 1.

6. With two exceptions, all the contributors to this book were participants in the Victoria conference.

7. "Asia Says Japan Is Top of the Pops," *Asiaweek* (January 5, 1996), p. 35.

8. Fosco Maraini, *Meeting with Japan* (New York: Viking, 1960), p. 370.

9. For an overview of Edo-period mass culture, see H. Paul Varley, *Japanese Culture* (New York: Praeger, 1973), pp. 113–138.

10. Quoted in Junko Hanna, "Manga's Appeal Not Limited to Japanese Fans," *Daily Yomiuri* (December 11, 1996), p. 3.

11. Frederik L. Schodt, *Dreamland Japan: Writings on Modern Manga* (Berkeley, CA: Stone Bridge, 1996), p. 198.

12. For the definitive English-language treatments of manga, see Frederik L. Schodt, *Manga! Manga! The World of Japanese Comics* (New York: Kodansha International, 1983); and Frederik L. Schodt, *Dreamland Japan, Writings on Modern Manga* (Berkeley, CA: Stone Bridge, 1996).

13. Mark Schilling, *The Encyclopedia of Japanese Pop Culture* (New York: Weatherhill, 1997), p. 11.

14. Fosco Maraini, *Japan, Patterns of Continuity* (London: Hamish Hamilton, 1972), p. 23.

15. Benjamin Fulford, "Comics in Japan Not Just Funny Business," *Nikkei Weekly* (February 17, 1997), p. 1.

16. Idealism, innocence, and romance may seem contradictory to the idea of "portraying the dark side of life" that was introduced in the preceding paragraph. Both are compatible, however, with the imperative "embrace life in all its dimensions." Just as the real world can be presented without the shackles of censorship or social pressure, so can dream worlds be expressed without being dismissed as naive or corny. Dreams and harsh reality—both are part of life.

17. The difference is well illustrated by a television interview with New York Yankees owner George Steinbrenner, which was dubbed for broadcast in Japan. Asked for his philosophy of life, Steinbrenner offered, "Nice guys finish last." The Japanese translator didn't understand this, but assumed it had a positive meaning and rendered it as "The nice person struggles through to the very last." From Gregory Clark, "Japanese Culture and Society." In *Doing Business in Japan: An Insider's Guide*, ed. Jane Withey (Toronto: Key Porter, 1994), pp. 56–57.

18. Schodt, *Dreamland*, pp. 89–90.

19. Ibid., p. 28.

20. Ibid., pp. 219–220.

21. Fulford, "Comics in Japan," p. 1.

22. Linda Chong, "Dateline: Tokyo," *United Press International* (October 5, 1995).

23. "Asia Says Japan Is Top of the Pops," p. 35.

24. "Japanese TV Drama 'Oshin' to Air in Cambodia," *Kyodo News Service, Japan Economic Newswire* (February 2, 1996).

25. Joshua Ogawa, "Japanese TV Shows Find Fans in Asian Region," *Nikkei Weekly* (December 23, 1996), p. 1.

26. Romero, "Asia Puts Some Pop Back," p. 1.

Part I

Popular Music

2

Can Japanese Sing the Blues?

“Japanese Jazz” and the Problem of Authenticity

E. Taylor Atkins

Sometime in the early 1950s, when the legendary bebop pianist Hampton Hawes was residing in Yokohama as the leader of a U.S. Army band, he had the following conversation with his protégé, Toshiko Akiyoshi (as recreated in Nat Hentoff's *The Jazz Life*):

> Akiyoshi: How do you play the blues that way? How can I learn to play them so authentically?
>
> Hawes: I play the blues right because I eat collard greens and black-eyed peas and corn pone and clabber.
>
> Akiyoshi [sighs]: Where can I find that food? Do I have to go to the United States to get it?
>
> Hawes [laughs]: All you need is the feeling. If you have the feeling, you could eat Skippy peanut butter and play the blues right. And if you don't have that feeling, you could eat collard greens and all that so-called Negro food all the time and sound corny.[1]

Hentoff may have taken some liberties with the wording here, but given the close and mutually respectful relationship Hawes and Akiyoshi enjoyed during the American's year-long sojourn in Japan, it is likely that they exchanged words of this nature more than once.

The conversation is symbolic on a number of levels. For one thing, it captures the essence of the Japanese jazz community's historical dilemma: how to achieve "authenticity" of jazz expression if one is not an American or, more specifically, a black American. In Akiyoshi's question there is an assumption that Hawes knows some secret that will provide access to this treasured "authenticity." Hawes' initial, teasing response playfully employs stereotypes to signify that authenticity is the exclusive province of people of his ethnic background. But they seem to agree that there is *some* solution to the dilemma, which could clear the hurdles of ethnic difference: Akiyoshi's question suggests the possibility that authenticity can be learned or acquired; and Hawes encourages Akiyoshi (whose playing he much admired) to believe that a Japanese with the proper "feeling" is as legitimate a jazz artist as anyone.

On another level, the conversation, as reconstructed by Hentoff, signifies a widespread notion of the nature of Japan's relationship with the United States in the postwar period: The Japanese comes to the American to learn, to adopt the American standard, and to emulate it. The paternalistic stance adopted by General Douglas MacArthur during the early Occupation is faithfully replicated here, with the wise American sage, whose virtue and power the Japanese disciple admires, teasing the disciple like a beloved child. We are reminded of the powerful image of the benevolent American GI, passing out gum, sweets, jazz, and democracy to Japanese children. Moreover, Hawes's assertion that anyone with the "right feeling" can play jazz recalls the Occupation-era assumption that America's culture was somehow "universal" and applicable to all peoples—with the "right feeling."

There can be no denying the power of America in twentieth-century Japan's cultural landscape. For Japanese, America has served as a model for both emulation and contrast. At various historical moments in the twentieth century, America's power over Japan has been manifested concretely in military, economic, and political terms. But the fascination with and the widely acknowledged sense of "yearning" (*akogare*) for things American suggest a different kind of "power," emanating neither from the barrel of a gun nor from the rhetoric of an imposed constitution, but rather from the inculcation of aspirations, standards, values, and ideas originating in America.[2] While there has always been resistance to political and cultural domination by the United States—resistance that has fueled fascism, pan-Asian imperialism, and leftist radicalism—the American presence in Japanese cultural life usually has been accepted, even welcomed, by consumers. In the democracy of the marketplace, America is a clear winner.[3]

Perhaps nowhere is America's cultural dominance in Japan more readily visible than in the realm of popular music. Japan's historical experience of jazz, in particular, has been strikingly intense, reflecting perhaps more than any other single art the tensions and ambivalence of Japanese-American relations in the twentieth century. Through the performance and discussion of jazz, Japanese have debated and refined their knowledge of America and of themselves. Japanese conceptualizations of jazz provide evidence of the conflicting impulses that have driven Japan's twentieth-century history, particularly the tensions between cosmopolitanism and nationalism (Is Japan truly part of the [Western] world, or is it an isolated, unique entity?), and the concomitant concern with purity and authenticity (If Japan borrows culture from the West, is that culture still authentically Western? If Japan borrows so much from other nations, what is authentically Japanese?). As we shall see shortly, such anxieties are compounded when jazz—a culture of American pedigree with its own rigid ideas about authenticity—is added to the mix.

Jazz is often touted as a "universal language,"[4] a vocabulary that can and does speak for people of diverse backgrounds and transcends national boundaries. Yet within the jazz subculture the (African) American exemplar is conspicuously privileged as the most "authentic."[5] When the authenticity and purity of jazz are determined by the ethnicity of the performer, jazz serves as yet another index of difference in a world increasingly partitioned into a collection of mutually hostile identities. The "universal language" metaphor therefore ruptures. Moreover, historical experience testifies that jazz has facilitated not only the integration of a global culture but also the fragmentation of the world into an unruly assemblage of competing nationalist identities. We could look at early-twentieth-century Germany, Japan, or Russia for evidence of this,[6] but we need look no further than America's own contemporary "culture wars" and identity politics, in which jazz itself has become both weapon and prize in a struggle to distinguish the cultural contributions of black Americans.

In Japan and other countries that have gone to considerable trouble to construct and cultivate distinctive national identities, jazz has presented a host of compelling dilemmas: What are the expressive possibilities of an "American" art in a non-American culture? Does a performer surrender his or her national or ethnic identity when performing jazz? Or is it possible to express that identity *through* the "American" art of jazz? If

Figure 2.1 **Reunion of Japanese musicians who performed in U.S. service clubs during the Occupation era. Raymond Conde (clarinet and vocals) and Gay Septet, with guest Satoru Oda (tenor sax), at Tokyo Kaikan, October 30, 1994.**

so, does such expression constitute a unique "national style"? Can such a "national style" be considered "authentic" jazz?

As an art form that has existed and thrived in both the United States and Japan since the 1920s, jazz became one field on which definitions of national self and other were tested and contested, and yet another yardstick by which Japan measured itself in comparison and in competition with America. Japanese often describe themselves as afflicted with a "complex" toward America; the word suggests a variety of emotions ranging from extreme self-consciousness to feelings of inadequacy or inferiority. It is a feeling with which many Japanese, particularly those who witnessed the Occupation, can identify, but it is particularly acute within the jazz subculture. The primary engine driving the music's historical experience in Japan has been the various attempts to assuage this "complex," and to find an expression that is authentically jazz yet authentically Japanese.

As anyone who has spent much time in Japan soon discovers, in a country that has borrowed so much from other peoples, a great deal of value is attached to the excavation of the indigenous or "Japanese," and to the differentiation of "rediscovered" customs, beliefs, or arts from the non-native. However, Japanese jazz artists have been in the rather awkward position of trying to authenticate themselves with reference to two very different standards—that of "jazz" and that of "Japanese culture." The dilemma of jazz artists was, in this respect, similar to that facing some of Japan's most distinguished modern writers, as described by Hisaaki Yamanouchi:

> How could Western culture and [Japanese] native tradition be harmoniously reconciled to one another when often it persuaded [the Japanese] to hate whatever of their own culture and themselves they had been reared to respect? They felt compelled to imitate [Western literature] and *thus* be authentic, a contradiction that obviously gnawed at their consciousness. Consequently they came to suffer from insecurity and identity crises. These circumstances are partly responsible for the many instances of mental breakdown and suicide among modern Japanese writers.[7]

Aside from the famous bebop pianist Shōtarō Moriyasu (1924–1955), whose artistic and personal frustrations compelled him to throw himself in front of a train, "authenticity anxiety" did not lead to widespread suicides among jazz musicians—although it was most certainly at the root of many drug habits.[8] The jazz culture in general was much more disengaged (and deliberately so) from the social concerns that tortured some of Japan's great literary figures. Moreover, concerns of authenticity have never completely obscured the sensuality, personal liberation, spiritual insight, and fun that artists and audiences alike have found in jazz. If Japanese jazz musicians and aficionados, to varying, individual degrees, have despaired of ever "authenticating" their work, they have continued to *play;* they simply enjoy playing too much to let nihilism set in.

Yet, although its centrality has varied significantly over the years, authenticity remains a key theme, not only in the history of jazz in Japan, but also in the study of Japanese popular culture in general. The debate over authenticity provides a crucial key to an understanding of Japanese conceptualizations of jazz, and of the social positions and artistic development of creative people (within and outside the world of jazz). By extension, it also illuminates the cultural identity crises that form a major theme of Japan's twentieth-century experience. Jazz, a form of culture to which authenticity is sacred, provides a unique lens for sharpening our awareness of the significance of "authenticity" in modern Japanese history.

This chapter discusses the concepts of authenticity as applied to jazz and to the idea of "Japanese culture," and then looks at some of the authenticating strategies jazz artists and aficionados have developed to cope with the dilemmas posed by jazz. One such authenticating strategy, the construction of a national style, is examined in depth. The idea of a unique and inimitable Japanese style of jazz—a "Japanese" identity expressed through an "American" art—illustrates the contradictions inherent in notions of ethnic differences. In this case, people who believe that ethnic groups have distinct, metaphysical "essences" have chosen a vehicle of expression—jazz—that is ostensibly alien to the essence of Japanese culture. At two crucial historical junctures, the Pacific War and the aftermath of the 1960s *Anpo* (Japan-U.S. Security Treaty) protests, artists and aficionados invested considerable effort to develop and explain "Japanese jazz" (*Nihonteki* jazz),[9] thus using a music regarded as quintessentially American to cultivate an independent, explicitly non-American (if not *anti*-American) sense of self. Finally, I conclude that these strategies of authentication have failed to convince the vast majority of jazz artists and aficionados that jazz performed by Japanese is as legitimate as that performed by black Americans. This failure demonstrates how the idea of authenticity subverts idealistic notions of jazz as a "universal language."

Race, Authenticity, and All That Jazz

If we think of "jazz" not only as a music but as a culture, with its own values, practices, fetishes, and hierarchies, we find that few cultures are as concerned with "authenticity" as jazz is. It is an obsession that potentially undermines the rhetoric of jazz as a "universal language," for "authenticity" implies particularism, not universalism. But what does "authenticity" mean?

Anthropologists—particularly those interested in how "authentic" Third World cultures represent themselves to First World tourists, or how historical sites and artifacts are presented to the public—have defined the concept of "authenticity" as verisimilitude, credibility, originality (as opposed to imitation), or authoritativeness. Anthropologist Edward Bruner points out that "authenticity" implies that someone has the power or authority to "authenticate" a representation; the concept of authenticity thus privileges one voice as more legitimate than another.[10]

Authenticity in jazz (or in any art, for that matter) implies that an artist must possess specific qualities—educational background, life experience, ethnic heritage, motivations, or artistic vision—which confer upon that artist the *right* not only to work unchallenged in a particular medium, but to establish the standard by which all others working in that medium will be judged. Those who are influenced by such work may be deemed "authentic" or "unauthentic" depending either on how closely they adhere to the aesthetic standards enshrined in the "original" or on how closely their personal profiles match the specific experiential, ethnic, or motivational qualities of the "original's" creator. The standards for determining authenticity may change or be contested, yet some such standard is always in operation and its power is significant.

Authenticity is "paramount" in jazz, and charges of "imitativeness, insincerity or inauthenticity" are the most "devastating" that a jazz artist can suffer.[11] There are a number of standards by which jazz performances and artists are judged for authenticity: a lack of deference to commercial concerns, reverence for "the tradition," and a hard-luck story of "paying dues." But ever since the days when French critics such as Hughes Panassié held up Louis Armstrong as an "instinctive" musical genius, a musical "noble savage,"[12] there has also been a powerful racial or ethnic dimension to concepts of authenticity. Even as we enter the twenty-first century, the old question "Can white people sing the blues?" remains a topic of hot debate.[13] America's leading blues periodical, *Living Blues*, maintains an editorial policy by which white blues artists (usually dubbed "blues interpreters") are ignored while increasingly obscure black blues artists (labeled "bluesmen") are given substantial coverage. The magazine was downright apologetic when it carried a cover photo of Adam Gussow, the white harmonica player from the blues duo Satan and Adam. Unquestionably, the belief that some combination of African ancestry and American nationality is a precondition for authentic expression in jazz and blues is still strong (if contested), and perhaps dominant. "In an age of renewed and heightened racial and cultural sensitivity," philosopher Joel Rudinow reflects, "such a critical stance seems paradoxically to be both progressive and reactionary. . . . It seems to embody, as well as any, the problematic of 'political correctness.'"[14]

In his controversial *Cats of Any Color* (1994), jazz critic Gene Lees points out that, while this ideology has been propagated by the highly visible and predominantly black "Young Lion" coterie and its spokesmen (primarily Stanley Crouch, Wynton Marsalis, and Herb Boyd), it also represents the thinking of many prominent white critics.[15] "[T]he blues is black man's music," the late Ralph J. Gleason wrote in 1968, "and whites diminish it at best or steal it at worst. In any case they have no moral right to it."[16] Indeed, the role of white musicians and critics in propagating this belief cannot be overstated. Bix Beiderbecke and Milton "Mezz" Mezzrow are but two examples of white artists who believed that their skin color and middle-class upbringings had to somehow be overcome if they were to become legitimate jazz artists. Mezzrow's classic autobiography, *Really the Blues* (1946), documents the clarinetist's quest to become a "white negro" for the purpose of playing jazz:

> We were Jews, but in Cape Girardeau they had told us we were Negroes. Now, all of a sudden, I realized that I agreed with them. . . . The Southerners had called me a "nigger-lover" there. Solid. . . . I knew that I was going to spend all my time from then on sticking close to Negroes. They were my kind of people. And I was going to learn their music, and play it for the rest of my days. I was going to be a musician, a Negro musician, hipping the world about the blues the way only Negroes can.[17]
>
> . . . Everything the Negro did, we agreed, had a swing to it; he talked in rhythm, his tonal expression had a pleasing lilt to the ear, his movements were graceful . . . every move he made was as easy and neatly timed as anything Mother Nature had put down on this earth.[18]
>
> . . . We [Eddie Condon's Chicago band] weren't in the same class with the Armstrongs and the Bechets, the Noones and the Olivers, and we might as well admit it and keep on studying. . . . [Our music] was just an imperfect reflection, like you get in a distorting mirror, of the only real jazz, the colored man's music. . . . We had to recognize where we derived from, and try all the time to be more authentic, purer, closer to the source.[19]

Many find it shocking that these racist ideas still have credibility. "I don't know what they mean by black music," trumpeter Doc Cheatham said in a National Public Radio interview. "I have never seen any black music. I've seen black notes on white paper." Dizzy Gillespie, a devout Baha'i who made a point of assembling multiethnic bands, objected to the notion that only black people can play jazz: "[I]f you accept that premise, well then what you're saying is that maybe black people can *only* play jazz. And black people, like anyone else, can be anything they want to be."[20] Jazz has usually been thought of as a relatively tolerant culture when it comes to racial matters. Yet issues of race and authenticity are as divisive in today's jazz world as they ever were. Working bands "voluntarily segregate" themselves; young black musicians have become marketable emblems of racial pride; and even institutions such as the National Endowment for the Arts' American Jazz Masters Fellowships and Jazz at Lincoln Center are suspected of "Crow Jim" (or "reverse racist") policies.[21]

The controversy has occurred in the context of a movement to retrieve and retell a history of black people in America and their contributions. The basic dispute in jazz studies centers around the question of which "race" created jazz, and therefore should "own" it. The quintessential "melting-pot" metaphor, as stated by Dan Morgenstern of the Rutgers University Institute of Jazz Studies, has been challenged in recent years. "I see jazz as an American music which came into being through the interaction between different musical cultural elements, and what was so fascinating about jazz was the mixture of European and African and Latin American and, you know, all kinds of Native American, all these elements coming together and out of that came a new music." Saxophonist Archie Shepp dismisses this view: "This is my music. I want to make that clear. . . . In my estimation, so-called jazz music is founded on African American blues idioms. Now what did Western music give to the blues? Except to give the people who sang it the blues?"[22] Shepp uses the phrase "African American" rather than "African" or "black," perhaps suggesting a concession to Morgenstern's melting pot, yet his concept of jazz is explicitly that of a "pure" music, untainted by "Western" influence, which can be *possessed* ("my music") by people of a particular ethnic background.

The idea that jazz is the exclusive cultural property of black Americans is widely accepted among musicians, fans, and jazz scholars around the world. It has crossed the Pacific to Japan largely intact. For two rising star trumpeters with whom I spoke, Issei Igarashi and Tomonao Hara (the latter a friend and protégé of Marsalis), the assertion "Jazz is black music" has become a mantra, if not a "party line." Most Japanese fans, by some estimates the largest per capita jazz audience in the world,[23] concur that jazz by black Americans is the "real thing"; at the very least many share a compulsion to categorize the music (an activity of which Japanese fans seldom weary) as "black jazz" or "white jazz."

The Japanese jazz audience is particularly well versed in the struggles of African Americans for liberation and for recognition of their contributions to American society and culture. Contrary to the image of Japanese as unrepentant racists, many are acutely sensitive to racial strife in America and sympathetic to the economic and social plights of black

Americans. This sensitivity to race issues and familiarity with the doctrines of Malcolm X and Amiri Baraka further predispose Japanese to favor the black nationalist orthodoxy regarding the "ownership" of jazz. Ironically, this consciousness embraces what is regarded as the inherently "rhythmical" nature of black people. People with whom I spoke during the course of research repeated this stereotype ad nauseam. The stereotype of the rhythmic black person is, in fact, intended as a compliment and a key to authentic jazz performance. The stereotype of the black person with a superior rhythmic sense is frequently invoked by American jazz artists as well,[24] which merely reinforces the legitimacy of such stereotypes in Japan.

Yet Japanese create and propagate as many stereotypes of themselves as they do of others. A best-selling literature of mass-market and academic publications, known collectively as *Nihonjinron (*discourses on the Japanese),[25] testifies to the uniqueness and purity of an unchanging "Japanese culture." Proponents argue that Japan's geographical isolation engendered "unique" systems of social relations, cultural values, and aesthetic sensibilities. Japanese and Western scholars have reacted by demonstrating that "Japanese culture" is an artificially coherent and monolithic category of relatively recent pedigree, contrived to suppress the very real differences, innovations, variations, complexities, and conflicts that have driven modern Japanese history.[26] Still, the power of the *idea* of "Japanese culture" remains formidable, as the popularity of Nihonjinron literature suggests. Paradoxically, scholars tend to overstate the "uniqueness" of this literature; Japanese are not alone in proclaiming their singularity and purity. In fact, "race thinking" has been a prominent feature of postwar jazz criticism.

When we bring together these two cultures—"jazz" and "Japan"—each with its own conceptions of ethnically determined purity and authenticity, we find an artistic community with a persistent compulsion to "authenticate" its own art. Generally speaking, Japan's jazz community has historically been ambivalent about the authenticity of its own jazz expressions, and to a lesser degree about the authenticity of its identity as Japanese. The importance of these dilemmas varies from person to person, of course, but they figure prominently in the testimonies of some of Japan's most respected jazz artists. Even Akiyoshi, who has been widely acclaimed as a distinctive composer and big band leader, concedes, "The history [of black artists] is longer. If your history is longer and liable to produce better players. . . . If you name who's the best player, they're black."[27] Acceptance of this myth has necessitated strategies of authentication that justify and legitimize the art of Japanese musicians as "real jazz." Yet the jazz community's historical development has coincided with moments in which nativist sentiments and conceptions of "purity" have been especially strong. Thus the jazz subculture, whose very identity was defined by a "foreign" art, could only endure such moments by authenticating itself as "Japanese."

Strategies of Authentication

Japanese jazz artists and aficionados have concocted a variety of authenticating strategies to cope with their unique conundrum. From a broad historical perspective, such strategies include: attempts to replicate the exact sounds of American jazz; study abroad in exotic locales such as Shanghai or the United States; apprenticeships in foreign bands; efforts to recreate the social and cultural contexts (e.g., the "hipster scene") in which jazz is produced; assertions of the basic affinity of the "colored races"; and efforts to "indigenize" or "nationalize" jazz by incorporating textures, instruments, or aesthetic principles from traditional musics and creating a national style of jazz, "which foreigners cannot imitate."

Obviously, the strategies used by Japanese jazz musicians and aficionados to authenticate jazz in Japan have been variegated and rooted in the demands of particular historical moments. They have also colored the music produced at those moments. Even a cursory listen to Japanese recordings of jazz from the 1920s and early 1930s, or from the first two decades of the postwar era, indicates that at these times musicians were listening closely to, and often attempting to duplicate, the feats of America's jazz giants. Recordings from the war years or from the late 1960s onward, however, demonstrate a willingness to tinker with jazz, to "indigenize" it, and even to forge a distinctive national style. Clearly the authenticating strategies and aesthetic imperatives at work differ according to the historical moments in which these recordings were produced. It follows that the authenticating strategies shifted with historical developments, particularly those that involved Japan's sense of self and its political and cultural relationship with the United States.

We can make brief mention of one such shift. In the immediate post-World War II period, which was one of national humiliation and American occupation, the dominant authenticating strategy involved not only the rote replication of the exact sounds and techniques of "modern jazz," as established by Americans, but also the creation of a Japanese "hipster" scene, with its own lingo, fashions, and attitude. Here the aim was to create an "authentic" jazz expression by reproducing the social and cultural contexts in which "real" jazz is produced. In much the same way that white musicians such as Mezz Mezzrow studied the language and mannerisms of black people ("I spent weeks studying Bessie Smith's slaughter of the white man's dictionary"[28]), Japanese beboppers adopted the ways of their hipster heroes (as best they could discern them from afar through American movies and through periodicals such as *Down Beat* and *Metronome*). The problem with the strategy in this case, as a number of musicians and commentators realized at the time, was that it subverted the authentication agenda rather than advancing it. The aesthetic principles of jazz demand that the artist take the music into uncharted terrain, that he or she follow no particular example and aspire only to an unknown art of the future. Japanese were thus in the humiliating position of having their own artistic future mapped out by Americans. In the late 1950s one Japanese critic, probably paraphrasing Douglas MacArthur, lamented, "The Japanese jazz world is still a twelve-year-old child when compared to that of the United States."[29]

The reaction against the tendency to imitate American jazz occurred in the wake of the so-called Anpo protests of 1960, which challenged the nation's security arrangement with the United States. The new authenticating strategy for jazz was conceived during a period of artistic effervescence and the search for a "national voice" in cinema, painting, drama, and composed music that can be labeled "nativist" or "neonationalist." The new jazz concept involved the incorporation of Japanese musical instruments and aesthetic principles, in a bold effort to create an inimitable national style of jazz. While many might regard this movement as yet another manifestation of the obsession with Japanese uniqueness (which it most certainly is), the drive to forge a "Japanese jazz" was also a protest against what many perceived as cultural domination by America. After years of artistic activity which, in their own estimation, had consistently failed to match the standards set by Americans, some prominent Japanese jazz artists were calling for *new standards*, which would render comparisons with American jazz meaningless. Thus, in contrast to the dominant authenticating strategy of the previous era, "authenticity" in the late 1960s did not derive from the mere mastery of the sounds and social contexts of American jazz, but from the incorporation of an amorphous, inimitable Japanese "spirit."

"Japanese Jazz" as National Style

Japanese jazz artists have consistently been subjected to the ultimate indignity in jazz—being known as the *Nihonban* (Japanese version) of some great American jazz artist. Fumio Nanri (1910–1975) made his reputation as "Japan's Satchmo"; Akira Miyazawa was recognized as Japan's most successful disciple of Sonny Rollins; and George Kawaguchi never ends a performance without "Drum Boogie," the anthem of his principal influence, Gene Krupa. Yet Japanese artists, of course, are well aware of the value of individual creativity in jazz and have thus been uneasy with their roles as "the Japanese version" of American artists. Veteran saxophonist Satoru Oda admits that he was bothered when he was billed as "Japan's Lester Young" at a performance in Ireland, but sighs that it was the most convenient way to "label" him for an audience unfamiliar with his work. He was much more pleased when another European festival described his music as "Asian jazz" in its promotions.

As Oda suggests, one solution to the discomfort of being recognized as the *kagemusha* (double) of an American jazz giant has been to transform the perceived ethnic "disadvantage" into a vehicle for an allegedly unique Japanese expression within the jazz idiom, something that would distinguish the music of Japanese artists from that of Americans. The result, it was argued, would be an inimitable national style of jazz that would express the "Japanese essence," a music that would be recognizably Japanese and constitute a unique contribution to the jazz oeuvre. The desire to assert a Japanese national identity through music was not unique to jazz. In fact, proponents of a national style of jazz could and did look for musical and philosophical inspiration from a number of classical composers, such as Tōru Takemitsu (1930–1996), Minoru Miki, Jōji Yuasa, and Yasushi Akutagawa, who were engaged in a "search for a voice within a universal musical language."[30] Judith Ann Herd describes this "neonationalist" upheaval as a quest for "an independent voice" free from "European cultural imperialism."[31] In a similar vein, Elizabeth Sesler-Beckman employs musicological analysis in an attempt to prove that a "Japanese essence" has been effectively incorporated into jazz:

> The Japanese musicians that emerged [between 1965 and 1970] were often playing a highly emotional and many times extreme music which

> did not, on the face of it, reflect such traditional Japanese values as love of order or quiet tranquillity. Yet it is my hypothesis that this musical movement represents the highest form of Japanese expression and that it is, in fact, a powerful example of Japanese culture flowering through the form of American jazz. It is here that a national Japanese jazz style emerges, and it is here that Japanese musicians have found the juncture where imitation of old forms has become something truly new and innovative. Musicians such as [Terumasa] Hino, [Yōsuke] Yamashita, [Masahiko] Togashi, and [Masahiko] Satō have successfully captured not just the trappings of traditional Japanese musical forms but the actual essence of *what it is to be Japanese* within their musical improvisations.[32]

While I would certainly concur with Sesler-Beckman's appreciation of these artists' music, it is essential that we question the assumptions of "ethnic essence" on which she bases her remarks: what exactly does it mean "to be Japanese"? Uncritical acceptance of the idea of a national style determined by the performer's ethnicity merely validates "race thinking."

For those who do subscribe to such notions, what constitutes "Japanese jazz?" There are about as many definitions as there are jazz musicians and fans in Japan. For some, Japanese jazz represents the fusion of the improvisatory, harmonic, and rhythmic elements of jazz and Japanese pentatonic scales, folk melodies, or instrumentation. Such musical experimentation first occurred in the mid-to-late 1930s, under the aegis of Ryōichi Hattori (1907–1993), but has continued sporadically throughout the decades (as we shall see momentarily). One of the most successful representatives of this approach is the *shakuhachi* (bamboo flute) master Hōzan Yamamoto, who has almost singlehandedly brought a new timbre to the tonal palette of jazz. Many proponents of a national style have pointed to Yamamoto as the ultimate example of an original artist who expresses the "Japanese heart" in a way that foreigners could not hope to emulate.

Of course, traditional Japanese musics such as *gagaku* (court music) and *min'yō* (folk songs) are no more linked to ethnicity than are jazz or Western classical music. Japanese jazz musicians have repeatedly confessed that mastering the vocabularies of indigenous musics did not come naturally to them, but rather required considerable effort, in spite of their supposed ethnic "advantage." Moreover, a number of non-Japanese—including saxophonists John Coltrane, Tony Scott, and Charlie Mariano, flautist Herbie Mann, and bassist Jamaaladeen Tacuma—have successfully incorporated Japanese folk melodies and instrumentation into their music. If Japanese jazz is no more than a musical fusion, it hardly constitutes an inimitable national style that comes naturally to Japanese and is impossible for foreigners to replicate.

The mere fusion of traditional Japanese musics with jazz strikes many proponents of a national style as too gimmicky and does not begin to do justice to their concept of Japanese jazz. For them, there is something much more intangible, even mystical, that distinguishes jazz performed by Japanese artists; a Japanese artist playing Tin Pan Alley tunes on the Western piano unconsciously expresses his or her ethnic identity as much as an improvising *koto* (a Japanese stringed instrument) player does. Jazz critic Shōichi Yui (1918–1998) and percussionist Masahiko Togashi, among others, have highlighted the importance of *ma* (space), the relatively long, pregnant intervals between notes, as a distinctive feature of Japanese jazz. Although Thelonious Monk, Miles Davis, and many other non-Japanese artists have accorded a great deal of respect to space in their music, proponents of Japanese jazz insist that whereas Monk and Davis were deliberately and unnaturally manipulating space within their music, the Japanese "sense of space" is "unconscious," "natural," and "unique." Togashi, who announced that he wanted "to try to create a music so that Japanese, foreigners, or anybody who hears it can feel that 'this is something peculiar to Japanese people,'"[33] emphasized a unique and unconscious sense of rhythm and space as a distinguishing feature that ensured the Japanese identity of his jazz. Regarding space, he said:

> In Oriental thought because there is existence [*yū*] there is nothingness [*mu*]. Because there is nothingness there is existence. . . . So by not playing a sound, you can make a combination of sounds, by making nothingness you create—totally different from Western thinking. So American and Japanese "concepts of space" are different.[34]
>
> Regarding my music, it's often written that one can feel a peculiar Japanese "interval" [*ma*] or "space" [*kūkan*], but in fact I'm not especially conscious that I'm creating such a thing; it's not an interval or space of which I have a theoretical grasp, it's not something I've completed studying. It's a condition that I first notice after it's been pointed out in writing, when I listen to it again myself. . . . These elements, the parts that I cannot explain theoretically, that is what I believe to be the Japanese natural sense.[35]

Aside from space, there are other ephemeral characteristics that supposedly make Japanese jazz distinctive. Saxophonist Satoru Oda has coined the term "yellow jazz" to connote an as yet undeveloped style, using what he calls Asian techniques, sounds, scales, and spirit, which Japanese and other Asians "have in their blood" and should develop further. Another conceptualization comes from stereo dealer Shūichi Sugiura and his wife Hitomi, activist jazz fans who reside in Okazaki outside of Nagoya. The Sugiuras insist that when they listen to a jazz performance they can identify the ethnicity of the performer.[36] For them, Japanese jazz is moodier and less energetic than American jazz. They believe that Japanese are basically a sad people (this from some of the cheeriest people I know) and that the sadness reflected in song forms such as *enka* (popular ballads) colors their jazz. Through the common language of jazz, the Sugiuras say, Americans and Japanese express themselves in ways that are determined by their respective backgrounds and that will be understood by their respective audiences. Shūichi used colors to illustrate his conception: jazz is red, Japanese culture is white, and Japanese jazz is pink.

It should be noted that Japanese jazz as a coherent national style is not a widely accepted concept among jazz aficionados, but even those who scoff at the idea feel that jazz as played by Japanese is subtly different, with the added implication that it is ultimately inferior to the American product. Shūichi Sugiura asserts that Japanese do not have the physical power to play jazz like Americans so they must play their own way. Jazz critic Masahisa Segawa contends that the "inferior" physique, lack of power, and smaller lung capacity of Japanese account for the lack of any "powerful" trumpeters in Japan's jazz pantheon. Saxophonist Jirō Inagaki cites experiences playing with Bud Shank and Lionel Hampton in which he and other Japanese musicians, operating on what he calls "Japanese time," played their parts too early compared with their American counterparts. Inagaki's son Masayuki adds that the Japanese rhythmic sense is impaired: they cannot play behind the beat or the chord for fear of "messing up."

Finally, there are those who believe that the very idea of a national style is inimical to the individualistic aesthetic basis of jazz, if not outright ridiculous. Avant-garde saxophonist and Stir Up! bandleader Sachi Hayasaka is one of many musicians who regard jazz as an individualistic music on which nationality or ethnicity has no bearing. Then there is Teruo ("Terry") Isono, a drummer, disc jockey, critic, former club owner, and former United States Information Service (USIS) employee, who scoffs at the very idea of Japanese jazz. It's all American music, he says, adding, "Japanese have no originality." To musicians such as Masahiko Satō and Masahiko Togashi, who have made the creation of Japanese jazz their missions, Isono offers the following words of advice: "It's impossible. It's unnecessary. Just quit it."

Necessary or not, there is a long history of such experimentation. Since the mid-1930s there have been several sporadic attempts to fuse the melodies and instrumentation of Japanese folk or pop songs with the improvisational spontaneity, harmonic structures, and rhythms of jazz, with mixed results. The popular composer Ryōichi Hattori pioneered this approach with such hit records as "The Mountain Temple Priest" and Noriko Awaya's smash hit "Farewell Blues." Hattori believed that the blues was universal and, paradoxically, that there was a blues unique to Japan. "I don't think that the blues, such as W. C. Handy's 'St. Louis Blues,' is the monopoly of black people," he reportedly said to his lyricist Kō Fujiura (1898–1979) in 1937. "Don't you think that a Japanese blues in Japan, an Oriental blues, is quite possible?"[37] No one person invented the idea of a "Japanese jazz," but certainly in the between-wars era few did as much to propagate the notion as Ryōichi Hattori. He strove to "emphasize the rhythm and maintain a jazz style," yet by choosing folk material (in the case of "The Mountain Temple Priest," a handball song) Hattori envisaged "a Japanese blues that uses the emotions of Japanese people as material."[38] In the years leading up to the war, a number of other composer-arrangers—many of them, such as Tasuku Sano and Shigeo Taira, students of Hattori—wrote and recorded jazz songs with more or less explicitly nationalistic themes. Perhaps the most artistically successful of these composers was Kōichi Sugii (1906–1942), whose King Salon Music Series presented sophisticated and swinging jazz arrangements of Chinese and Japanese folk tunes. The records were put on the market to coincide with Japan's aggressive efforts to subjugate China, under the banner of pan-Asian unity.

Perhaps because of its associations with wartime nationalism, "indigenized" jazz was not a popular concept in the early postwar era. There were sporadic examples of recordings that blended Japanese pops and folk songs with Dixieland, Glenn Miller-style swing, or George Shearing-style "West Coast cool"—American jazzmen such as Tony Scott, Charlie Mariano, and Herbie Mann encouraged and even participated in such excursions themselves—but such experiments were usually dismissed in the jazz press as mere novelties or as overtly commercial attempts to attract listeners who preferred Japanese pops to "foreign" music.

Japanese jazz did not become fashionable until the triumphal performances by the Shiraki Hideo Quintet (plus koto trio) at the Berlin Jazz Festival in November 1965, and by the Sharps and Flats big band at the Newport Jazz Festival in July 1967. Before the Newport concert, Sharps and Flats bandleader Nobuo Hara conveyed a sense of the performance's significance: "It's a dream come true . . . but my shoulders are very heavy. I'll be carrying the hopes of Japanese jazz." He aspired to "show the Japanese people that a Japanese band has the power to play with the best. And it could give encouragement to the many Japanese jazz musicians who are having difficulty."[39] Hara planned a program of Japanese folk songs, rather than the band's usual Count Basie-Woody Herman fare, which he hoped would impress an American audience demanding a distinctive sound from a jazz band. Clearly a program of traditional Japanese songs would garner more attention and, it was hoped, respect for Japanese artists. Thus the idea of a national style was developed as a crucial strategy for constructing a distinctive musical identity and winning over skeptical audiences.

Arguably the most prominent voice proclaiming the advent of a national ethnic style of jazz was that of jazz critic Shōichi Yui. Having first advanced the possibility of a Japanese jazz in the hopeful days of the late 1950s, Yui began articulating a more fully conceived theory in the late 1960s, when Japanese musicians were starting to attract unprecedented favorable recognition at home and abroad. In a 1969 essay in *Jazz Critique*, Yui wrote:

> From Hideo Shiraki to Nobuo Hara, Japanese musicians invited to foreign jazz festivals, each with their own creativity, are using Japanese scales, *koto*, and *shakuhachi*, performing a unique jazz that other peoples cannot imitate, and garnering great acclaim. "We will not be accepted for imitating and playing the same things foreigners play," they say. "That made us painfully aware that Japanese musicians should create a Japanese jazz."
>
> Right now this is a new global trend that is coming to rule jazz. Even in America, blacks are aiming for black jazz, whites for white jazz; and in Europe, as well, in Spain and West Germany different national hues using the diction of jazz are being worked out. It is certainly reasonable that Japanese musicians are in a hurry to "create Japanese jazz."
>
> Now, thinking calmly, what in the world does the term "Japanese jazz" indicate? If it means jazzing [songs like] "Yagi-bushi" or "Sōran-bushi," [such attempts] have been tested since the early Shōwa period and they have all experienced merciless failure. They may have all been Japanese-Western compromises, but they have never been "Japanese."

> One hundred years after Meiji, the course of modernization that our nation has pursued has been accomplished only by abandoning precious Japanese traditions and taking in Western culture in large quantities. . . . [W]hat do we have to prove that we are real Japanese? Nothing.

Yui argued that Japanese should follow the example of black Americans, who had recently demonstrated renewed pride and interest in the "lost" traditions of their ancestral homelands in Africa, and search for a "clear solution" to the question "what is Japanese?"[40]

In a roundtable discussion to commemorate the second All Japanese Jazz Festival in 1969, Yui clarified his conception of Japanese jazz in an exchange with fellow critics Yōzō Iwanami, Masaichirō Ono, and Kiyoshi Koyama.

"When one says 'Japanese jazz,'" Ono began, "one immediately thinks of jazz arrangements of Japanese folk songs, but Japanese jazz is the Japanese artist's expression of the Japanese heart through the Esperanto [universal language] of jazz. It is jazz that eats rice."

Yui replied that "using scales from Japanese folk songs, or playing 'Yagi-bushi' with a four-beat rhythm" was not necessarily the only way to distinguish a national ethnicity in Japanese jazz. "The problem is," he went on, "what is Japanese?"

> When I listen to Toshiko Akiyoshi play the piano, I know that something comes out that is peculiar to Japanese, I know that it's not an American, but it's difficult to explain what that something is. I think that [composer] Tōru Takemitsu is the most Japanese of the great composers produced by Japan in the twentieth century, but what I like about his music is not, for instance, his use of the *biwa* (lute) or *shakuhachi* but the fact that he has created music that really has the heart of Japanese people. If you ask what that is, in Tōru Takemitsu's case, it's his serious regard for "space" [*ma*]. Foreigners seem to have a sense of what is called "space," but not this. A temple bell always sings "*garan garan garan*." A Japanese temple's bell only makes one sound. The sound it makes reverberates and fades among the mountains. Before and after that there is a tremendous void, and if you're Japanese you feel that in your gut. Tōru Takemitsu's compositions call on that Japanese sympathy. . . . That [sense of space] is an element that must appear in various forms in Japanese jazz.
>
> What impressed me as an example of a Japanese jazz performance in which that element appeared was Masabumi Kikuchi's piano solo on

> Charlie Mariano's composition "Rock Garden of Ry)an Temple." *That* is a Japanese person's piano solo. Kikuchi's solo on this song has the so-called Japanese sense of "space," and constitutes a performance that the world's pianists probably couldn't imitate if you made them.[41]

Yui's emphasis on the amorphous concept of "space" echoed roughly contemporaneous neonationalist discussions within Japan's classical music community regarding the incorporation of "traditional" aesthetic principles. Composer Ikuma Dan, in particular, emphasized *ma* (thinking in silences) as one principle on which a new national style would be based.[42] Dan, a member of what he himself called the "nationalist school" of composers (along with Yasushi Akutagawa and Toshirō Mayuzumi), expressed a vision which is echoed in Yui's formulations:

> It is not enough to write Japanese-sounding compositions using Western forms and harmonies. Those who have tried to do so have had no real or lasting success. The purpose of the composer, first of all, must be to write good music, and this we are not likely to have through mere rearrangement of traditional music for Western instruments. Something new, but at the same time fundamentally Japanese, must be created. . . . Western musical forms are based on Western ideals of logic and symmetry. These are not necessarily Eastern ideals. The East has its own ideals, and it is in relation to them that truly oriental musical forms must be evolved. In such forms will the Japanese Western-style music of the future be cast.[43]

Yui's definition of Japanese jazz was similar in that it went beyond previous conceptualizations of national style as a self-conscious combination of Japanese melodies and instrumentation with jazz harmonies and rhythms. Yui regarded Japanese jazz as more than merely playing "Autumn Leaves" on the koto. In this respect he echoed the composer Tōru Takemitsu, who once said, "I must not be trapped by traditional instruments any more than by all other kinds." For Takemitsu, "Japanese music" should be no mere manipulation of techniques, instrumentation, and scales, but rather a "living order that combines the fundamentally different musical phenomena of the West and Japan."[44] Yui contended that Japanese performers, even when working with Western instruments and Tin Pan Alley material, betray their ethnic identity by displaying a "unique" and unconscious sense of melodic construction, rhythm, and space. This "ethnicization" of jazz was, moreover, a universal phenomenon that Yui observed in the jazz of other nations.

His theory thus maintained a faith in the much-proclaimed "universality" of jazz as a language, while incorporating nationalistic themes of fundamental ethnic difference and Japanese exceptionalism to distinguish Japanese jazz and accentuate its originality.

Whereas Shōichi Yui conceived of national style as a universal trend, emanating naturally from the global movements toward postcolonial liberation and ethnic pride, others regarded it as the artist's fundamental responsibility. Keyboardist Masahiko Satō exhorted Japanese musicians to "create a music that only Japanese can play."[45] His joint performance workshop with *shakuhachi* player Hōzan Yamamoto, entitled "Opening Untrodden Space," (August 1970), was an attempt to "produce an untrodden space, which no one but Japanese musicians can discover." What is striking about this concept is its explicitly exclusionary agenda; the goal was a music that "only Japanese can play," that "foreigners cannot imitate." Whither the "universal language"?

Revolutions are perhaps necessarily exclusionary, and what Japanese jazz artists were speaking of was nothing short of revolutionary. They sought no less than the articulation of new aesthetic standards that would legitimate their music without reference to an American model. After decades of playing by (and, in their own judgment, too often failing to meet) the aesthetic principles established and enshrined by the American jazz pantheon, Japanese jazz artists and aficionados were attempting to formulate a new aesthetic for judging their own work, which did not entail comparing it with American art.

This attempt at an aesthetic revolution also entailed, in part, a much more profound quest for a deeply expressive, *Japanese* artistic language analogous to the blues. Well versed in the work of Amiri Baraka (whose *Blues People*, written under the name LeRoi Jones, remains the pivotal black nationalist statement on jazz and blues) and the emerging literature on blues as the basic primary expression of black Americans, Japanese musicians and aficionados in the late 1960s sought a parallel vocabulary that matched the richness they found in the blues, which communicated a singular Japanese experience the way the blues was said to communicate a singular African-American experience, and on which they could base their future artistic explorations. The idea of a Japanese analogue to the blues was made to seem plausible through flexible ideologies of ethnic affinity and difference. Particularly during this period in which Japanese jazz aficionados identified themselves with radical, antiwar, and pro-civil rights politics, some commentators argued for the basic affinities of the freedom-seeking "colored races" against the colonizing "white race." Japanese and black Americans, Yui contended, shared a history of cultural humiliation in the face of white Euroamerican accomplishments: "While we were catching up with European cultures," he said at a 1971 conference in Warsaw,

> we were astonished at everything being upside-down from ours. We were ashamed, because we realized we had lived in the least advanced country for many years. Then what we did was to throw away our traditional customs and instead we absorbed more advanced customs from overseas.
>
> This reminds me of the Negro culture in the United States. Just two years after the Negro slaves were emancipated in the United States, Emperor Meiji became the Emperor of Japan. So, the Japanese people and Black American people started for the New World, of which they never knew, almost at the same time. In their musical tradition, both did not have a harmony conception. Moreover, the music they had was on the pentatonic scale. . . . And those two peoples had to abandon their old traditions, of which they were ashamed when they compared them to the old European traditions. Subconsciously, this historical coincidence has induced us to feel some affinities between the Japanese and American Black people.
>
> That is why we Japanese can easily understand everything the American Black people are doing.[46]

Japanese jazz, thus conceived, became the "yellow man's cry" against white American domination.

If Japanese—"yellow Negroes" in the words of the eminent poet Shūji Terayama (1935–1983)[47]—had a natural affinity and a shared history of white oppression with other "colored" peoples, then did it not stand to reason that "yellow Negroes" had a deep emotive vocabulary analogous to African American blues, an artistic language of resistance to the subsuming and homogenizing forces of white cultural imperialism? Pianist Yōsuke Yamashita's famous "blue note studies" in the late 1960s stemmed in part from this desire to discover and develop a basic emotive vocabulary that would render the American standards of authenticity superfluous. Success in such a quest promised finally to bring down the persistent referential aesthetic, by which the jazz performed by Japanese was said to consistently fail to meet the standards set by Americans. Rather than abrogate the idea of authenticity completely, advocates of Japanese jazz sought to erect a new standard, one which no one but ethnic Japanese could meet or fully appreciate. Rather than challenge the idea of ethnically determined legitimacy, the Japanese jazz movement adopted its assumptions and used them to its advantage.

A great deal of creative energy was expended in this quest, not to mention some adventurous music. Yet today, while there is considerable respect for the "progress" that Japanese jazz artists supposedly made in the 1960s, the authenticity of the music of that period is questioned in Japan because it is *not enough like American jazz*. Most Japanese artists and fans I spoke with regard the use of Japanese instruments, melodic scales, or folk songs as an annoying contrivance that is too distant from the "black" soul of the music. The marketplace reflects this prejudice: virtually all the classic recordings from the heyday of "neonationalist" jazz, such as Togashi's *We Now Create* and Satō's *Palladium*, are now out of print and unavailable. The jazz market today thrives on reissues of American recordings and on the proselytizing efforts by Japan's "young lions," the so-called Jazz Restoration in Japan, to return to the classic sounds and aesthetic principles of American jazz from the 1950s and 1960s. This is partially due to the fact that nostalgia is profitable in the jazz market in particular and in Japan's popular culture in general, but it is also because Japanese jazz musicians have yet to convince purity-minded audiences in their home country that their music is as legitimate as any American's.

The Failure of Authenticating Strategies

By any standard, we must conclude that strategies of authentication have failed to convince the majority of Japanese artists and aficionados that their music is the real thing. In the average jazz fan's imagination, Japan remains a voracious consumer of creative jazz, but hardly a producer of such. Japanese, the conventional wisdom goes, are thoroughly well-informed about jazz and provide enviable support for the music. But they just can't play it right. The following entry from Kōdansha's *Japan: An Illustrated Encyclopedia* neatly sums up the stereotypes and prejudices with which many view jazz in Japan:

> One Western genre that has firmly established itself within the Japanese music scene is jazz. Japan is home to an important and highly profitable market for jazz, boasting numerous clubs, some of the best jazz magazines in the world, and a steady core of avid fans. Major international

> jazz figures play extensively in Japan's clubs and concert halls. The flourishing scene has also produced native musicians like saxophonist Watanabe Sadao, regarded as the patriarch of Japanese jazz, Hino Terumasa, and Watanabe Kazumi, and jazz fusion groups Casiopea and T Square. Yet while many of Japan's jazz artists display marvelous technical ability, few display any real originality.[48]

This treatment is so full of clichés that it barely merits commentary. But what it lacks in descriptive veracity is compensated for by the bald-faced insight it gives us into common thoughts about jazz in Japan. When we read it we start to understand why Japanese artists have felt the need to authenticate Japanese jazz. We understand why the committed musician had to go to Shanghai in the 1930s, or to Boston's Berklee School of Music in the 1980s and 1990s, to earn a reputation as a legitimate jazz artist. We start to see why "young Japanese musicians leave the richest jazz market in the world—Japan—to find work and to study in America," and why, in the view of Japanese audiences, jazz does not "seem 'authentic' unless it's played by Americans." And we grasp the "craze . . . for performers from the United States, who therefore naturally demand the highest prices they can get—much more, 'sometimes ten times as much,' than most could command in their own home country—and thereby drain the coffers of performance and recording fees that might go to Japanese musicians."[49] But does this mentality explain why Japanese artists perpetually suffer the indignity of being considered the "Japanese version" of American artists? "They're [the jazz critics] always calling some Japanese musician the 'Japanese Coltrane' or the 'Japanese Miles Davis,'" pianist Kichirō Sugino has said. "They won't let the young people who *are* creating original music have any credit for it."[50] Why are the contributions of Japanese artists still largely unacknowledged, by their audiences *and* by themselves?

The short answer to these questions is "race thinking": powerful, socially constructed beliefs in national character and in the racial or ethnic "ownership" of culture. Rudinow identifies two arguments that represent race thinking as applied to blues and jazz: the proprietary argument and the experiential access argument. The proprietary argument allegedly rectifies what Baraka called "The Great Music Robbery."[51] The proprietary argument claims that the music belongs "to the African-American community and that when white people undertake to perform the blues they misappropriate the cultural heritage and intellectual property of African-Americans. . . ." The experiential access argument says "in effect that one cannot understand the blues or authentically express oneself in the blues unless one knows what it's like to live as a black person in America, and one cannot know [this] without being one. . . . Members of other communities may take an interest in this experience and even empathize with it, but they have no direct access to the experience and therefore cannot fully comprehend or express it."[52] For many people, this experiential access argument excludes anyone who does not have firsthand knowledge of what it is like to be black in America. "Never was a white man had the blues," Leadbelly is quoted as saying, "'cause nothin' to worry about."[53] Few who have engaged in this debate have thought in terms other than black and white (literally and figuratively), but we may assume from the premises of both the proprietary and the experiential access arguments that if white Americans can't play the blues, Japanese have no hope.

There is another stereotype or example of race thinking that inhibits the authentication of jazz by Japanese: the persistent illusion that Japan is a "nation of imitators," psychologically incapable of originality and socialized to devalue creativity. "In our models of cultural exchange," Ian Littlewood muses, "the West figures as virile originator, Japan as wily imitator."[54] It is a stereotype in which far too many Japanese themselves believe, one that hardly does justice to the artistic legacies of Murasaki Shikibu, Chikamatsu Monzaemon, Akira Kurosawa, Sesshū, Yasunari Kawabata, Bashō, and Toshiko Akiyoshi. It is, in fact, a stereotype of relatively recent pedigree, rooted in the Japanese state's persistent efforts since the mid-nineteenth century to achieve parity with Western nations by studying and following their examples. The "imitator" stereotype remains powerful today; it lies at the heart of frictions between Japan and the United States over technology transfers, and underlies calls for national education reform. It also "explains" why Japan's most accomplished and popular jazz artists are identified as the "Japanese version" of someone else.

The "nation of imitators" is an offensive stereotype, but it is rooted in some very concrete historical and social realities: the consensual value of conformity in Japan; the education system's willful failure to encourage critical thinking; the historical legacy of centuries of "cultural borrowing"; and the primacy of the "school" in Japan's artistic and musical tradition. "The West believes in the personality," musicologist Eta Harich-Schneider has written, "[t]he East believes in the school. A work of art is evaluated in the West by its degree of independence and originality; in the East as a perfect specimen of a type." To achieve the aesthetic ideal of "a perfect specimen of a type," music education (including the Suzuki violin method) has for centuries focused on mastery of *kata* (form), which leads to the pupil's understanding of the internal principles.[55]

Harich-Schneider's formulation is oversimplified at best, glossing over the fact that Western aesthetic *practice* (if not theory) often rewards formula or technical virtuosity at the expense of artistic "originality" or "soul." "Originality" and "soul" themselves are problematic and difficult to judge. What some listeners regard as "original" may be little more than the manipulation of old tricks in new ways. Even the most "original" of jazz artists betray the influence of *somebody* in their own work, and all "original" jazz artists are recognizable for melodic and rhythmic signatures on which they fall back at every performance. Moreover, the differences between Japan's artistic traditions and those of the jazz world appear even less significant when one considers that jazz is subdivided into stylistic schools or sects, founded by a few exceptional musicians whom all other musicians within the style revere; and that, especially since the 1980s, all young jazz artists are expected to be familiar with and master the musical principles of Charlie Parker, Duke Ellington, Thelonious Monk, and a few select others. Mastery of the now-mainstream language of bebop is considered essential before a musician can legitimately explore alternative avenues of expression.

This is, in reality, not much less constricting than the traditional music training regimen in Japan. In both cases, there are masters, there are students, there are established curricula and practice procedures, and there are expectations of individual achievement within those boundaries. Jazz musicians, no more and no less than musicians in other traditions, face the paradox of appearing to be in "the tradition" while still doing "their own thing." When one considers the realities behind the stereotypes, it seems indefensible for so many critics to argue that the notion of a "'perfect' way of doing things," conducive to the development of flawless technique and formula rather than of individual expression and novelty, is peculiar to Japanese society. Tom Pierson, a pianist and composer who abandoned New York City for the safer streets of Tokyo in 1991, turns the stereotype of the "imitative" Japanese on its head in his critique of America's neoconservative Young Lions ("kittens," in his words): he calls Wynton Marsalis "a Japanese jazzman, in the worst sense of the word."

Figure 2.2 **Aki Takase's Oriental Express at Jazz Inn Lovely in Nagoya, July 23, 1994. The musicians are trombonist Hiroshi Iaya, Aki Takase on piano, and Nobuyoshi Ino on bass.**

In sum, one reason that Japanese jazz artists are not regarded (in some cases, do not regard *themselves*) as "authentic" is that they are thought to be "imitators" rather than "innovators." Masahiko Satō recalls a time in the late 1950s and early 1960s when "Japanese jazzmen were pretending to be someone else [and] [t]here was no shame in it," when Japanese musicians meeting for the first time asked one another, "By the way, who are you imitating?"[56] Takashi Yasumi, a jazz pianist who played in the University of Minnesota Jazz Band and currently works for the Japan-United States Education Commission, regards his own improvisations as nothing more than an assemblage of licks he has heard by American artists. He admits to a certain prejudice against Japanese jazz artists, claiming that they have masterly technique but express themselves poorly through improvisation.

Yasumi's prejudice against native artists is hardly unique, judging from the number of times even the most generous and cooperative of my informants laughed at the very idea of an American historian studying jazz in Japan. They often asked, "Why did you go to the trouble of coming *here* to study jazz, when you're from the homeland of jazz [*jazz no honba*]?" Most believe that Japanese have contributed nothing of substance to the music and therefore merit little attention, especially from an American. In the end, the principal reason for this deeply ingrained "authenticity complex" is the persistent system of beliefs in the fundamental and immutable racial and ethnic differences between Japanese and Americans. It is an intractable mentality equating authentic jazz with American nationality and African descent, and convincing Japanese musicians that their own ethnonational identity impedes their potential as innovative, authentic jazz artists.

****

In closing, as someone who appreciates and performs music, I admit to having my own very strong aesthetic convictions and opinions of what is legitimate or authentic in art. My experiences—listening to and talking with Japanese jazz artists and aficionados—lead me to the conviction that, to the extent that the concept of authenticity has any value at all, ethnicity has no place in determining it. This may seem a rather noncontroversial position, but in this age of identity politics and resurgent ethnic nationalism (as if it ever went away), debates over authenticity and cultural identity are more intense than ever. In the jazz world, in particular, there is an obsession with identifying and filtering the "pure" or "authentic" core of the music from the eclectic contexts in which it was actually created. (Yes, it may be a crime that Paul Whiteman was once known as the "King of Jazz," but how can we deny his overwhelming influence in the 1920s and 1930s?) More often than not, those artificial boundaries correspond closely to markers of ethnic difference. It is possible to acknowledge the African American roots of jazz and blues music, and even to argue that the most influential and imposing artistic legacies are those of black artists, and yet still to reject the widely held notion that authenticity is a virtue peculiar to those of African ancestry. One historical crime—robbing black artists of their rightful profits and credit for creating this music—does not justify another: denying the significance of nonblack artists in shaping jazz. Authenticity as a concept renders the idea of jazz as "universal language" into a meaningless cliché, for it merely serves to reinforce ideologies of ethnic difference.

My feeling is that the personal experiences, discipline, depth of feeling, imagination, and artistic vision of the individual musician—however complex and difficult to gauge they may be—should be the only real criteria for judging his or her art. Those who delight in identifying music based on the ethnicity of its producers—black, white, Japanese, or otherwise—are well advised to remember Duke Ellington's famous quote: "There are only two kinds of music, good and bad." By Ellington's standards, some of the best, and most authentic, music on the planet right now is being made in Japan, by groups such as Stir Up!, Fumio Itabashi's Mix Dynamite, Aki Takase's Oriental Express, and others. Their music is significant not because it is Japanese, black, white, or anything other than original in conception and lovely in execution. Jazz can only become a "universal language" when we abandon our current conceptions of authenticity. Jazz can represent the similarities in human experience as well as the differences. That is why it matters.

Interviews

Toshiko Akiyoshi, February 5, 1996.
Nobuo Hara and Aiko Tsukahara, April 11, 1995.
Tomonao Hara, October 20, 1994.
Sachi Hayasaka and Toshiki Nagata, July 15, 1994.
Issei Igarashi, July 23, 1994.
Jirō Inagaki and Masayuki Inagaki, April 12, 1995.
Teruo Isono, May 2, 1995.
Fumio Itabashi, August 20, 1994.
Hideto Kanai, April 27, 1995.
Yasunori Kaneko, October 9, 1994.
Satoru Oda, January 14, 1995.
Tom Pierson, September 15, 1994.
Masahisa Segawa, August 22, 1994.
Hitomi Sugiura and Shūichi Sugiura, July 20, 1994.
Takashi Yasumi, July 6, 1994.
Shōichi Yui, September 12, 1994.

Discography

1. Dixie Kings, The. *Dikishii Nippon min'yō.* King SKG-27, 1963.
2. Hara, Nobuo, and Sharps and Flats. *Sharps and Flats in Newport.* Nippon Columbia XMS-10019, 1969.
3. Ryōichi Hattori. "Wakare no burūsu." Nippon Columbia 29834A, 1937.
4. Ryōichi Hattori. "Yamadera no oshō-san." Nippon Columbia 29300A, 1937.
5. Inomata Takeshi and the Westliners, Sawada Shungo's Double Beats, and the Fujita Masaaki Quintet. *Jazz of the Four Seasons.* Polydor SLJ-59, 1964.
6. Ono Shigenori and the Blue Coats. *Guren Mirā sutairu—Nippon no mūdo.* Nippon Victor SJL-5088, 1964.
7. Ono Shigenori and the Blue Coats. *Guren Mirā sutairu ni yoru Nippon no senritsu.* Nippon Columbia PS-5070, 1965.
8. Yoshiko Sakai and the Victor All-Stars. *Nihon min'yō wo jazu de.* Nippon Victor LV 293, 1962.

9. Masahiko Satō. *Palladium*. Toshiba Express EP-8004, 1969.
10. Tony Scott. *Music for Zen Meditation*. Verve V6–8634; CD reissue 817209, 1964.
11. Hideo Shiraki. Quintet. *Japan Meets Jazz*. Saba/MPS 15065ST (West Germany). *Matsuri no gensō—Berurin no Shiraki Hideo kuintetto*. MPS/Columbia Y5–2320–MP and Teichiku SL3002 (Japan), 1968.
12. Masahiko Togashi. *We Now Create*. Nippon Victor SMJX-10065, 1969.
13. Various Artists. *Pioneers of Japanese Jazz*. King KICJ 192, 1994.
14. Hōzan Yamamoto, with Hara Nobuo. *New Jazz in Japan*. Nippon Columbia YS-10022, 1968.
15. Hōzan Yamamoto. *Beautiful Bamboo Flute*. Philips FX-8510, 1971.
16. Hōzan Yamamoto, and Kikuchi Masabumi. *Ginkai*. Philips BT-5319, 1970.
17. Yōsuke Yamashita. *Mokujiki*. Nippon Victor VICJ-23009, 1970.
18. Yōsuke Yamashita. *Dancing Kojiki*. Sadaneri Shobō DANC-3, 1995.
19. Toshiko Yonekawa and Okuda Munehiro's Blue Sky Orchestra. *O-koto no jazu*, 1958.

Notes

1. Nat Hentoff, *The Jazz Life* (New York: Dial, 1961), p. 73.

2. H. D. Harootunian, "America's Japan/Japan's Japan." In *Japan in the World,* eds. Masao Miyoshi and H. D. Harootunian (Durham, NC: Duke University Press, 1993), pp. 199–200.

3. See Joseph J. Tobin, *Re-Made in Japan, Everyday Life and Consumer Taste in a Changing Society* (New Haven, CT: Yale University Press, 1992).

4. Richard C. Kraus challenges the conceit that Western music possesses a "universal" appeal, and argues that its "considerable aesthetic attractions are reinforced by the West's political and economic domination of the world." See Richard C. Kraus, *Pianos and Politics in China, Middle-Class Ambitions and the Struggle Over Western Music* (New York: Oxford University Press, 1989), pp. 191–195.

5. I believe similar assertions could be made with regard to subcultures that embrace rockabilly, blues, hip-hop, folk, reggae, and other "ethnic" music.

6. See Michael H. Kater, *Different Drummers: Jazz in the Culture of Nazi Germany* (New York: Oxford University Press, 1992); Paul Oliver, "Jazz Is Where You Find It: The European Experience of Jazz." In *Superculture: American Popular Culture and Europe*, ed. C. W. E. Bigsby (London: Paul Elek, 1975); Frederick S. Starr, *Red and Hot: The Fate of Jazz in the Soviet Union,* rev. ed. (New York: Limelight, 1994); Taylor E. Atkins, "The War on Jazz, or Jazz Goes to War: Toward a New Cultural Order in Wartime Japan." In *positions: east asia cultures critique,* vol. 6, no. 2 (Fall 1998), pp. 345–392.

7. Hisaaki Yamanouchi, *The Search for Authenticity in Modern Japanese Literature* (Cambridge, England: Cambridge University Press, 1978), p. 4.

8. Drummer Shimizu Jun frankly recounted his own search for authenticity through drugs and living with black Americans, "I fell into the illusion that I, too, could become [black musicians'] equal as a player. . . . I set out to immerse myself among the first-class jazzmen through drugs. . . . Another appeal [of drugs] was that no matter how many hours I played I never felt tired. . . . When I was doing drugs, ideas I that couldn't believe were mine would gush out like a fountain. Perhaps for

a moment, [drugs] liberated [me to overcome] the inadequacies of feeling and technique which usually suppressed my subconscious rhythmic sense." Quoted in Shūji Terayama and Reiko Yugawa, eds., *Jazu wo tanoshimu hon* (Tokyo: Kubo Shoten, 1961), pp. 244–251.

9. While some use the term "Japanese jazz" to refer to jazz performed by Japanese, I use it specifically to designate the concept of a jazz that is uniquely and quintessentially Japanese.

10. Edward M. Bruner, "Abraham Lincoln as Authentic Reproduction: A Critique of Postmodernism," *American Anthropologist,* 96: 2 (1994), pp. 399–400.

11. Irving Louis Horowitz, "Authenticity and Originality in Jazz: Toward a Paradigm in the Sociology of Music," *Journal of Jazz Studies* 1:1 (1973), pp. 57–58.

12. John Gennari, "Jazz Criticism: Its Development and Ideologies," *Black American Literature Forum* 25 (1991), p. 466.

13. Joel Rudinow, "Race, Ethnicity, Expressive Authenticity: Can White People Sing the Blues?" *Journal of Aesthetics and Art Criticism* 52:1 (1994), p. 127.

14. Ibid.

15. Gene Lees, *Cats of Any Color: Jazz Black and White* (New York: Oxford University Press, 1994), p. 193.

16. Ralph J. Gleason, "Can the White Man Sing the Blues?" *Jazz and Pop (*August 1968), p. 28.

17. Milton "Mezz" Mezzrow and Bernard Wolfe, *Really the Blues* (New York: Random House, 1973), p. 18.

18. Ibid., p. 146.

19. Ibid., pp. 153–154.

20. Quoted in Lees, *Cats of Any Color,* p. 189. Gillespie's views are all the more significant because he was one of the pioneers of bebop, a musical revolution that many musicians, scholars, and critics (far too many, in fact, to cite comprehensively) have interpreted as a racially motivated attempt to "keep the white boys off the bandstand." Lees correctly points out, in *Cats of Any Color*, that: "To suggest that men of such genius would devote their energies and thought to so small and negative a purpose is a confession of ignorance. . . . It was not in the great and glorious heart of Dizzy Gillespie to do something so mean" (p. 218).

21. Ibid., p. 190.

22. Morgenstern and Shepp were both quoted in Dean Olser, "Jazz Musicians Discuss Racism in the Jazz World," *All Things Considered* (National Public Radio, January 10, 1996).

23. Bruce Ingram, "Frisco FMer Jazzes It Up with Live Broadcast to Japan" *Variety* (July 1, 1988), p. 45.

24. James T. Jones IV, "Racism and Jazz: Same as it Ever Was . . . or Worse?" *Jazz Times* (March 1995), pp. 55–56.

25. Peter N. Dale, in *The Myth of Japanese Uniqueness* (London: Croom Helm, 1986), points out three basic premises that underlie these widespread and persistent belief systems: "Firstly, they implicitly assume that the Japanese constitute a culturally and socially homogeneous racial entity, whose essence is virtually unchanged from prehistorical times down to the present day. Secondly, they presuppose that the Japanese differ radically from all other known peoples. Thirdly, they are consciously nationalistic, displaying a conceptual and procedural hostility to any mode of analysis which might be seen to derive from external, non-Japanese sources" (p. ii).

26. Tessa Morris-Suzuki, "The Invention and Reinvention of 'Japanese Culture,'" *Journal of Asian Studies* 54 (1995), p. 768; and Marilyn Ivy, *Discourses of the Vanishing, Modernity, Phantasm, Japan* (Chicago: University of Chicago Press, 1995), p. 4.

27. Quoted in Jones, "Racism and Jazz," p. 55.

28. Mezzrow and Wolfe, *Really the Blues,* p. 112.

29. Ichitarō Ōkura, "Nippon no biggo bando tenbō," *Swing Journal* (November 1959), p. 15. MacArthur's notorious remark was, "Measured by the standards of modern civilization, [the Japanese] would be like a boy of twelve as compared with our development of forty-five years." Quoted in Sheila K. Johnson, *American Attitudes toward Japan, 1941–1975* (Washington, DC: American Enterprise Institute for Public Policy Research, 1975), p. 52.

30. Hilary Tann, "Tradition and Renewal in the Music of Japan," *Perspectives of New Music* 27:2 (1989), p. 44.

31. Judith Ann Herd, "The Neonationalist Movement, Origins of Japanese Contemporary Music," *Perspectives in New Music* 27:2 (1989), p. 120, 154; see also Thomas R. H. Havens, *Artist and Patron in Postwar Japan* (Princeton, NJ: Princeton University Press, 1982), p. 16.

32. Elizabeth Ann Sesler-Beckman, *Jazz Is My Native Language: A Study of the Development of Jazz in Japan* (M.A. thesis, Tufts University, 1989), p. 95; emphasis in original.

33. Masahiko Togashi, "Nippon no jazutte nan darō," *Swing Journal* (April 1975), pp. 114–115.

34. Masahiko Togashi, "Hatashite donaki tabitachi ni mukete," *Jazu hihyō* 17 (1974), p. 125.

35. Masahiko Togashi, "Nippon no jazutte nan darō," p. 115.

36. I am often asked if I tested the Sugiuras on this point. I declined to do so, believing that such a test would not really prove anything. The ideology that conditions their assumptions is what I find interesting. Proving their "ethnic listening" skills right or wrong would not serve the aims of this study.

37. Ryōichi Hattori, *Boku no ongaku jinsei* (Tokyo: Chūō Bungeisha, 1983), p. 140.

38. Ibid., p. 149.

39. Quoted in Dave Jampel, "Japanese Jazzmen Invading Newport, Bandleader Nobuo Hara Seeks 'Moment of Truth' at Wein's Fest Classic," *Variety* (June 14, 1967), p. 50.

40. Shōichi Yui, "Nipponteki jazu," *Jazu hihyō* 6 (1969), pp. 28–29.

41. Yōzō Iwanami et al., "Zadankai, 'Nippon no jazu' wo kataru," *'69 All Japan Jazz Festival—19th Swing Journal Poll Winners* (Tokyo: Swing Journal, 1969), pp. 25–28.

42. Ikuma Dan, "The Influence of Japanese Traditional Music on the Development of Western Music in Japan," *Transactions of the Asiatic Society of Japan*, 3d series, vol. 8 (1961), p. 201.

43. Ibid., pp. 216–217.

44. Quoted in Havens, *Artist and Patron in Postwar Japan*, pp. 183–184.

45. Quoted in Kiyoshi Koyama, "Zoku, Nippon no jazu wo kangaeru," *Swing Journal* (November 1968), p. 71; and Kiyoshi Koyama, "Shinshun tokubetsu zadankai—1970 nendai no jazu wo kataru," *Swing Journal* (January 1970), p. 93.

46. Yui, "Jazz in Japan," pp. 43–44.

47. Shōichi Yui et al., "Wareware ni totte jazu to wa nanika?" *Ongaku geijutsu* (August 1968), p. 26.

48. Keith Cahoon, "Popular Music in Japan," *Japan: An Illustrated Encyclopedia* (Tokyo: Kōdansha Ltd., 1993), p. 1287.

49. "Jazz in Japan, Have You Heard the Latest?" *Japan Update* 12 (1989), p. 21.

50. Quoted in "Jazz in Japan, Have You Heard the Latest?" p. 21.

51. Baraka uses the "Great Music Robbery" to describe "the 'cover' and 'cooperation' relationship of the [white] bourgeoisie to black music and to black culture in general. . . . [T]he half-hip white, certainly as the twentieth century has unrolled, appropriates black style as an *attribute*. . . . We are now told magnanimously that R&B *influenced* Rock and Roll. Whew! My friends, Rock and Roll *is* Rhythm and Blues! We realize Fats Domino, Chuck Berry, etc., could never get as rich and famous as Elvis Presley and company who are written about as if they had actually *originated* something rather than copied." Quoted in Amiri Baraka, "The Great Music Robbery," *The Music: Reflections on Jazz and Blues* (New York: Morrow, 1987), pp. 328–330.

52. Rudinow, "Race, Ethnicity, Expressive Authenticity," pp. 132–133.

53. Quoted in Gleason, "Can the White Man Sing the Blues?" p. 28.

54. Ian Littlewood, *The Idea of Japan, Western Images, Western Myths* (Chicago: Ivan R. Dee, 1996), p. 96.

55. Eta Harich-Schneider, *A History of Japanese Music* (London, Oxford University Press, 1973), pp. 547–548; and William P. Malm, "Layers of Modern Music and Japan," *Asian Music* 4:2 (1973), p. 3.

56. Quoted in John Schofield, "Pianist Infuses Jazz with Japanese Spirit," *Wall Street Journal* (October 8, 1991), p. A20.

3

The Marketing of Tears

Consuming Emotions in Japanese Popular Song

Christine R. Yano

Tears—lovers parting, longing for home, broken hearts. These images may be found in popular songs around the world. In Japan, those tears form the nucleus of *enka,* the popular ballads which have been dubbed the heart and soul of Japan. Originating in the early twentieth century and continuing to be newly created and appreciated today, enka dwell on the melodramatic, the maudlin, and the sentimental. Combining Western instruments with Japanese scales and vocal techniques, enka sound continually old; a 1993 hit is easily mistaken for a 1953 one. What helps erase the gap is not only the sounds, but also the sights and, more importantly, the sentiments of the genre. Amid the tumult and complexity of today's Japan, as the nation wrestles with scandal, recession, and natural disaster, these affairs of the heart dredged up from a recreated past seem wonderfully simple, direct, and elemental. What ties a listener to them is not so much a melody or a turn of phrase as the baring of the heart, the private made public. In the large commercial industry that is Japan's music business, enka produce tears for sale.[1]

I chose to study enka from among the various genres of Japanese popular music for two reasons. First, emotions in enka run particularly high. Enka are a form of *naki-bushi* (crying songs), songs whose merit rests upon eliciting tears. This chapter explores those tears, analyzing who does the crying, why, and to what commercial or public gain.

Second, more than any other popular song genre in Japan, enka has been dubbed the national music. Both within and outside the music industry, the genre's reputation as *Nihon no uta* (song of Japan), as *dentō no oto* (the sound of Japanese tradition), and as an expression of *Nihonjin no kokoro* (the heart and soul of the Japanese), thrusts enka into the spotlight of what it means to be Japanese. According to enka's producers as well as its consumers, the emotions in enka are characteristically Japanese, drawing upon a long history of tear-drenched sleeves. The degree to which enka's tears are unique may be debatable, but it is clear that the enka has become part of Japan's collective imagination and historical memory. Enka is a story Japanese tell about themselves to themselves.

Tears flow in enka for two primary reasons: failed romance and longing for home.[2] This essay focuses mainly on romance enka, since these constitute the majority of enka songs today. Of the 115 songs from the 1950s to 1990s that were analyzed in this study (selected from among current playlists, songbooks, and popularity charts), approximately 80 percent sing of failed romance. We begin with a look at the consumers of enka and then discuss the many conventions that characterize the creation, performance, and promotion of enka music. Finally we turn to the emotions conveyed in enka lyrics, examining the appeal of this music and what it reveals about traditional ideas about women, men, and romance in Japan.[3]

The Market for Tears

It has been said that the "old age" end of Japan's media market is characterized by the "consumption of tradition."[4] Indeed, enka fulfills this axiom; its fans tend to be older Japanese, many of whom claim to have turned to this music only after reaching the age of 40. The most common explanations given for this are that: (1) after having accrued a certain amount of life's experiences, one comes to appreciate the complexity and deep sadness of the songs, and (2) as a Japanese person gets older, it is "natural" that he or she turn increasingly to things Japanese, including enka. These explanations combine ideas of maturity, wisdom, and experience together with notions of racial and cultural identity and aesthetic preference. In doing so they suggest that those Japanese who do not like enka are either insufficiently experienced, particularly in life's hardships and sorrow, or not true to their innate Japaneseness. The Japaneseness of enka is also an attraction for enka's younger fans; a sushi apprentice in his twenties explained that he liked enka rather than rock music in the same way that he likes rice rather than bread.

It is widely believed that enka fans constitute not only a life-stage group—experienced, older Japanese—but also a class and regional group. According to its reputation, enka is most popular among blue-collar workers and in rural areas. This belief overlooks the many urban office workers who sing enka nightly in *karaoke* (sing-along) bars and "boxes" (private rental booths). But by maintaining a class and regional basis for its popularity, in myth if not in strict fact, enka becomes exotic. Blue-collar workers and rural areas are seen as an "other" Japan that coexists side by side with the white-collar, urban world of Japan's international achievements, and that represents a truer, more fundamental, indigenous Japanese culture.

Enka's detractors, on the other hand, who include intellectuals and younger people, dismiss this blue-collar, rural genre as an anachronism in modern Japan, and claim that its place in present-day society is not central but peripheral. Both sides to this argument place enka in the same spot, but they differ as to how realistic or meaningful that spot is in the Japan of the twenty-first century.

Patterns of Tears

Producing and marketing tears in Japan involves a considerable amount of repetition and redundancy. The expressions of enka—musical, textual, and visual—are constructed from set patterns and formulas, several of which are detailed below. Although formulaic expression is not uncommon in popular music industries throughout the world, it finds particular resonance in Japanese expressive forms through a concept known as *kata* (patterns), which refers to conventions that are used repeatedly in the production or practice of an art form. Kata is also employed in traditional Japanese arts such as martial arts, flower arrangement, tea ceremony, and *kabuki* (popular drama). It is thanks to kata that a new enka song sounds like, and in fact is, a recombination of old songs.

Kata are used on several levels in the production, performance, and marketing of enka. The music itself is produced by assembling new combinations from a well-established repertoire of musical formulas which includes characteristic scales, rhythms, guitar riffs, saxophone interludes, chord progressions, and *kobushi* (vibrato-like vocal ornamentations). Japanese electronic keyboard manufacturers such as Yamaha and Kawai even include an "enka" sound, alongside such standards as bossa nova, samba, ragtime, polka, hard rock, and reggae, in the menus of push-button musical styles built into their instruments. Listening to the results of selecting the enka button on an electronic keyboard is sadly disappointing, but a listener versed in the musical kata of enka need hear only a second or two of an introductory passage to recognize most songs of the genre.

Likewise, many songs are recognizably enka simply by their titles. Among the enka analyzed in this study, for example, the following dwell on drinking and sorrow: “Ame Sakaba” (Rainy Night at a Bar), “Ame Yo-zake” (Sake on a Rainy Night), “Izakaya” (A Bar), “Izakaya ‘Fujino’” (Bar ‘Fujino’), “Kanashii Sake” (Sorrowful Sake), “Omoide-Zake” (Sake of Memories), “Sakaba” (A Bar), “Sakaba Hitori” (Alone at a Bar), “Sake Yo!” (Sake!), “Suika” (Drunken Song), “Tejaku-zake” (Pouring Myself Sake), and “Yoi-gokoro” (Drunken Heart). Within Japan’s popular music world, songs with *sake* (liquor) or *sakaba* (bar) in their titles may be generally predicted to be enka.

The textual formulas used to create the lyrics of enka rely on a stock set of words, expressions, and scenarios. In my study of 115 songs, the word used most frequently is *yume* (dream), which appears 93 times in 59 songs. Other frequently sung enka words are *kokoro* (heart/soul), *namida* (tears), *sake*, *onna* (woman), and *koi* (love). These words, strung together, provide a broad and accurate overview of the enka world: A woman or man alone at a bar drinks in order to blunt the pain of heartache, and as the person drinks the lover’s face becomes visible, as if in a dream. Other scenarios that appear in enka with kata-like regularity include the whistle of a boat or train leaving and visions of a countryside hometown far away.

Japan’s enka singers have their own kata of stylistic flourishes, which they use in delivering these mostly sad songs. Not unlike the presentation of country and western music in the United States, professional enka performance has little room for spontaneous expression. Rather, every move is carefully choreographed, from the slow raising of microphone to mouth just before the first note is sung, to the smallest nuance of breathiness, the lifting of one heel, the facial distortion caused by emotions barely under control, and finally, in some cases, actual tears streaming down the singer’s face as the song reaches its climax. These tears—shed by the character in the song, the singer on stage, and, often, the listener in the audience—are no less heartfelt because they are a cliché. On the contrary, the very patternedness and predictability of lyr-

Figure 3.1 **One of today's most accomplished tear shedders: enka star Sayuri Ishikawa**

ics and performance make of the tears a waiting moment, artfully suspended and deeply felt.

Predictability and repetition are also heavily employed by enka's marketers to promote the songs. Enka audiences like to hear the familiar, rather than the novel, and so promoters saturate the market with repeated playings of a single song. At promotional events, a new song may be performed repeatedly in order to *mimi ni hairu* (get the song in the listeners' ears). At enka concerts, new songs are mixed together with old hits, inevitably including a singer's debut number—this sometimes more than twenty years after the song was popular. At karaoke gatherings and on radio programs, the enka sung and requested are just as likely to be old hits as current ones. These repeated listenings have the effect of erasing the intervening years, producing not just nostalgia for the past but also a comforting feeling that the past has never left, in spite of the outward changes surrounding everyone's lives.

Men, Women, and Romance in Enka

The stories that enka lyrics tell are among the most revealing kata of this musical genre, not necessarily of the reality of contemporary Japan

Figure 3.2 **Veteran enka star and singer of "Matsuri": Saburō Kitajima**

but of some traditional views on love, home, society, and the feelings and behavior of men and women in romantic relationships. But before turning to the mainstream romance enka, and lest the reader get the impression that enka offer nothing but teardrops and heartache, let us take a quick look at two common types of nonromance enka.

Some enka songs are celebrations of manhood, which is defined by hard work (often on ships in stormy seas), physical endurance, and spiritual connection to the gods. Sung by male stars such as Takashi Hosokawa and Saburō Kitajima, these songs feature faster tempos, greater rhythmic drive, and less refined vocal ornamentations than romance enka. The emotions surrounding this version of manhood mingle with sweat.

> Men bearing the festival palanquin, yes,
> On their shoulders were living life [to the fullest].
> God of the mountains, god of the seas,
> We truly thank you for this past year.

> The snow swirls around the young men in white loincloth.
> Festival! Festival! Festival! It's a festival for the year of
> abundance.
> These young men, permeated with the smell of the earth—
> Their hands are treasures. . . .
> Burn! The life of a man is one of sweat and tears.
> I am living to the fullest.
> This is a festival of Japan!
>
> "Matsuri"

Also common, and much less upbeat, are tearful enka of longing for one's hometown.

> This is the time of year when the snow begins to blow in
> Tsugaru, isn't it?
> Is everyone fine there? Is everything all right?
> I long for my furusato [hometown], where we sang the . . .
> childhood song—ah! . . .
> So many years have passed since I left there.
> Shall I go home? I want to go home.
>
> "Bōkyō Jonkara"

The vast majority of enka songs, however, deal with failed, or at least frustrated, romance. Further, it is most often the woman's romantic sorrows that enka sing of. Although there are also plenty of enka about men suffering the pain of a broken heart, women's songs outnumber men's by a large margin—over two to one in this study's sample.[5] Female singers also outnumber male singers; a 1991 listing of professional enka performers contains nearly twice as many women as men.[6] Statistics on enka consumption are more difficult to come by, but women far outnumber men in enka fan clubs. On the other hand, men dominate certain clearly targeted segments of the enka market, such as truck drivers, to whom middle-of-the-night enka radio programs cater.

The composers and lyricists of these tear-filled songs, as well as the industry's managers, record producers, and promoters, are overwhelmingly male. Thus it is men who create and shape these products, which somehow find resonance in the emotional lives of female singers and listeners. Interestingly, it is also quite common for male singers to sing women's songs, using female language forms and expressing the

Figure 3.3 **Enka superstar Misora Hibari (1937–1989), considered Japan's greatest postwar singer**

woman's feelings, and, conversely, for women to sing men's songs. Such cross-impersonation turns these gender-specific songs into a kind of kata that is accessible to and performable by members of either sex. It also suggests that while women and men are different, it is not unnatural for them to understand and even role-play each other.

The melodramatic stories that enka tell rest upon patterned structures of gender and romance. "She" is an object of beauty, passive in her attractiveness. "He," by contrast, is the viewer of beauty, active in shaping the world around him. Even though most enka revolve around the woman, this does not suggest that she is empowered. Usually, it is the man who controls the action, which often consists of leaving, while the woman passively accepts the unhappy hand that fate has dealt her. This man-woman dichotomy is sometimes complicated by a tension between the individual lovers and society, with the lovers being pulled by their passion into actions that violate public duties and values. To illustrate these patterns and ideas, let us take a brief tour of the world of enka romance through the lyrics of its songs.

One distinctive aspect of romance in enka is its ephemerality. Likened to bubbles on the surface of water, the short-lived brilliance of fireworks, or cherry blossom petals scattering in the wind, romance is pictured as poignant and beautiful in its very passing. At its extreme, romance may be as fleeting as a one-night stand.

> Even if we had but one night together,
> I was happy, because I loved you.
> "Koi Moyō"

The interpreter of this brief encounter is the woman, who fabricates lifelong happiness out of a one-night fling, love out of passion, commitment out of whim. For her, the single night becomes the basis of a love that will last forever. Though this love is built upon a fleeting moment of happiness, its beauty made all the more precious by its perishability, it also gains respect for its single-mindedness and its loyalty.

Another frequent feature of romance in enka is its reliance upon fate.

> We were connected even before we were born. . . .
> This is the red thread of fate that I feel.
> Therefore, we will be together until death.
> "Inochi Kurenai"

> Our love's destiny guides us,
> Bobbing and floating down the wintry river.
> "Shigure-gawa"

So often painted as a river, fate is an unchangeable force with a predetermined course governing life and love. Women and men can do no better than to follow, staying afloat, accepting its course as their own.

The ways in which men and women love are as patterned as the brevity of romance and its shaping by fate. In general, men love passionately and leave abruptly. Women, on the other hand, love loyally and longingly.

> For a man, love is a mere passing storm;
> But for a woman, love drifts on in a paper boat.
> "Kami no Fune"

> A man's love is the tenderness of a single night.
> But a woman's love lasts until the day of death.
> "Nakase Ame"

A woman stays, asking little else but to be in the presence of her man.

> When you are with me I need nothing else.
> I can live just by your smiling face.
> "Inochi Kurenai"

A woman clings.

> Even if I cling to you, begging you not to forsake me,
> Your flickering visage
> Grows distant, grows distant.
> "Nakase Ame"

A woman also waits.

> I wait for you, as does the primrose flower
> Wait for the seed to sprout.
> "Meoto-zaka"

By contrast, men leave.

> Without saying where he was going,
> He left aboard the ship at dawn.
> Even if I strain my eyes to see on board the
> rain-soaked deck,
> I cannot see a thing with my eyes full of tears.
> "Please, tell me why!"
> I call out, but the gong of the ship's departure drowns
> me out. . . .
> He left without telling me anything.
> Please, do not go, do not go,
> Do not go!
> "Namida no San-bashi"

Before men leave, they lie and cheat. Astonishingly, women still love.

> In your [man's] deceitful embrace I feel warm.
> "Amagi-goe"

> Even if a man's love is merely an act,
> A woman remains faithful to him.
> "Yoi-gokoro"

In many enka, romance fails because of the acts of the individuals involved. In other enka, however, it is society's norms, rules, and morals that keep men and women apart.

> Alone at a bar, I drink sake
> Which tastes like tears of parting.
> I drink, and long to forget his face, but
> When I drink, his visage floats before me in my glass. . . .
> I cry with bitterness toward a world
> which keeps me apart from the one I love.
> "Kanashii Sake"

The reasons for social censure include barriers of class and public mores. In many cases, romance in enka is illicit, with one or both lovers married to other people.

> Even if I love you, even if I love you . . .
> Ah, you are someone else's wife.
> Even if our love blooms red, it is a winter flower
> That blooms in sadness at the inn of sasanquas.
> "Sazanka no Yado"

Romance under these circumstances must be conducted in secret, shielded from the watchful guardians of public morals.

> In early spring we will follow the Yoshino route,
> Driven out of town because of our love. . . .
> Hiding from the eyes of the world, we will ply our boat. . . .
> Without knowing our destination, we find the ripples of
> Gossip harsh on our boat of leaves.
> "Kinokawa"

For a woman, parting is rapidly transformed into *miren,* or lingering affection, something rarely found in men.

> How are you, my dear?
> Day by day the cold weather gets worse.
> Although I will never see you wear it,
> I knit this sweater for you, enduring the cold.
> Is this the lingering affection of a woman's heart?
> I long for you from the inn in the north country.
>
> "Kita no Yado Kara"

> You, who have a wife,
> Become distant with me.
> This brings such pain to my heart which loves you.
> Rain, wash this pain away.
> Ah, but I cannot help this lingering affection.
> Sake on a rainy night.
>
> "Ame Yo-zake"

Such lingering affection, considered foolish yet inevitable, gives women a kind of moral currency as an exemplar of loyalty. *Miren* also lends the woman an exquisite and touching beauty, based on an aesthetic that values pathos and evanescence. Finally, the *miren*-bound woman exemplifies passivity; her heart will not let go, yet her role as a woman will not let her do anything about it.

This is a volatile mixture. In a tumult of emotion, she loves and hates at the same time.

> Loving you can also mean hating you.
>
> "Kizuna-gawa"

> I run my fingers through my hair . . .
> And when I look in the mirror, I start to cry.
> My feelings of love are matched by
> My growing feelings of hate.
> A flower is a flower, whether strewn about or freshly in bloom.
>
> "Midare-bana"

She longs, and in the longing kindles her own passion. At the mercy of forces beyond her control, her bodily desire ties itself into knots of powerlessness.

> My lips . . .
> Will not forgive you, yet long for you.
>
> "Koi-bune"

> I long to see you, I long to see you.
> I can see the boat [which will take me to you], but I cannot cross over to it.
>
> "Mujō no Umi"

> My body is so lonely, my body is so lonely.
>
> "Koi Banka"

It is little wonder that enka songs so often focus upon women, as women rest at the structural center of emotional turmoil. Tied down by cultural prescriptions of passivity, women inevitably end up bound for sorrow. They become avatars of suffering, their tears paraded as badges of sincerity, loyalty, and loss.

These images are expressed as well in advertisements for the songs and performances of female enka artists. Enka ads show women in unusual or dramatic poses far more often than they do men. Close-up photos are common, as are ads with women lying down, kneeling, or crouching. In one poster, a female singer is shot from directly above, lying with her long hair splayed and her kimono spread (though not revealing). These and like depictions sell women as victims, and their tears for the high drama and inner turmoil they represent.

A "Wet" Oasis in a "Dry" World

Enka presents a world in which Japanese are at their teariest, at their most vulnerable, and, according to some, at their most Japanese. These melodramatic packages of emotion may not reflect everyday life, but they are at least partly grounded in a common Japanese "heart" in which trial and tears are an inevitable part of life, bearing the unbearable is a virtue, and empathy for those who suffer and cry is humanizing and good.

Enka also provide a counterpoint to the "good wife, wise mother" model for women upon which the modern Japanese nation is said to have been built.[7] Most enka songs are dominated not by model wives and mothers, nor by male heroes, but by mistresses and bar hostesses. By painting sympathetic portraits of these women, and by creating tearful bonds of empathy between singer and audience, enka glorify actions—illicit love affairs, fleeing from social scorn, hiding from the eyes of the world—that run counter to idealizations of family, village, and nation. At the same time, however, these female antiheroes display some of the very same virtues that the traditional female model wears: sincerity, loyalty, and devotion.

The tears and suffering that enka glorifies—indeed almost celebrates—may also make more bearable the difficulties its fans face in their own real worlds. Whether in romance, family, or workplace, daily life is full of trials, barriers, and insults. In enka, as in contemporary life in Japan, one accepts the flow of fate, suffering, persevering, sometimes letting private tears flow unchecked.

More broadly, enka provides comforting reassurance that Japan has retained the capacity to cry amid what many perceive to be the "evils" of modern life: urban anonymity, electronic dehumanization, and waning loyalty. The concept of "wet" versus "dry" is frequently invoked in Japan to distinguish the modern, logical, and Western—considered "dry"—from the premodern, emotional, and Japanese—the "wet." Enka, with its plenitude of emotions, is unabashedly "wet." For its consumers, it provides precious redress for the "dryness" of technology-dominated, information-filled lives.

Notes

1. For more on the history of the enka genre, see Linda Fujie, "Popular Music," in *Handbook of Japanese Popular Culture*, ed. R. Powers and H. Kate (New York: Greenwood Press, 1989); Nobuo Komota, Yoshifumi Shimada, Tamotsu Yazawa, and Chiaki Yokozawa, *Nihon Ryūkōka-shi (Sengo-hen)* (Tokyo: Shakai Shisō-sha, 1980); and *Nihon Ryūkōka-shi (Senzen-hen)* (Tokyo: Shakai Shisō-sha, 1981).

2. For more on the history of tears in Japanese popular song, see Munesuke Mita, *Social Psychology of Modern Japan*, trans. Stephen Suloway (London: Kegan Paul International, 1992).

3. Field research for this paper was conducted in Tokyo from 1991 to 1993 with the support of a Japan Foundation Dissertation Fellowship and a Crown Prince Akihito Scholarship, for which I am extremely grateful. I would also like to acknowledge

the support I received from the Edwin O. Reischauer Institute of Japanese Studies at Harvard University during the period this paper was written. Many fond thanks go to Takie Lebra, Judith Herd, Harry Urata, and Hisashi Noda for their support and guidance.

4. Lise Skov and Brian Moeran, "Hiding in the Light: From Oshin to Yoshimoto Banana," in *Women, Media and Consumption in Japan,* ed. L. Skov and B. Moeran (Honolulu: University of Hawaii Press, 1995), p. 8.

5. The song's gendering is usually clear from the language used and the stereotypical situation. Of the 115 songs in this study, 76 are women's, 33 are men's, 4 are duets, and 2 are ambiguous.

6. Orikon Co., *Orikon Nenkan 1992 Nenban* (1992 Oricon Yearbook) (Tokyo: Oricon, 1992).

7. See Gail Lee Bernstein, ed., *Recreating Japanese Women, 1600–1945* (Berkeley: University of California Press, 1991).

4

Open Your File, Open Your Mind

Women, English, and Changing Roles and Voices in Japanese Pop Music

James Stanlaw

Introduction

These days in Japan, there is a new fad which is perhaps indicative of how relations between men and women are radically changing. At the trendy Juliana's nightclub in Tokyo—which boasts more than 50,000 patrons a month—dozens of scantily dressed Japanese women jump on stage and bump and grind to the latest hot dance music. Most of these young women are "Office Ladies" (OLs), the female clerical labor force. After work, they (literally) shed their company uniforms or office attire for the skimpy, tight-fitting skirts or leather bras of the bar scene. However, these "Juliana girls," as they are sometimes called, are not there to be picked up. Though no scientific survey has yet been conducted on this timely topic, it appears that nine times out of ten they go home alone. What the Juliana girls are there for is to be looked at and admired—but not to be touched. They tease the starry-eyed men looking at them on the dance floor or up on the stage, and they savor their sexual power. In the office, or at home, there is usually some male who has control over them in some fashion or other. Here, the meek and subservient OL blossoms, relishing her superiority and control—albeit temporary—over the admiring (and frustrated) men. Her taunts, in a sense, are her revenge.

In the world of Japanese popular music, a similar transformation seems to be taking place. Women are no longer bound by the whims of male songwriters or publicity handlers, and many are going off in new musical directions of their own. Woman pop vocalists are offering new ways of viewing the relationships between men and women, and in their songs are providing new, alternative models of how women can view themselves and behave.

This chapter presents some of these female vocalists and songwriters, and shows how they are singing in a new women's "voice." Established veterans as well as some newer performers are introduced, along with the reasons major changes in Japanese music are taking place. It is also argued that a linguistic device—the judicious use of both English words and English loanwords—contributes to the new style and rhetoric of female-produced pop music in Japan.[1]

The Face of Women in Japanese Popular Music

We begin our discussion of the role of women in Japanese popular music with a brief survey of the roots of popular music in Japan and the styles that are today considered to fall into the category "pop music." We then examine how "idol" singers are cultivated and promoted, focusing on two examples of best-selling favorites: Seiko Matsuda, perhaps the most successful woman in the idol genre, and PRINCESS PRINCESS, a rock band composed of young women that is especially popular among teenage girls.

Popular Music in Japan

Popular music in Japan is broadly labeled *kayōkyoku,* but "popular" music in any country is always hard to define. Rather than give a dictionary definition, it might be useful to mention some of the styles, traditions, and influences that have led to the development of kayōkyoku and the genres of kayōkyoku in which the female artists discussed in this chapter work in: "idol songs," "new music," theme songs, and Japanese rock.

Legend has it that *Amaterasu Ōmikami,* the ancient Sun Goddess of Japan, hid in a cave in a fit of rage and turned the world into darkness. To coax her out, the minor gods arranged for a performance of an erotic dance at the entrance. It apparently worked. *Saru-gaku* (literally, monkey music), a precursor of the famous Nō theater, is said to have come from this primordial dance. The "Juliana girls" can probably trace their roots back to this event as well.

Through the centuries, Japanese music split into two streams, the ancient court music of the royal classes known as *gagaku* (elegant music), which is played basically the same way today as it was in the past, and the folk music of the lower classes, known as *min'yō* or *zokkyoku*. The distinction between min'yō and zokkyoku is not always clear, but zokkyoku usually refers to earthy types of songs about lost love, good sex, or delicious *sake* (rice wine), while min'yō is more serious music on themes such as work and harvesting the fields.

During the Edo period, several narrative genres of singing became popular, including *naniwabushi* (solo storytelling and singing accompanied by the shamisen, a three-stringed Japanese instrument), which remains popular today. In the late nineteenth century, the mixing of Japanese folk songs with Western instrumentation and harmonies resulted in *enka* (a kind of "Japanese country and western") which is still very popular, especially among Japanese male office workers drinking in bars after work. Western music, of course, has been imported into Japan for 150 years, and by the 1920s popular music had become informally divided into two categories: music imported from America and Europe, and styles created in Japan. The name given to the latter was kayōkyoku. Today kayōkyoku, broadly defined, includes enka as well as "idol songs," "new music," theme songs, and Japanese rock. Idol songs are Western-style made-in-Japan versions of light rock, ballads, folk songs, or standards; this is the genre most popular among Japanese teenagers and young adults today. Older or more sophisticated audiences enjoy "new music," a style started in the late 1970s and noted for more complex melodies and harmonies, and more interesting and clever lyrics. Theme songs of all kinds—from films, television shows, and even TV commercials—are extremely popular in Japan, as is a wide variety of rock and roll, from local heavy metal to imported and imitated avant-garde styles.[2]

The Early Days of Japanese Female Pop Music: O-Nyanko Club and the Production Company System

In the area of mainstream Japanese popular music, until recently it was very difficult for women to become successful merely because they had talent. Usually they had to be "discovered," or "developed." The most common entry into the entertainment field for girls was through the production company system. A production company would take a young woman, sometimes no older than 12 or 13 years old, and groom her for potential stardom. She would be instructed not only in the proper way of singing a pop song, but also in how to laugh and smile, pose for a camera, and reply with innocuous banter to interviewers' questions. In short, she would be shown how to act innocent, yet sexy. Around her seventeenth birthday, her company would sponsor her debut, when she would release a demo tape and/or give her first public performance. Depending on her talent and appearance—but as often as not, also on proper backing and promotion—the budding starlet might become a new teenage idol singer—a young professional who, with some luck, would last past her twenty-first birthday. Like the seasons, hundreds of new idol singers, male and female, appear annually. The competition is fierce, and only a few become successful professional singers of note.

One example of the discovery method to stardom was the O-Nyanko Club (Kitten Club) of the late 1970s and 1980s. These high school and college girls, thought to be as pretty as little kittens, often appeared on evening television programs such as *All Night Fuji TV,* sitting around in bikinis or less. Instead of names they each had a number, and were referred to accordingly. They also sang, and one O-Nyanko Club song, "Sailor Fuku o Nugasanaide" (Don't Take Off My Sailor Suit), became quite famous, setting new lows for political incorrectness with its reference to the sailor-suit school uniform worn by Japanese junior high school students. By even the most generous of pre-1990s standards, the song's enjoyment-of-rape innuendos were degrading. Though this song was sung by women, using female language and speech styles, it was written by men, and it reveals several Japanese male sexual fantasies, such as sailor-suit fetishes and sexual encounters with very young women.[3]

Seiko Matsuda, the Classic Idol Singer

Probably the ultimate idol singer has been Seiko Matsuda, known simply as *Seiko-chan* (Little Seiko) to her fans.[4] There was no bigger singing sensation throughout the 1980s than Matsuda, though with her squeaky nasal voice and slightly off-key intonation, there were dozens of technically better vocalists. Also, like most idol singers, she did not write her own material. It was her presentation of self—her hesitant smile, big fawn eyes, and costuming—that primarily accounted for her huge popularity. (See Figure 17.1 in Chapter 17.) A typical Seiko-chan song was her 1983 hit, "Squall":

I wish shining days いつも夢に見ていたので
I wish shining eyes めぐり逢える素敵な瞳
Oh, squall こんな気持ちは
Oh, squall はじめてなの
焼けた肌つきさすように
Oh, squall 砂が燃えるわ
. . .

I wish shining days
I've always seen them in my dreams
I wish shining eyes
To come across beautiful eyes
Oh, squall, this kind of feeling
Oh, squall, it's my first time
Feels like it's piercing my sunburnt skin
Oh, squall, the sand is on fire
. . .

There is little to remark upon in this song, other than the abundant use of English loanwords and phrases, which is discussed below. The depth of feeling and range of emotion in idol songs typically does not venture much beyond the "girl meets boy and lives happily ever after" variety, though the inverse variant, "girl loses boy and will be miserable forever," is also occasionally found. Still, these songs are technically well produced, are arranged with a great deal of polish, and have catchy, if innocuous, melodies. Since the 1980s, there has been a gradual increase in the level of musical sophistication found in idol songs, one reason being the contributions of a number of extremely gifted songwriters and lyricists, such as Yumi Matsutōya (introduced below) and Mariya Takeuchi.

PRINCESS PRINCESS and a New Japanese Consumer Culture

Not all Japanese pop music is performed by solo idol singers, of course. There are groups of all kinds, and one of the most popular in recent memory is the five-member female rock band PRINCESS PRINCESS. By the mid-1990s, PRINCESS PRINCESS had been a teenage favorite for almost four years, the equivalent of several millennia according to the standards and fickle tastes of young Japanese pop music fans. It is often noted that modern Japanese culture is becoming more "Westernized," "bourgeois," and "consumer oriented." No song demonstrates this better than PRINCESS PRINCESS's megahit, "Diamonds." "Diamonds" is a meditation on life, love, and maturation, even though the members of the band are barely into their twenties. In the song, a young woman tells of growing up, of how music moves her, and how she longs to experience more than what she sees on television.

Dipping my bare feet in the cold fountain, I look up at the
  skyscrapers,
Just wearing clothes I like, I'm not doing anything bad.
Flying around the city with gold handlebars.
I'm hooked on having a good time.
I want to see scenes I can't know from TV.
Burn into my memory the beat of my heart the instant the
  [phonograph] needle hits the record.
That's a lovely collection, I want to add more and more to it.
Even if I'm sleepy, even if people don't like me, even as
  I get old, I can't stop.
They're diamonds! Ah . . .
Several scenes . . . Ah . . . it's hard to express . . . they're
  treasures!
What I felt then, ah . . . that premonition, it was the real thing.
Ah . . . it's that kind of feeling that's moving me now.

I fell in love several times, I even remember the order,
I got good at kissing, but
Whenever I make that first phone call, I still tremble.
Even buried under a mountain of presents, struggling to
  get free, I can't die yet.
I was born greedy. The party is just beginning.
Lock in the love potion that flows into my ears.
I won't sell this for any coin.
I won't give it to you even in exchange for love.
I fasten my seat belt, turn the propeller,

Figure 4.1 **PRINCESS PRINCESS**

> Give the earth a kick, I'm taking off!
> There are nights when I long to start over,
> To go back to when I was a child and didn't know anything.
> The feelings I felt then were the real thing.
> What moves me now are diamonds.

The singer's memories, visions, and feelings from the past are today's diamonds, gems that she still sees with crystal clarity and would not sell for love nor money. At the same time, though, as with Marilyn Monroe, diamonds turn out to be a girl's best friend, with today's material objects overshadowing more youthful visions. When she declares at the end that what moves her now are diamonds, she may be speaking quite literally: At the 1992 Japanese "Grammies," the manager of PRINCESS PRINCESS presented each member of the group with an expensive diamond necklace in honor of this song hitting number one on the charts.

New Faces and Sounds of the 1990s

The previous section may suggest that mainstream Japanese popular music is static and uncreative, with artists—especially female artists—performing mundane and superficial songs. For better or worse, however, the face of Japanese pop music has been altered rather drastically over the last decade, as simple-appearing idols performing banal and uninspired songs are gradually being replaced by more adventuresome and daring vocalists and songwriters. In this section we look at some of the ways that Japanese pop music is changing, and particularly at how women singers are involved in these innovations.

Yuki, of the Judy and Mary Band

The progressive group sound, represented by trios and other ensembles such as the Judy and Mary Band, Access, Mr. Children, the B'z, and Kome Kome Club, made a resurgence in the 1990s after lagging behind less daring 1980s groups such as Hikaru Genji and The Checkers (both now defunct). Many contemporary groups are unique, and some of the more interesting new music is being produced in this format.

The main songwriter and vocalist of the Judy and Mary Band, which had become quite popular in Japanese rock and alternative circles by the mid-1990s, is a young woman who calls herself simply Yuki. By all accounts, Yuki is a self-proclaimed tomboy, shedding most vestiges of traditional Japanese pop music femininity. In fact, she criticizes those women who use their feminine wiles to achieve what they want. In a 1995 interview in the pop music journal *GIRLPOP* titled "Onna no Buki!?" (Women's Weapons!?), she outlines some of her views of contemporary femininity.[5]

Yuki argues that women are the more natural—even animal-like—members of the human species. She argues that, in fact, contrary to popular belief, women are generally stronger than men; they are physically tough, and in spite of what you may hear in many contemporary songs, they handle failed relationships better than men do. When men reach their thirties or forties, they tend to become really immature; women, in contrast, become increasingly more realistic as they age. Enthusiastically, Yuki claims that "When the end of the world comes, the only survivors will be women and the cockroaches" (p. 27).Women can, and do, control men, who are really quite naive and simple-minded. But it is this naiveté and purity that

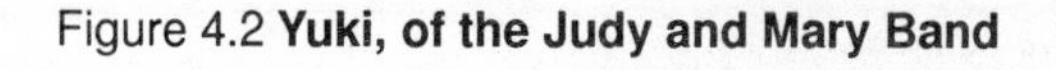

Figure 4.2 **Yuki, of the Judy and Mary Band**

actually makes men cute, giving them an almost helpless nature. When asked if she would be willing and able to support a husband, Yuki answers "Certainly!" without hesitation. Being competent, and feeding and taking care of men, is actually more feminine than saying you can't do anything.

Yuki gets really peeved by women who use tears to manipulate others. She herself is very emotional and sometimes cries, of course, but she never uses crying to obtain something. She feels that one of the major faults of males is that they cannot express themselves. Even if they do harbor deep feelings, they think it is necessary to hide them. Women, on the other hand, are comfortable with a wide range of emotions, and can express them in nondebilitating ways. Such emotions can be seen in this excerpt from the Yuki-penned song "Chiisana Koro Kara" (Ever Since I Was a Child).

小さな頃から　叱られた夜は
いつも　聞こえてきてた
あの小さなじゅもん
静かに流れる　時にいつの日か
あたしは眠れる森に連れ去られてた
小さな頃から　見えない力で
あたしを強くさせる
あの小さなじゅもん
たくさんの傷と争う夜にも
抱きしめるたびに　いつも震えて響く
. . .

Ever since I was a child, on nights when I was
scolded,
I could always hear it, that small *jumon*.
As time flowed quietly by, before I knew it
I had been taken to a forest where I could sleep.
Ever since I was a child, with its unseen power
It gives me strength, that small *jumon*.
Even on nights of struggling with many hurts
When I embrace it, its words echo, trembling.

This song offers more feeling than story. A *jumon* (spell or incantation) is often intoned when one wishes for something. When the young woman Yuki sings of feels unhàppy or afraid, she finds refuge in her jumon. Its comforting sound takes away her fear, makes her feel that she is not alone, and assures her that if she sleeps a little, morning will come again.

Miki Imai: Remaining Popular, Yet True to Oneself

Miki Imai is one of Japan's most popular female singers, especially among women up to the age of 30. Imai was never really an idol, even as a teenage star. Unlike many female singers, who seem to be naturally

Figure 4.3 **Miki Imai, as shown on the cover for the CD *flow into space***

photogenic and anxious to pose for the camera at any opportunity, Imai is camera shy. In fact, she does not have enough self-confidence to feel comfortable with color photos; most of her album portraits are in black and white. At the time of the release of her 1996 album *Mocha—Under a Full Moon,* she had been a star for over half a dozen years. Such a sustained success is unusual for a young singer. That she is popular among teenage women is also remarkable, as her music is not especially geared to them; she writes and sings in a more jazz-oriented "new wave" type of style that typically appeals to a more musically sophisticated adult listener.[6]

One of Imai's early hits was "Boogie Woogie Lonesome High Heel," a song about a woman—perhaps an OL—who decides to forget about all her troubles and just dance the night away. She spends the evening in a dance hall, exchanging jokes and bantering with men—"I'm hard to pick up, but go ahead and try!" The "Japanized" English title describes her feelings in a way that neither Japanese nor standard English could alone: "Boogie Woogie" covers dancing, and appeals to the Japanese ear, as similar onomatopoetic expressions abound in the Japanese language; "Lonesome" conveys the singer's mood of isolation; and "High Heel" alludes to the song's setting, a time and place—at night in a ballroom—where formal dress is the norm.

The range of expression and emotion that Imai puts in her songs strikes a chord in the hearts of younger and older women alike, which accounts for her popularity among different age groups. For example, "The Days I Spend with You," from her 1993 album *flow into space,* describes how the winter constellations looked so different when she was with her lover. She and he had talked about their dreams and encouraged each other in every way, but one night, with their relationship unraveling, he simply said good-bye. The world moves on, time flows, and she is alone:

. . .

あなたを愛し　あなたに抱かれ　あなたと笑い　あなたと泣いて
夜明けを歩き　明日へ願い　夢を見た

I loved you, I held you, I laughed with you, I cried
with you.
We walked in the dawn, we dreamed of tomorrow.

Miki Imai's popularity across generations shows that young Japanese women will buy something besides standard Japanese or American pop, and hints at a growing sophistication in taste and sense of self on the part of female Japanese singers and listeners alike.

Nana Konda, Idol Singer in Transition

Nana Kondo represents the new wave of pop idol singers of the 1990s. She made her formal debut in 1994 at the age of 20, and is more in the traditional idol vein, both in repertoire and in presentation, than Miki Imai. She and several other young singers are extending the boundaries of the idol category by foregoing the "cute" route to idol stardom and exploring alternative avenues to pop music success.

Kondo's 1996 album *N/S* (North/South) features her favorite song "+1" (pronounced "plus one"). She gave the song this name because she always tries to walk ahead and push herself. Kondo places great importance on doing things her own way, and at her own pace. She didn't call the song "+10" because she does not yet feel she is doing things perfectly; "+1," she says, is a good compromise between pushing herself to be better and demanding more than is possible at the moment. Kondo is also a self-described "optimist," in the sense of "doing her best." She advises her fans not to compare themselves to others, but to "Just compare yourself to the yourself of yesterday." She believes in reincarnation, and definitely wants to be reborn as a woman. She cherishes the special feelings that only women have, and encourages women to come to her concerts so they can share them together.[7]

The star production system still churns out a new crop of idol singers each year, but more and more young women, like Nana Kondo, are finding their own way with a new feeling of assurance. Part of this new confidence may come from the success of earlier idol singers, such as Seiko Matsuda, who have also forged their own trails and survived the pressures and difficulties of going against standard practice in Japan's tradition-bound pop music establishment.

Seiko Matsuda: Idol Singer Transformed

As mentioned above, Seiko Matsuda is one of the most popular idol singers of all time. She has been at the forefront of Japanese pop music for well over a decade and a half, which amounts to several lifetimes as the careers of idol singers are measured. Unlike most idols, who disappear into oblivion, or to the "sexy shot" back pages of men's magazines, Matsuda has taken great pains to reinvent herself and her image. As she was the exemplar of the cute and innocent idol figure of the 1980s, her transformation, and the independence she has gained from handlers and production companies, is remarkable.

In the late 1980s Matsuda tried the unthinkable—to gain exposure to an American audience. This has been notoriously difficult for Japanese pop artists to do, and only once has a Japanese song penetrated the thick-skinned American market. That was in 1963, when the late singer Kyū Sakamoto's tune "Ue o Muite Arukō" (I'll Walk Looking Up)—released in the United States under the silly title "Sukiyaki"—was a *Billboard* number one single for several weeks. Like Japanese baseball players, few Japanese pop artists have been able to successfully cross the wide cultural barrier of the Pacific.[8]

To help gain exposure and legitimacy with American listeners, Matsuda teamed up with Donnie Wahlberg and the New Kids on the Block, a Boston-based soft-rock group that was extremely popular with American teenagers in 1990. She recorded several singles and videos with the New Kids, but they themselves fizzled out at the height of their stardom (due to internal differences and Wahlberg's problems with the public and the law).

Even with such marketing precautions, there was little doubt that Matsuda was taking a great risk in making a career move that was almost destined to failure. Seiko herself was no doubt quite cognizant of the possibility that American audiences would dismiss her as just an exotic attraction at best, or a New Kids' groupie at worst. But she had already flaunted the pop music establishment back in Japan. After a widely publicized romance with heartthrob movie and singing star Hiromi Gō, she married actor Masaki Kanda and had a child a year later. However, instead of retiring quietly into the background after her marriage, to be brought out of mothballs now and then as a kind of musical elder stateswoman on special occasions, Matsuda refused to go the way of most over-21, married-with-child idol singers. She continued doing film work and sought new musical projects. Some of her filming took her to Hawaii and the U.S. mainland, where she met progressive American musicians.

Matsuda's American debut was unremarkable. Using only her first name as her moniker, her videos and one album (titled simply *seiko*) enjoyed barely moderate success, even though she sang in English, was backed by a major American label (Columbia), and had the support of many established names in the business, including singer Gloria Estefan and songwriter Quincy Jones. Back in Japan, she was the subject of gossip and rumors among fans and in the media. The lowbrow Japanese magazine *FOCUS* reported that she had a secret boyfriend, "Jeff," and things became worse when "Jeff" showed up in Japan trying, in Kato Kaelin-like fashion, to cash in on his one fleeting moment of notoriety.

However, it is likely that Matsuda has come out a winner through all this. Her brief flirtation with American stardom was probably less a serious attempt to achieve success in the West than a chance to grow musically, learn new styles, and meet different performers. Also, this venture gave her a hiatus from being the center of attention in the pressure-cooker Japanese pop music world. Simply put, she bucked the system and survived. She now directs her own career and projects, and has taken charge of her business affairs in a way that few Japanese female

Figure 4.4 **Seiko Matsuda, as shown on the cover of her U.S. CD *seiko***

artists ever have. She is no longer Seiko-chan. As one informant put it, "Seiko . . . she's really pretty smart."

A New Voice: English as a New Rhetoric in Japanese Pop Music

No doubt the reader has noted the presence of English words in some of the lyrics presented so far. Actually, English loanwords have been commonly used in modern Japanese for over a century, and no Japanese could carry on even the most elementary conversation today without using them.[9] However, in the linguistic register of popular music, English loanwords and phrasings are especially abundant. I suggest that this is not coincidental, and that Japanese female songwriters in particular are using English to avoid some of the linguistic restrictions placed upon women by the Japanese language. Out of dozens of possible examples, let me now introduce three singer-songwriters who make particularly effective use of English in their lyrics.

Figure 4.5 **Yūming (Yumi Matsutōya)**

The "New Music" of Yūming

Yumi Matsutōya, or Yūming as her fans call her, is said to be the voice of a broad new generation of Japanese young women in their twenties, thirties, and forties.[10] As one informant said, "Yūming speaks to all Japanese women." A brilliant songwriter and performer, Yūming not only writes her own material but also is in demand to write for other performers. She wrote many of Seiko Matsuda's hit songs and has done the soundtracks for several successful films. According to her autobiography *Rouge no Dengon* (The Message of Rouge), Yūming was a middle-class girl who had an artistic and introverted adolescence. Her songs are a substantive cut above the simple boy-girl idol music most often heard on Japanese radio and television.

Yūming's single from the early 1990s, "Dandelion," includes some of the interesting images for which she has become famous. In the song's lyrics, a woman speaks philosophically to a friend about the friend's newfound love. This love, she says, will travel like a tiny dandelion seed over the winter, will endure the cold and then bloom again, even though, like a dandelion seed, it is tiny and seemingly powerless.

. . .

きみは dandelion
傷ついた日々は　彼に出逢うための
そうよ　運命が用意してくれた
大切な lesson
今　素敵な lady になる

. . .

You are a dandelion.
Those days when your heart was hurt
Were important lessons that fate arranged for you
In order to meet him.
Now you've become a lovely lady.

The use of the English word "dandelion" as a metaphor both for the friend who has fallen in love and, further on in the lyrics, for love itself is quite effective. "Dandelion" captures well the fragility of interpersonal feelings and of love, which, like the dandelion seed, can either grow into a bright flower or fall on barren ground and wither. There is also the feeling that a dandelion is something quite ordinary, a pretty flower certainly, but by no means rare or beautiful. This makes love seem ordinary as well, though still special and able to convey strong feelings, just like the unsophisticated letter the woman receives from her parents back home which brings tears to her eyes. Had *tanpopo* (the Japanese word for "dandelion") been used instead, the song would sound more like a folksong, with a country girl in love with a country boy, but use of the English word means that any city OL can relate to the song. Yūming herself told me she used the word "dandelion" because she liked the image she felt it gave of an English hillside; she wanted to throw in a little fragrance of Western culture.

"Dareka ga Anata o Sagashite Iru" (Somebody Is Looking for You) is one of Yūming's later ballads, from around 1994. This song is high-tech in both melody and lyrics and is so interesting, and so creative in its use of English, that it is worth examining in its entirety.[11]

誰かがあなたを捜しているわ
この夜明けに
流れる monitor くり返される code number

合鍵を使いしのび込んでみた
あなたの部屋には
ぬぎ捨てた pajamas 飲みかけの beer つけたままの computer

誰かがあなたを edit してる
program に ghost がいるわ

誰かがあなたを狙っているわ
闇の中で
しゃべり出す answer phone 急に光って動く fax

mouse をたたいて access したら正体がわかる
あなたを蝕む恋の virus を早く消してしまおう

OPEN YOUR FILE, OPEN YOUR MIND
かくさないで ghost がいるわ

fiber の迷宮で loop から出られない
彷徨えるあなたを救い出すために
mouse をたたいて私の code を input したら
あなたにまとわる恋の virus に laser を浴びせる

OPEN YOUR FILE, OPEN YOUR MIND
まだまにあう ghost がいるわ

OPEN YOUR FILE （誰かがあなたを）
OPEN YOUR MIND （探しているわ）
かくさないで ghost がいるわ

Somebody is looking for you.
In the middle of the night . . .
A glowing monitor . . . a repeated code number.
Using the duplicate key, I sneak into your room and find
pajamas on the floor, unfinished beer, the computer left
running.
Somebody's editing you.
There's a ghost in the program.
Somebody is targeting you.
In the dark. . .
An answering machine starts to speak, a fax machine
suddenly lights up and begins moving.
If I click the mouse and access it, I'll find its true
character revealed.
Let me quickly erase the love virus that's infecting you.

OPEN YOUR FILE, OPEN YOUR MIND
Don't hide, there's a ghost!
Wandering in a maze of fiber . . . caught in a loop. . .
To rescue you, I click the mouse, input my code,
and beam the laser on the love virus that hovers over you.

OPEN YOUR FILE, OPEN YOUR MIND
It's not too late, there's a ghost!

OPEN YOUR FILE (somebody is . . .)
OPEN YOUR MIND (looking for you)
Don't hide, there's a ghost!

Of course the liberal use of English is not surprising in a song featuring computer imagery. Even in everyday Japanese, English words (given Japanese pronunciation) are used for "monitor," "code," "computer," "program," "fax," "virus," and "file," as well as for many other ordinary items such as "pajamas" and "beer." Yet the use of so much English, including the "pure" English refrain that punctuates the choruses and the end of the song, is especially effective in creating not only a feeling of modernity and electronic wizardry but also a mood of apprehension and intangible fear. These "alien"—that is, non-Japanese—words work much better than more familiar Japanese terms could, to lend the

Figure 4.6 **Dreams Come True (Masato Nakamura, Miwa Yoshida, and Takahiro Nishikawa)**

song the impersonal and alien air that so aptly conveys the idea that an unseen but clearly present virus is stalking and infecting the singer's boyfriend. Of course, while the song's techno-imagery suggests that the lurking danger is a computer virus, it is in fact a "love virus" that threatens to steal from the singer the heart and mind of her boyfriend. This juxtaposition of "dry" impersonal technology with the "wet" human emotions of love and jealousy works well. With her typically gentle humor and clever use of language, Yūming has created an exotic world, but one that we can understand and even be drawn into.

Dreams Come True: Innovation in the Mainstream

Dreams Come True is one of the most popular music groups in Japan at the present time. Their phenomenally successful 1992 album *The Swinging Star* was one of the best selling CDs of all time in the country. Composed of two male instrumentalists (Masato Nakamura and Takahiro Nishikawa) and a strong female vocalist and lyricist (Miwa Yoshida), Dreams Come True is particularly popular with female audiences. The group is known for covering a variety of musical styles—including reggae, swing, and salsa, as well as Japanese pop standards—but it always makes any vehicle into something especially its own.

One of Dreams Come True's strongest attributes is their unique song writing. Their songs' lyrics, like those of Yūming, often include creative and effective uses of English. A 1995 single, for example, is titled "Sankyū," the Japanese pronunciation of the English "thank you." This song presents a woman's feelings about her impending breakup with a man. The woman senses that the man wants to leave her, but that it is very hard for him to tell her this. She comes to his rescue by saying she is grateful for all that he has done for her—for their shared laughter, for his presence, for today. By conveying her appreciation with the English loanword "sankyū," rather than the Japanese *domo* or *arigatō* (Japanese words for "thank you"), she makes the situation seem less tragic than it is. If she were to use the word "arigatō" instead, things would sound much more serious. She does appreciate his kindness, but appreciating too deeply seems not to be her style, and the borrowed English term "sankyū" is perfect for capturing this "lighter" feeling.

The members of Dreams Come True sometimes write and perform entire songs in English. Here are some of the lyrics from their 1994 number, "Winter Song."

> The way you came into my life,
> filling every day with laughter
> Almost blinded by the snowflakes on my face
> Despite the chill
> I feel the warmth of your embrace
> Intoxicated now, I stagger like a fool
> I feel that surely I could float away. . . .
> I want to show you everything
> I see, the way I'm feeling
> I need to be with you tonight

Two things are worth noting. First, this is well-written, poetic English, quite unlike the many examples found in Japanese pop music of English words and phrases that are thrown into a song to lend a "modern" or "hip" flavor but that otherwise make little sense. The lyrics of "Winter Song" are the product of a collaborative effort between Miwa Yoshida and Englishman Mike Pela, with Yoshida first producing a literal translation from the Japanese and Pela then smoothing out the English to make it sound natural when sung to the music. Second, the lyrics suggest that it may be easier for a Japanese woman to express strong personal emotions, such as these, using English rather than Japanese. Westerners teaching English in Japan often find that their Japanese students will say certain things in English that they would hesitate to say in Japanese, at least in part because using a foreign language lifts them out of a Japanese context, liberating them from some of the conventions and discomfort that are attached to certain words or subjects in Japanese. The idea that English may be especially liberating for female Japanese artists, who would be hard pressed to state things so explicitly in their native tongue, is explored further below.

The Independent Road of Shōnen Knife

One of more interesting of the several all-girl alternative rock bands in Japan at present is Shōnen Knife ("young boy knife"). The members of Shōnen Knife are former OLs who began playing in the mid-1980s, more as a hobby than as a serious attempt to achieve stardom. The band consists of two sisters, Naoko Yamano on guitar and Atsuko Yamano on drums, and Michie Nakatani on keyboards and bass, with all three doing vocals.

Shōnen Knife has achieved an international following, particularly after performing as the opening act on a tour of the American supergroup Nirvana in 1993. (A "Shōnen Knife" Internet search produces numerous pictures of, and home pages dedicated to, the group.) In 1994 the group even released a record in the United States on Virgin Records titled "Rock Animals," based on their 1993 recording in Japan. (The Japanese version of this CD has both Japanese and English songs, while the American version includes only the English songs.) The subjects of Shōnen Knife's songs are certainly unique, ranging from a fight between a cobra and a mongoose to concrete animal statues in a park. They also display a confident and playful attitude toward men. The song "Quavers" tells about a woman's adoration for a man, but in a funny, tongue-in-cheek way, and with a melody and background vocals that give the lyrics a sarcastic flavor:

He's my PRINCE, he's my GOD
But it's so complicated
He's my HERO, he's my IDOL
But I'm so dizzy of him
I wanna be his MADONNA

I wanna be his PRINCESS
I wanna be his HEROINE
I'd be happy just to be with him

But men can be more than gods and heroes to Shōnen Knife. As these lyrics from the song "Butterfly Boy" show, males can also be insects, to be captured:

Hey you say you were a butterfly
I see you in a peaceful field
Hey you say you were a butterfly
I see you in a beautiful garden
I wanna catch you catch you catch you
Butterfly Boy

The picture of the woman firmly in the driver's seat comes through clearly in the wacky but clever "Johnny, Johnny, Johnny," Shōnen Knife's song about the "regular boy" who lives next door. Johnny is "the nicest boy in town" because "he's good at archery" and "real good at ping pong"; he's "the cleanest boy in town" as "he's good at dominoes"; and finally he's "the best boy in town" because "he's good at bowling." Here, the glorious achievements men are so proud of are tartly dismissed with wit and humor by Shōnen Knife. But Johnny should not feel downcast because, still, "He's the coolest boy! Ha!"

The Future of Women and English in Japanese Pop Music

It is obviously difficult to predict the directions that any kind of popular music may take, and this is especially true in the Japanese pop music field, where so many diverse domestic and foreign influences are at work. Optimists see great potential for creativity and experimentation, especially in the roles that women might play. Others are less confident; one informant lamented, "There used to be a lot of great female singers around. There just aren't anymore."

No doubt the female artists themselves are still working to expand their musical frontiers and discover what roles they might have to play in any "women's revolution" in Japan. At the same time, in their daily lives they face many of the same problems that the typical OL does: how to reconcile career and home life, how to achieve personal satisfaction while meeting family obligations, how to manage life in both the public and the domestic spheres. By their own standards, many Western women would be disappointed by some of the choices that Japanese women make, both as private citizens and as public entertainers. For example, Yuki, the feminist tomboy of the Judy and Mary band that we met earlier, is noted for wearing beautiful traditional kimonos on stage during her concerts. Yet, in the magazine interview cited earlier as well as in other magazine layouts and album covers, she is often provocatively photographed in these same kimonos, in a style reminiscent of some of the erotic woodblock prints (*shunga*) of earlier centuries—this in spite of her claim that she wants to construct a new image. It is important, though, to be cautious in comparing the style or form of feminism in one country with the style or form that it may take in another. Definitions vary as to what constitutes "liberation" or "freedom," and different people have different agendas and timetables. What might be problematic in North America—say, using scantily clad women to sell cars—might not be seen as important in Japan, where different concerns—for example, how to improve relationships between mother-in-law and daughter-in-law—may be considered more critical.

Regardless of the specific road that Japanese pop music and the female performers and songwriters who are pushing it forward take, however, it seems likely that the use of English will continue to help guide it to its destination. Particularly for female artists, English offers avenues of poetic representation, individual creativity, and emotional expression that are, at least to some extent, closed off by some of the restrictions imposed by everyday Japanese.

In medieval Japan, men and women led in many ways quite separate linguistic lives. Men, the literate and literary half of the population, generally wrote in the Chinese language—the medium of religion, government, and classical literature. At least they knew Chinese writing. Women, on the other hand, did not learn Chinese, or the Chinese characters or writing system. This did not hold women back artistically, however, for they developed a very effective "feminine" voice using native Japanese. While men wrote publicly in a largely imported idiom of Chinese and Sino-Japanese characters, women recorded their private thoughts in an indigenous Japanese vocabulary and writing system. This resulted in the creation of several marvelous literary forms—most notably the many famous poetic diaries and the novel—which were unique in world literature at that time. The best-known example, *Genji Monogatari* (The

Tale of Genji), written by the Lady Murasaki Shikibu around 1000 A.D., is generally considered to be the world's first true novel, as well as one of the finest flowers of all Japanese literature, past or present.

Today, of course, Sino-Japanese characters and their "Chinese" readings, along with indigenous Japanese and an ever-expanding set of English loanwords, are universally used in Japanese speaking and writing, by male and female, young and old. Still, it may not be coincidental that so many of the pop songs written and sung by Japanese women feature the extensive use of English or English loanwords. It is well known that there are marked linguistic differences between men's speech and women's speech in Japan. Because of these differences, there are some things that are simply quite difficult for women to express using "pure" Japanese. In such cases, English or English loanwords offer a way to circumvent some of the sociolinguistic limitations of Japanese.[12] They provide Japanese women not only with another "voice," an additional and different symbolic vocabulary with which to express their thoughts and feelings, but also with a rhetorical power that was unknown to them previously, and that is suited for the growing power and stature that women are gaining in Japanese society. In this way, the use of English helps to endow female-created Japanese music with new alternatives and potentials for women, and these, through the popularity of the music and the artists, in turn give encouragement to Japanese women who are pioneering new roles and ways of living and being in society. As the songs and artists introduced in this chapter show, the available artists for such an undertaking are abundant, and are more than competent for the task.

Notes

1. For their valuable help in discussing this essay with me and in checking translations, I wish to thank my friends, informants, and self-proclaimed experts in Japanese popular music: Mayumi Kano, Naoko Kisaichi, Ayako Kurosu, Kaori Mori, Michiko Sano, Reiko Takiguchi, and Mitsuko Yano. My longtime friend, collaborator, and colleague at Keio University, Dr. Kyōko Inoue, as always, helped in many ways, including providing me with key recordings and journals. Wakako Kusumoto at the University of Illinois also discussed key points with me. Without the help of these persons, this chapter could not have been completed. It is only my inherent obstinacy that has prevented me from following all their suggestions and making this a better work.

2. For other overviews of Japanese popular music, see James Stanlaw, "Not East Not West, Not Old Not New: Trends and Genres in Japanese Popular Music,"

World & I 4:11 (1989), pp. 621–633; James Stanlaw, "Dancing in the Park: Takenoko Zoku, Rock and Roll Zoku, and Band Zoku," *World & I* 5:9 (1990), pp. 630–642; James Stanlaw, "English Images and Metaphors in Japanese Popular Music," in *Facing East/Facing West: North America and the Asian Pacific Region in the 1990s*, ed. Nelson Hilton (Kalamazoo: Western Michigan University Office of International Affairs, 1993), pp. 400–408; and Steve McClure, "Pop Music in Japan: A Beginner's Guide," *Mangajin* 94 (June 1994), pp. 14–19, 48, 50, 52.

3. These themes are common in other popular media as well, especially men's magazines and comic books.

4. Tatsuo Inamasu, *Aidoru-gaku* (Studies in Idol-ology) (Tokyo: Chikuma Shoten, 1989).

5. *GIRLPOP* 13 (May 1995), pp. 23–30.

6. From the music magazine *Best Hit* 7 (1989), p. 182.

7. "Better Days, Better Morning," *GIRLPOP* 13 (May 1995), pp. 88–93.

8. A number of jazz and classical artists, such as Seiji Ozawa, Sadao Watanabe, and Keiko Matsui, have been successful in the United States. Popular musicians have generally not fared so well. Female singers Hiroko (Minato) and Akiko Yano have had American CD releases with limited success. Okinawan folk and pop music seems to have done better; Shōkichi Kina has several CDs in circulation, and the septuplet Shang Shang Typhoon released a CD in 1996 with moderate success in the "world music" category.

9. James Stanlaw, "Japanese and English: Borrowing and Contact," *World Englishes* 6:2 (1987), pp. 93–109; James Stanlaw, "English in Japanese Communicative Strategies." In *The Other Tongue: English Across Cultures*, ed. Braj B. Kachru, 2d ed. (Urbana: University of Illinois Press, 1992), pp. 178–208; James Stanlaw, "'For Beautiful Human Life.' The Use of English in Japan." In *Re-Making Japan: Everyday Life and Consumer Taste in a Changing Society*, ed. J. Tobin (New Haven, CT: Yale University Press, 1992), pp. 58–78.

10. Kenji Hatakeyama, *Kuwata to Yūming* (Kuwata [Keisuke] and Yūming [Matsutōya Yumi]) (Tokyo: San-Maku, 1990).

11. In the original Japanese lyrics of this and other songs presented in this chapter, most of the English loanwords are written using *katakana* (the phonetic Japanese syllabary used for writing foreign words). They are written here using *romaji* (roman letters) for easy identification by those who do not read Japanese.

12. See Stanlaw, "English in Japanese Communicative Strategies" and "HIKARU GENJI Monogatari: The Poetics of English in Japanese Song and Verse." In *The Poetics of Japanese Literature, Proceedings of the Midwest Seminar on the Poetics of Japanese Literature*, ed. R. Thomas (Purdue University, 1992), pp. 131–152.

5

A Karaoke Perspective on International Relations

Hiro R. Shimatachi

Karaoke is arguably Japan's greatest musical contribution to the world, and certainly its best known. Since its invention in the mid-1970s, the electronic sing-along system has won over millions of amateur crooners around the world. But karaoke remains largely an Asian phenomenon, enjoying far greater popularity in the nightclubs and living rooms of China and Myanmar than in those of Norway or Canada. The disproportionate receptiveness of East and West to karaoke reveals significant contrasts in socialization and value systems—Asians emphasize participating and "making a sincere effort," whereas Westerners tend to view karaoke as a kind of talent contest from which the less musically gifted had best abstain. Nevertheless, karaoke's merits as a form of entertainment as well as an important tool for doing business in Japan are gaining recognition in the United States and Europe, and it is no exaggeration to say that karaoke, as a part of today's global pop culture, holds out the promise of improving relations between the two civilizations.

Karaoke and Consensus Building

For Asians, it has been said, karaoke is an electric geisha—a modern invention that plays the socializing role traditionally performed by a hostess, who employs her entertainment skills to draw out guests and establish camaraderie. Westerners, on the other hand, tend to see an evening of karaoke as a talent contest rather than as an opportunity to enhance communication. In his book *The Electric Geisha*, Kunihiro Narumi asserts that differences in the socialization rituals of Japanese and Westerners account for these varying views of karaoke: "Unlike

Western parties, where people usually entertain themselves with conversation and dancing, Japanese gatherings often slide into venues for guests to display their lesser-known talents."[1]

When practiced in a Japanese cultural context, karaoke epitomizes *ringisei*, a method of conducting meetings in which participants aim to achieve consensus rather than score points. Ringisei-style consensus building should not, however, be mistaken for self-effacing conformity. As psychiatrist Takeo Doi writes in his best-seller, *The Anatomy of Self*, ringisei is rather "an instinctual sense that the support of the group is indispensable for the individual,"[2] and this sense pervades Japanese-style karaoke.

In Japan the good salaryman is also a good karaoke participant. He is never so horrible a singer as to irritate his colleagues, yet he is not necessarily vocally blessed. Having practiced a wide repertoire of songs, he is prepared to accommodate any audience with his talents, however limited. If he is called upon to play the role of the host, he may be the first to step up to the microphone, but he will wait until everybody has had his turn before he selects a second round of songs. He has already memorized his boss's favorites and chooses one of these to save his superior the appearance of being overly eager. He may elect to sing medleys by popular singers to allow others to join in. If spirits start to sag, he might wail a nostalgic tune in falsetto. Like a good emcee, finally, he can be counted upon to make appropriate compliments or jokes after each person's performance to show appreciation.

Singing for Success

A karaoke master is likely to be successful in business, according to research by Daniel Goleman, a former Harvard University psychologist. In his landmark work *Emotional Intelligence: Why It Matters More Than IQ*, Goleman focuses on the behavior of individuals in group settings and reaches conclusions of no little interest to practitioners of karaoke. He introduces the concept of an "emotional quotient" (EQ) expressing, among other factors, nonverbal sensitivity—the ability to "read" a social situation and act appropriately. Goleman's research shows that people with a high EQ tend to be more successful at work and in relationships. The kind of karaoke-competent salaryman described above would, according to this thesis, need only to apply his superior social skills on the job to move ahead. On the basis of evidence provided by personnel executives, Goleman argues that "IQ gets you hired, but EQ gets you promoted. Those workers who were good collaborators and networkers and popular with colleagues were more likely to get the cooperation they needed to reach their goals."[3]

But for the noninitiated—or the emotionally challenged—karaoke can be a daunting proposition. Indeed, karaoke overturns the stereotypes of the nonexpressive, inscrutable Oriental and the outgoing, flamboyant Westerner. In a karaoke club, these roles are reversed: If he is anything less than a Pavarotti, the Westerner is the one who shies away from the spotlight, while the Asian takes command of the situation.

To respond to the needs of those business people who want to sing their way to better relations with their Japanese counterparts, karaoke courses are now offered in many Asian and American cities. What is stressed above all is the importance of participation—not singing amounts to the cardinal sin of refusing to join the group. Another faux pas to which foreigners are alerted is singing English-language songs familiar to Japanese. Songs that one's hosts are likely to sing themselves—"My Way," "Yesterday," or anything by Elvis Presley, for example—should be avoided. Explains a bicultural business consultant, "The chances are you've chosen the one song they can sing in English and taken away their opportunity to impress you." Short of memorizing a Japanese song, he recommends Beatles tunes like "Eleanor Rigby," songs that are too fast paced for a typical Japanese to master yet are still well known.

Participation versus Exhibition

Mastering karaoke is not necessarily a shortcut to sealing a business deal, but it is in any case an activity that enhances one's emotional intelligence—a universal virtue in the business world. Westerners should abandon any embarrassment over a lack of vocal talent, because in karaoke it is not the most musically gifted who are most highly regarded. To the contrary, someone who dominates the microphone is likely to be branded a showoff. Simply put, *doryoku* (sincere effort) rather than ability is what Japanese value in a karaoke singer.

That this is so is made clear by the karaoke contests that can be found on Japanese television almost any day of the week. Objectively skillful singers represent only a minority of those selected to appear; they are accompanied by adorable children, funny old men, chatty middle-aged women, and strangely dressed teenagers, all of whom sing without compunction and are appreciated for their contribution to the entertainment.

Westerners grow up with the mentality that those without talent should remain on the sidelines, and karaoke illustrates that this lesson is internalized relatively early in life. In Tokyo teenagers like to get together at cheap karaoke "boxes" (small rooms with a karaoke system), where everyone, regardless of singing skills, takes a turn with the microphone. Among karaoke-inclined young people of the same age in San Francisco, "freestyling" is popular: a small group gathers around a microphone and spontaneously creates a rap song. One member begins the rap, then passes the microphone to the next. The recipient must continue the rap in perfect rhythm and rhyme before passing it along to the next person. Usually the participants are joined by friends who watch and cheer them on. Although Japanese-style karaoke is not as creative as freestyling, everyone can take part, regardless of talent; in freestyling there is an obvious distinction between those with talent and those who remain spectators. In this sense, Japanese are better than Americans at practicing the American ideal of "all are created equal."

Notes of Discord—Or Harmony?

Despite its value as a source of entertainment and means of building camaraderie, karaoke has at times been the target of artistic and other criticisms. Karaoke has been blamed for lowering the quality of Japanese music. The music industry, the argument runs, is forced to churn out simplistic tunes that are easy for sing-along sessions because karaoke hits mean big profits. Indeed, "serious" musicians sometimes dismiss karaoke as not being music at all. The legendary late Asian songstress Teresa Tang, for instance, disdained to sing karaoke-style medleys. Other critics have even gone so far as to label the lack of artistic creativity in Japanese society the "karaokization" of its culture.

In the rest of Asia, furthermore, karaoke has not necessarily contributed to consensus building. Although Asians quickly made the sing-along system one of their most popular pastimes, they seem to enjoy karaoke primarily because it can be practiced in cramped quarters and because it offers a way to release the accumulated stress of urban life. Among many, the Western idea of karaoke as a talent contest prevails. A Canadian working in Hong Kong relates that, after he won the karaoke contest at his company's annual Christmas party, several Chinese co-workers refused to speak to him for weeks. The latter were well-practiced karaoke artists who were miffed about losing out to a foreigner who, despite the inferior quality of his vocals, impressed the audience by crooning a popular song in Mandarin.

Nevertheless, compared to the Walkman and the boom box, two earlier

Japanese innovations in the domain of audio technology that swept the world, karaoke must be seen as a positive social development. In short, the Walkman isolates and the boom box domineers—but karaoke unites.

The Walkman culture can be seen on the crowded commuter trains of Tokyo and Osaka, where headphoned riders sway in complete self-absorption. It is a culture of noncommunication, lacking courtesy and interaction. The boom box, on the other hand, might be seen as a representative of certain "Western" patterns of behavior: aggressively assertive, at times to the point of distracting and irritating others. Too many boom boxes blasting away in a public place mean cacophony and chaos. The boom box articulates the language of friction—shouting rather than communicating.

By building consensus among participants and stressing listening as well as expression, karaoke brings people together, establishing a middle ground between isolation and domination. While karaoke can be a forum for discord, in such a setting even this conflict of egos can be the first step toward genuine communication. As the popularity of karaoke continues to increase in both East and West, it may portend deeper understanding and amelioration of relations between these two cultures.

Western circles have not been slow to recognize this possibility and, more generally speaking, the aforementioned social virtues of karaoke. Writing in *The Electric Geisha*, Narumi noted that when karaoke was presented at the New Town World Forum in Osaka, a group of Germans were interested in the idea of using the sing-along system as a means of developing community spirit in apartment complexes where people feel isolated or alienated from their neighbors.[4]

It can thus be seen that Japan's sociocultural influence on today's global pop culture should not be underestimated. Although this culture is widely interpreted as a creation of the United States and Europe, Japan is making a notable contribution as a provider of electronic hardware and musical software, and karaoke holds out the potential of becoming an especially important catalyst for this process of cultural unification.

Notes

1. Kunihiro Narumi, *The Electric Geisha* (Tokyo: Kodansha International, 1994).
2. Takeo Doi, *The Anatomy of Self*, trans. Mark A. Harbison (Tokyo: Kodansha International, 1986).
3. Daniel Goleman, *Emotional Intelligence: Why It Matters More Than IQ* (New York: Bantam, 1995).
4. Narumi, *Electric Geisha*.

Part II

Comics and Animation

— 6 —

Japanese Comics and Religion

Osamu Tezuka's Story of the Buddha

Mark Wheeler MacWilliams

Contemporary Retellings of the Buddha's Story

Buddhism is a living religion. It lives because it continues to speak to the vital concerns of ordinary people today. The story of the Buddha in Buddhism, like the stories of Jesus in Christianity and of Muhammad in Islam, has something important to say. Narration, the telling of a story by a particular storyteller to a particular audience at a particular time, is what gives the story of the Buddha its continuing vitality for modern audiences.

If we want to study living Buddhism today, then the stories of the Buddha from classical scriptural sources, such as the Theravada *Nidanakatha*, the Sarvastivadin *Mahavastu*, or the Mahayana *Buddhacarita,* should not be the focus of our study. The fact of the matter is that ordinary people usually do not know these scriptures. Difficulties of access, readability, and length put them out of reach of most people. Rather, it is the modern stories of the Buddha's life, those which make Buddhism come alive for a modern mass audience, that we should study. What new stories do I mean? In the West, for example, there is the novel *Siddhartha* by Hermann Hesse (1922) or, more recently, Bernardo Bertolucci's exquisite movie *The Little Buddha* (1994). There is also a third important contemporary version of the Buddha's story: the *manga* (comic book) story *Budda* by Osamu Tezuka.

Some might be surprised that it is a comic book rather than a novel or movie about the Buddha that has reached a large Japanese audience, but in Japan manga dominate the mass culture marketplace as an entertainment medium read by all ages and classes of people. As Ian Reader, a scholar of Japanese religions and popular culture, has noted, manga "are simply too fascinating, colorful, and rich a literary medium to be left solely to children."[1] In Japan one can find manga on most any theme imaginable, and while most cater primarily to a niche audience—boys, girls, men, or women—they also have a large crossover readership. Manga books and magazines are sold everywhere: in bookstores, at train station kiosks, and in vending machines. They are read in barbershops, on trains (during the daily commute), in coffee shops, and at home—places where they serve as handy sources of entertainment. Some recent statistics point to the dominance of manga in Japan's mass media and their sizable influence on society. In 1995, manga accounted for 40 percent of all books and magazines sold in Japan. A total of 1.9 billion manga books and magazines were sold, about fifteen for every person in Japan, comprising $6 to $7 billion in total sales.[2]

Osamu Tezuka's Budda

Budda was written and drawn by Osamu Tezuka (1928–1989), the man revered in Japan as the "god of comics." Over the course of an amazing career—Tezuka not only worked as a manga artist but also directed numerous animation projects, created production companies, and was a licensed physician—he penned over 150,000 pages of manga which are found in over 500 separate works.[3] Tezuka is perhaps best known as the creator of the *Tetsuwan Atom* (Astro Boy) comic that was serialized in Japanese newspapers from 1952 to 1968 and spawned the Japanese, and now Western, fascination with robot heroes.[4] Tezuka is also famous for pioneering *story manga* (comics with a novelistic format and complex plotting that run to thousands of pages in length). Story manga have been the mainstay of Japanese comics in the postwar period.

Budda dates from what manga critic Chiei Go calls Tezuka's "mature period." It first appeared in serialization in August 1972 and continued to be published in a number of manga magazines, all tied to Ushio Shuppansha, a publishing company with close associations with the Japanese Buddhist sect Sōka Gakkai, over a twelve-year period until 1983. Today *Budda* is sold in book form, its seven sections making up a twelve-volume set totaling 2,886 pages, Tezuka's longest story manga.[5] The manga magazines in which *Budda* was serialized, *Kibō no Tomo* (Friend of Hope), *Shōnen Warudo* (Boys' World), and *Komikku Tomu* (Comic Tom), are a clue to its intended audience, for these magazines catered to young teenage boys. That being said, however, it should be noted that large numbers of crossover adult readers certainly have read and continue to read *Budda* as well.

The circumstances surrounding *Budda*'s origin show that Tezuka actually had a diverse readership in mind. *Budda* was born when another of Tezuka's projects, his experimental monthly manga magazine *COM*, folded in 1972. His adult-oriented masterpiece *Hi no Tori* (Phoenix), a long story manga dealing with deeply religious themes, had been serialized in *COM*, and Tezuka was invited to continue its serialization in Ushio Shuppansha's publications. However, Tezuka decided to do a more youth-oriented adventure manga for Ushio instead, and the result was *Budda*. Thus, even while *Budda* is an adventure tale filled with battles and acts of heroism and tragedy, it also focuses on serious "adult" themes—love and death; the quest for truth, goodness, and the meaning of life; and what some have called Tezuka's own humanistic interpretation of the Buddha's spirituality.[6] Since being printed in book format in 1993 by Ushio Shuppansha, *Budda* has gone through twenty-two printings and sold over nine million copies.[7] This does not include the number of magazines sold during its serialization nor the number of copies of the first hardcover edition published by Aizō Shuppansha in 1987 and 1988. Given its publication history, it is no exaggeration to say that millions of Japanese have read at least some of *Budda*.

Tezuka knew the Buddha's story well, as he was well read in the Buddhist scriptures. *Budda* sometimes has the feel of a *kyōyō manga* (educational comic), with its occasional panels of historical summaries and its detailed maps of India and Nepal at the end of each volume.[8] *Budda* does in fact recount the basic story of the Buddha's birth at Lumbini near Kapilavastu, his life as a prince of the S'akya people, the Four Sights (seen by the Buddha-to-be on his trip outside the palace: a sick man, an old man, a corpse, and an ascetic), the great departure or renunciation and life as a *s'ramana* (ascetic), his awakening at Bodhgaya, his life as a teacher of the *Dharma* (the Buddhist natural and moral law), and his final *parinirvana* (enlightenment, release from suffering, and rebirth) at Kus´inagara. In this, Tezuka's own illustrations often closely parallel traditional devotional images of these key moments in the sacred biography (Figures 6.1 and 6.2).

Figure 6.1 **Budda as an ascetic, starving before Sujata**

Yet, in *Budda* Tezuka also deliberately changes the Buddha's story to make it more appealing and more relevant for a modern Japanese audience. This chapter describes five major changes that Tezuka makes in his retelling of the Buddha legend: (1) he turns the story into an adventure tale; (2) he visualizes it through manga iconographical conventions; (3) he contextualizes it to make it into a Japanese story; (4) he uses nature to convey human emotion and a sense of the spiritual; and (5) he reorients the story to address some of the key emotional problems faced by young Japanese boys today, in particular the fear of losing one's mother, of becoming separated from her warm, nurturing, and indulging presence. Tezuka's Budda is a hero because he is ultimately able to cope with the loss of the maternal intimacy of childhood. His life becomes one long search for an all-encompassing sense of selfless love that unites him with all things, a notion that is in line with the Mahayana spiritual ideal of the *bodhisattva* (one who, out of compassion, forgoes nirvana in order to save others) and which Tezuka may have felt is needed in today's competitive and materialistic Japan.

Turning Buddha into *Budda*—Popularizing a Sacred Story

Tezuka's *Budda* differs from conventional accounts of the Buddha's life. In response to a "religion boom" in Japan in recent years, some Buddhist groups have tried to capitalize on the popularity of manga by pub-

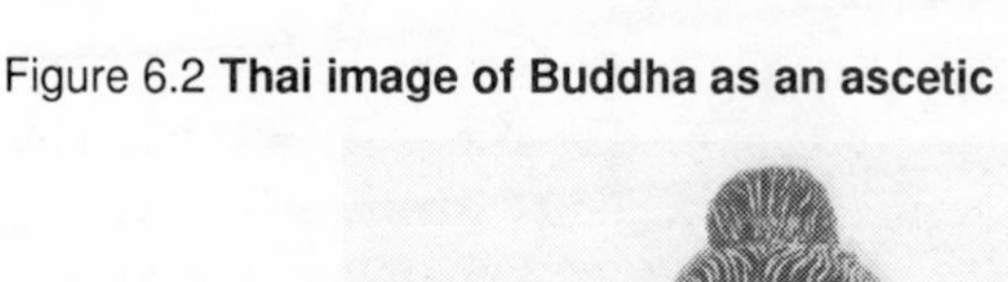

Figure 6.2 **Thai image of Buddha as an ascetic**

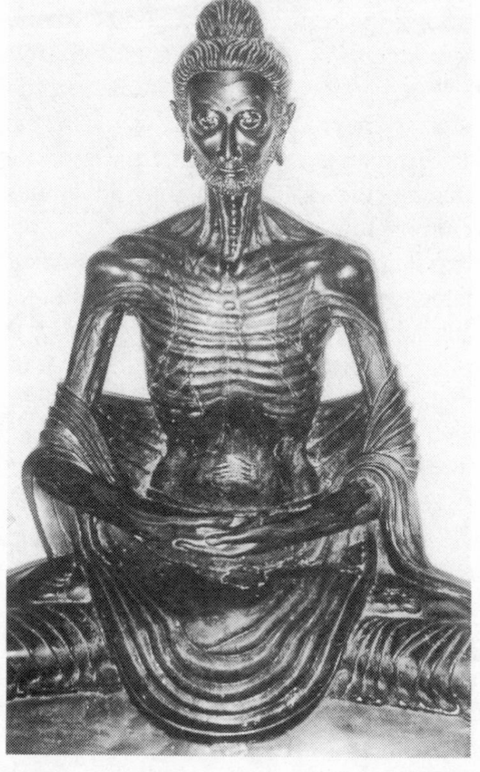

lishing *Bukkyō kaisetsu manga* (Buddhism-teaching manga). These are manga produced either explicitly for proselytization, that is to teach the basic Buddhist doctrines, or as educational manga designed to get students interested in the history of Buddhism. Both of these types tend to closely follow Buddhist scriptures, much as religious comic book projects in the West strive to "translate" scripture from the written word to the visual medium of comics. Such comics do not usually add new scenes, dialogue, or characters that are not found in the original sacred scriptures.[9]

Tezuka, however, did not draw *Budda* as a tool for explaining abstruse Buddhist doctrines; within its twelve volumes, Tezuka offers few explanations of Buddhist technical terms or even of such basic teachings as the Four Noble Truths. Nor is *Budda* simply a comic book rendering of the orthodox scriptural account.

Tezuka is first and foremost a storyteller, with his own story to tell about the life of the Buddha. Though he did not lower himself to the level of cheap sensationalism to gain market share, Tezuka was quite comfortable working in the mass entertainment marketing niche that manga occupies in Japan's postwar popular culture, and he craved commercial success. Manga are read for pleasure, and so Tezuka endeavored to create stories and characters that would fascinate his readers. One reason that *Budda* is a manga masterpiece is that it offers what Japanese consumers demand—a compelling adventure story that most anyone would enjoy reading for pleasure.

As a manga artist, Tezuka had no reservations whatsoever about inventing new characters to add excitement to his story. In his afterword to *Budda*, Tezuka admits, somewhat apologetically, that he does this even when it means going beyond the letter of Buddhist scripture. Tezuka's alterations are especially evident in the beginning of *Budda*. For example, the first two volumes contain the scriptural account of the conception and birth of Budda (as Tezuka calls the Buddha in his manga), yet most of these pages are filled with the swashbuckling tragedy of the boy-hero Chapura and his mother, both of whom Tezuka creates as slaves who suffer horribly from the inhumanities of an unjust Brahmanical caste system. These volumes interweave an action-packed story about their struggle to survive poverty and war with the fortuitous appearance of the newly born Shiddaruta (or Siddhartha, the Buddha's real name; after his enlightenment his followers called him the Buddha, which means Enlightened One). Chapura's complex story, which extends for over 200 pages, ends with his miraculous adoption by the warrior general Buda Shōgun, his innocent but illicit love affair with the Kosara (or Kosala, an Indian kingdom) princess Marikka, his battle to prove himself by force of arms against the cruel Handaka, warrior *extraordinaire* (and Tezuka invention) from the Koriya Kingdom, and finally his execution by his patron, Buda Shōgun. Chapura dies for having the gall to pretend to be a warrior when he was after all nothing but a slave.[10] Chapura's destruction, with its bleak picture of how human life can be demeaned into something that is nasty, brutish, and short, serves as a dramatic yet purposeful prelude to Budda's own story, for it is this same world that Budda works tirelessly to change throughout the rest of the manga.

Tezuka also adds characters who become crucially important in Budda's own life. One example is the girl pirate Migeera, whom Shiddaruta meets after secretly slipping out of the palace for a romp outside. Migeera is a shocking addition to the story. She is an outcast who becomes Shiddaruta's first love, in place of the high-born Yashodara who fulfills this role in Buddhist scripture. Defying their caste differences, Migeera later boldly enters the palace to fight for Shiddaruta, where she ends up being brutally tortured, blinded, and finally exiled by Shiddaruta's father, King Suddodana. The king is appalled by his son's infatuation with an outcast, an association which threatens Shiddaruta's accession to the throne. Following this, Shiddaruta gives in to his father's demands and marries Yashodara out of duty. As love grows, he falls into deep emotional conflict over his loves, his duty, and his budding religious aspirations. In this way, Tezuka transforms Shiddaruta's subsequent flight from the palace from a story about a person who tires of a life of meaningless sensual indulgence into a story of high adventure and low tragedy.

Tezuka also adds action sequences to *Budda* that frequently take the story beyond traditional scriptural accounts, and which add adrenaline-pumping excitement to the drama. For example, he adds a thrilling and shocking twist to the original tale of Ajase (or Ajatas´atru), the son of King Seeniya (or Bimbisara) and an actual figure in the Buddha legend who ruled during the last eight years of the Buddha's life and conspired with the Buddha's rival Daibadatta (or Devadatta) in a plot to kill the Buddha. Tezuka portrays Ajase as an insanely jealous child who hates Budda because of his own father's unstinting devotion to him, and because it has been prophesied that Budda will kill King Seeniya in order to ascend to the throne. In a sequence filled with suspense, Ajase becomes an assassin, shooting Budda in the stomach with an arrow one day as Budda is about to give his daily sermon (Figure 6.3).

Tezuka also embellishes episodes involving famous disciples. One example is the story of Ananda, who according to the Buddhist tradition was the Buddha's favorite and his personal attendant. In Buddhist scripture, all we know about Ananda's past is that he was dedicated, as a son of a S'akya family, to serve in the Buddha's retinue. Tezuka makes Ananda's conversion more interesting by filling in the details. In the manga version, prior to meeting Budda, Ananda is a merciless brigand, consumed with lust for murder and himself invincible because he is under the protection of a female serpent deity. Even Tezuka admits that he "went to extremes" in this portion of the story.[11] Ananda's tale, though, like those of Migeera and Ajase, adds moments of high drama to the narrative, helping make *Budda* a can't-put-it-down page turner with exciting characters, suspenseful plot lines, and keep-'em-guessing end-

Figure 6.3 **Budda wounded by Prince Ajase's arrow**

ings that keep readers coming back—and purchasing more of the magazines carrying the series—to see what happens next.

Visualizing the Buddha's Story through Manga Conventions

Manga is an intensely visual medium that, like the Japanese *haiku* (seventeen-syllable lyric poem), does not so much describe as directly present "the fragile essence of appearance."[12] *Budda* is a "visualized narrative"—to borrow Frederik Schodt's term—of the Buddha's life.[13] What this means is that the artwork plays more than the ancillary role of simply illustrating the meaning of the text. As Eri Izawa points out, image and text are equally important in manga, merging together into a powerfully synthetic whole.[14] Tezuka achieved this by creating his own cinematic style of manga artwork. In his autobiography, *Boku wa Mangaka* (I Am a Manga Artist), he writes about his dissatisfaction with the conventional manga of his time, which were drawn from the audience's viewpoint. In these manga, the story panels were like a stage play being viewed from the seats in a theater. Such an audience-centered manga, with its flat and unchanging perspective, could never deliver the punch, the psychological power, or the atmosphere that Tezuka wanted in his comics, and so Tezuka borrowed the cinematic effects he had discovered in German and French movies. Mixing together far-away shots, close-ups, and angled perspectives, and employing a variety of transition types—action to action, subject to subject, moment to moment, and aspect to aspect[15]—Tezuka and other artists following him create filmlike action sequences that can be scanned quickly.[16] An example of this in *Budda* is the depiction of Prince Ajase's assassination attempt, shown in Figure 6.3. This series of panels begins with close-up and aspect-to-aspect transition shots followed by a short action sequence with the arrow suddenly moving from the forest where Ajase is hiding to strike its target, Budda's stomach. Employing a repertoire of cinematic effects such as these, Tezuka powerfully draws the reader-viewer into this and other dramatic moments in his story.

Another feature of Tezuka's visualized narrative is his handling of the image of the Buddha. Icons have always played an important role in Japanese Buddhism, and statues and paintings of the Buddha still remain visually powerful symbols that make the abstruse and spiritually exotic doctrines of Buddhism more readily comprehensible to the Japanese. Tezuka's image of the Buddha, though, has special visual impact, for three reasons.

First, it offers a Buddha image that shocks the reader because of its unconventionality. Tezuka's Buddha is not an unmoving statue or the *Sambhoga-kaya* (divinized devotional image), a glorious form endowed with the thirty-two marks of the great man. Budda is instead a human being—alive, breathing, and posing in ways that are visually striking precisely because they are so different from the typical statues of the Buddha sitting in the lotus position. An example of this occurs in volume 9, in a scene in which Budda jumps into a river in order to save a disciple from being eaten by voracious crocodiles.[17] This swimming

Figure 6.4 **The troubled Budda gazing into the heavens**

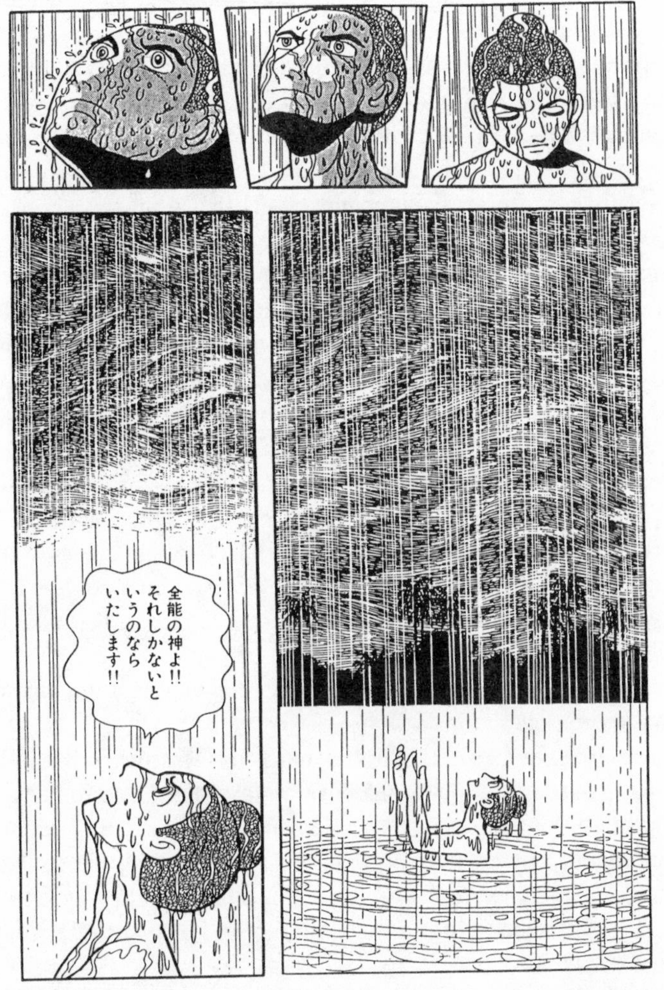

Budda, seen doing the breast stroke in a river just as you and I might, reveals Tezuka's essentially humanistic treatment of his subject. Throughout *Budda*, Budda is treated less as a god than as a fully human man who struggles through life trying to make sense of it all, not unlike the reader, sometimes falling into despair when he can find no answers to his questions about the meaning of life and death, even from the heavens (Figure 6.4).

Second, Tezuka offers an image with which his young target readers can easily identify. As *Budda* was first serialized in *shōnen* (boy-oriented) magazines, it comes as no surprise that Budda is very youthful. Even at the moment of his enlightenment, attained according to Buddhist tradition when he was 29, Tezuka's Budda looks like a youngish boy. It is not until volume 10, two-thirds of the way through the story, that he begins to age, becoming a full-fledged adult whose features resemble those of the statues of him familiar to most Japanese.

Third, Tezuka deliberately makes the young Shiddaruta into a cartoonlike abstraction. Tezuka is a master at making the faces of his heroes and heroines more iconic than realistic. His minimalist approach in drawing Shiddaruta's youthful visage, using sparse lines with little detail, has the effect of making him appear more generic than individualistic. As comics theorist Scott McCloud argues, such a simply drawn face creates a "vacuum into which our identity and awareness are pulled."[18] This allows readers to mentally place themselves in the story by visually identifying with Shiddaruta-Budda's character (Figure 6.5). This is where the power of manga lies; by animating the Buddha's image and making him eternally youthful, Tezuka allows his young readers to read themselves into the scene psychologically and iconographically in a way that would be impossible for someone watching actor Keanu Reeves play Buddha in *The Little Buddha*.

Contextualizing the Story for a Japanese Audience

Of course, Tezuka's key problem in retelling the Buddha's story is to overcome its "otherness," its distance from the real worlds and lives of its readers. As religions historian Wendy Doniger has noted, "it may well be that it is the very nature of classics to be other, to refer back to a lost golden age and to speak with an archaic diction that we must strain to understand. We sense instinctively that our classics were born long ago in a galaxy far, far away."[19] This distance is readily apparent in actual Buddhist scripture. The Buddha's story takes place in geographically distant India, not in Japan. Buddha was an Indian ascetic who lived in a foreign Vedic-Brahmanical culture and spoke a hybrid dialect of Sanskrit; he was not Japanese. He lived 2,500 years ago in a technologically simple age, not in the high-tech world of today. All the translations of Buddhist scripture, including the most readable, preserve archaic diction that is difficult for the modern reader. Faced with all this, what tack can Tezuka or any modern author take to reduce this feeling of otherness? How can the classic story of the Buddha's life, which on the surface seems so remote and alien, be made to feel familiar and relevant to a modern Japanese audience?

Figure 6.5 **Shiddaruta drawn iconically as a young boy**

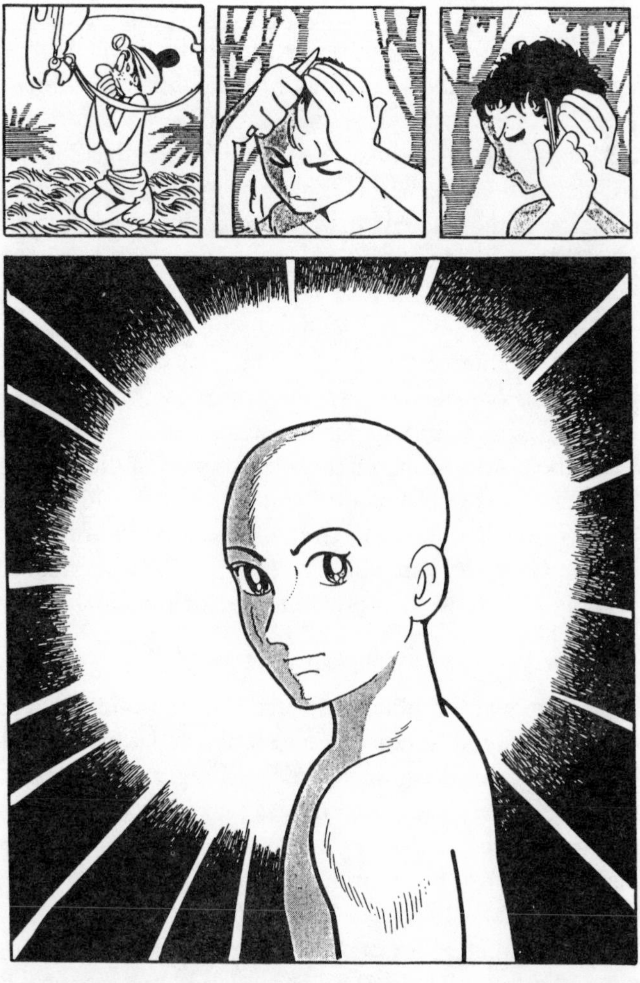

Bernardo Bertolucci takes one approach in *The Little Buddha* by juxtaposing the Buddha's legend with life in the modern world. Set in the present, *The Little Buddha* tells the story of Jesse, a young American boy from Seattle, Washington, whose life changes dramatically when he meets Tibetan lamas who come from Bhutan to Seattle to find the reincarnation of their former teacher. They believe Jesse to be that person, and in the course of the movie gradually tell him Buddha's story to help guide him back to his former spiritual life as a Buddhist holy man. In the movie Bertolucci deliberately intersperses scenes of the Buddha's spiritual biography with his narration of Jesse's everyday life in modern Seattle. The exotic tale of the Buddha's search for spiritual freedom, which initially seems totally irrelevant to Jesse's own life, becomes a master narrative for interpreting Jesse's life by the end of the movie. When Jesse travels to a Tibetan monastery in Bhutan, gorgeously filmed in warm reddish and brown earth hues, he moves directly into the Buddha's story as it is lived by the modern Tibetan lamas. In doing so, he escapes a spiritually vacuous life in contemporary America, symbolized by cold and silent skyscrapers filmed in bluish hues, a maze of superhighways which seem to go nowhere, and his parents' stylishly empty modern house, a "palace" on top of a hill overlooking the Seattle skyline. In sharp contrast to this world, the Buddhist world of the Tibetan monastery, initially so unreal compared to life in Seattle, becomes a meaningful alternative and a refuge from the emptiness of the modern, urban West.

In *Budda,* Tezuka takes a different tack from Bertolucci's. Whereas Bertolucci juxtaposes classic story and modern life, keeping them separate until Jesse journeys to the East at the end of the movie, Tezuka fuses the two together from the start, using the magic of the manga medium to fabricate one seamless reality out of the ancient Buddhist and modern Japanese worlds. Part of Tezuka's genius is his ability to insert modern symbols, characters, events, and details into the archaic setting of the story without creating anachronisms that seem "out of place." By drawing in features from the modern world, Tezuka draws out the Buddha's relevance for today.

Budda contains many examples of such narrative fusion. To illustrate the famous Fire Sermon about how human life burns with the fires of craving, Tezuka tells the story of a boy who goes to the big city with dreams of getting rich quick. The plot resembles Kenji Mizoguchi's famous movie *Ugetsu*, itself a postwar cinematic retelling of an eighteenth-century ghost story by Akinari Ueda. In *Budda*, however, Tezuka preserves the story's in-the-past, "once-upon-a-time" setting while giving the scenes a contemporary flavor in a variety of ways. The big city the boy travels to is a dazzling "20th B.C. Fox," an ancient Hollywood cityscape in lights (Figure 6.6). Excited by city life, the boy proves to be a "type A" personality who starts his own restaurant business. He tries to outcompete his rival, whose restaurant name "Rairaidai Hanten" sounds like a Japanese fast-food chain, by lighting up his marquee with thousands of candles, a move that ends in disaster when his restaurant catches fire and destroys the entire city. This version of the story makes

Figure 6.6 **An ancient city—"20th B.C. Fox"**

もうひとつ
話をしよう
むかし むかし
ある栄えた町があった
その町はにぎやかで
いつも明るく
ともしびが
燃えていた……
20B.C
FOX

the Fire Sermon meaningful by giving it a contemporary feel. The burning city, associated with modern Hollywood but orientalized artistically to suggest a Japanese locale (with Japanese lettering on the signs and Japanese architecture), brings home the point that craving is at the heart of the hustle and bustle of "go-go" urban life in modern Japan. This same idea is expressed by a panel showing a nuclear mushroom cloud and a world on fire seen from space, frightening and contemporary images of what the fires of craving can do to us today.

Images also abound that strike even closer to home. One scene in the story of Ajase finds the young prince at home, seemingly doing his homework after a hard day at school. Ajase's mother, however, much to her dismay, discovers what he is really up to; she catches her son in the act of reading a porno manga (Figure 6.7).

"If you're going to read comics," she scolds, as any boy's mother might, "at least read something wholesome like Disney or Mickey Mouse!"

There are also school scenes that are readily familiar to any Japanese boy. In one panel, the god Burafuman (Brahma) is explaining to Shiddaruta the interconnectivity of all life. The drawing has Burafuman posed like a junior high school science teacher using slides and a pointer,

Figure 6.7 **Prince Ajase caught in the act of reading porno**

and the picture on the board looks like something from a sex education class dealing with sperm and the fertilization of eggs (Figure 6.8). Tezuka also includes scenes that deal directly with social issues of special concern to his young audience. When *Budda* appeared in serialization in the 1980s, *ijime* (bullying) in schools was a growing problem, and Japan faced an increasing incidence of suicide among children who were being ostracized and tormented by their schoolmates for being different.[20] To consider this issue, Tezuka includes a long episode about the childhood tragedy of Daibudatta, a rival of the Buddha in Buddhist scripture who plotted to assassinate him. While giving Daibudatta the same role in *Budda*, Tezuka adds a section that offers an explanation of why Daibudatta is so evil: During childhood, Daibudatta was cruelly bullied by school classmates, whom he eventually kills in revenge.

Tezuka also makes allusions to contemporary cinema. Famous movie characters make guest appearances in *Budda*, such as ET (from the movie *ET*) and Yoda (from *The Emperor Strikes Back*), who show up as monks in the *sangha,* or Buddhist order (Figure 6.9). Another example is Daibudatta's persuading the monks to choose him as their leader; as they vote for him, they raise their hands into the sky like the Hindus worshipping the extraterrestrials in Steven Spielberg's *Close Encounters of the Third Kind.*

Tezuka employs many contemporary symbols, often in humorous

Figure 6.8 **Burafuman teaching Budda about the interconnection of life**

Figure 6.9 **ET and Yoda as members of the Sangha**

ways. For example, when Prince Ajase falls for the Greek slave girl Yuderica, he does so both figuratively and literally in a panel where a large heart, the symbol of his "crush," crashes down on him, causing him to fall flat on his face (Figure 6.10). Tezuka also resorts to commercial symbols for comic effect. Sujata, the woman who saves Budda from starvation by offering him some milk porridge, is also the brand name of a "Swiss" coffee creamer marketed in Japan in television commercials. In *Budda* she appears as a cute little blond Swiss girl, true to her commercialized form (see Figure 6.1). Tezuka also uses his own symbol, one that any fan instantly recognizes. Tezuka's trademark is his *hyōtantsugi* (literally, "patched gourd"). This figure has a tendency to randomly appear in much of Tezuka's work, often with no apparent connection to the plot (Figure 6.11). The hyōtantsugi was first drawn

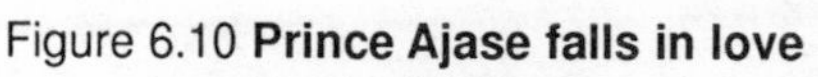

Figure 6.10 **Prince Ajase falls in love**

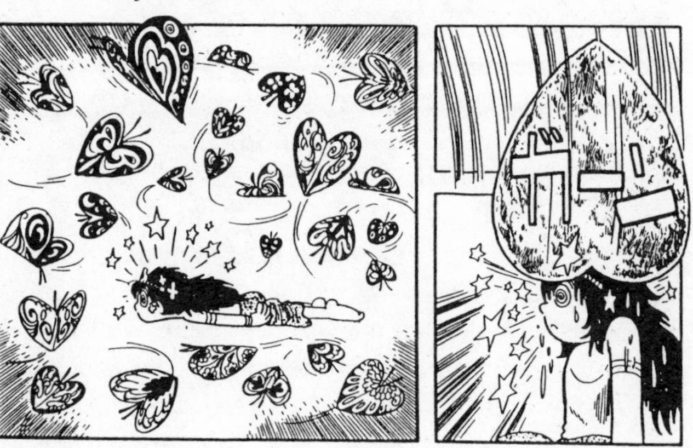

Figure 6.11 **Hyōtantsugi with the words "this has no connection [with the story]"**

by Tezuka's younger sister when they were both in elementary school, and Tezuka adopted it as his own and began to include it in his manga beginning with *Kurubeki Sekai Uchū Daiankoku Hen* (The Coming World, The Darkness of Space) in 1951.[21] In *Budda*, the hyōtantsugi often shows up at moments of great dramatic tension. For example, it appears as the symbol of slavehood in volume 1, when young Chapura lifts up his foot to show a hyōtantsugi mark. This dramatically reveals his true background: He is a slave, not a warrior, and as such is ineligible to become Budda Shōgun's heir. The hyōtantsugi appears again at

Budda's last meal, as a symbol, with its piglike features, of the pig meat Budda is given by Cunda at the Mango grove, which causes his death by food poisoning.

Using Nature to Express Human Emotion and the Sense of the Spiritual

One key to *Budda*'s commercial success is that, like best-sellers anywhere, it evokes feelings that appeal to a mass audience. One way that Tezuka does this is by deliberately expropriating Walt Disney's "feel-good" anthropomorphic view of nature. One of the great attractions of any Disney movie, from *Bambi* to *The Little Mermaid*, is the way nature, especially animals of the wild, is anthropomorphized; the nonhuman world becomes an extension of the human one, and the animals that inhabit it take on human characteristics and express the gamut of human emotions. Tezuka himself loved American animation and claims in his autobiography to have seen *Snow White* over fifty times and *Bambi* over eighty times. Tezuka clearly borrows from Disney's mostly benevolent view of the natural world, presenting in *Budda* happy scenes of cute little furry animals surrounding the hero (Figure 6.12).

Tezuka goes beyond Disney to explore the darker side of life and human nature as well. *Budda* deals primarily with the psychological complexities of life, delving deeply into many adult themes: facing the fear of death; dealing with the consequences of morally inexcusable acts; and living with life's ambiguities, particularly those concerning the meaning of existence. Budda himself, as well as many other major characters in the story, is constantly plagued by intense and unresolved feelings of guilt, anxiety, and frustration in the face of what seems to be life's essential meaninglessness. Tezuka uses nature as a medium for expressing these feelings, filling nature with sad, dark, and sometimes even dangerously violent expressions of human emotion. In his rendering of the Great Renunciation, for example, Shiddaruta's horse Kanthaka is seen standing behind Yashodara, both wife and steed showing grief over the loss of their beloved master (Figure 6.13). Even more typical is Tezuka's reliance on stormy weather to create an atmosphere of foreboding, especially in key scenes. In one example (not found in scripture), the Kosara Prince Ruri (Vidudabha), half-mad from the shame of being born of a slave mother and from the guilt of having burned her to death, strikes Budda, who is trying to get him to squarely face what he has done.

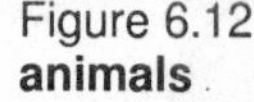

Figure 6.12 **Shiddaruta walking in the jungle surrounded by Disneyesque animals**

The scene in which Prince Ruri collapses before Budda after exploding in anger and drawing his sword to kill him is beautifully drawn against the backdrop of a darkened palace, as is the dark night outside with its terrifying thunderstorm, which mirrors the Prince's black psyche and the perilous moment where Budda's life hangs in the balance (Figure 6.14).

Nonhuman dimensions of nature are also prominent in *Budda*. Though Tezuka was enamored of Disney, he was also a Japanese artist steeped in a religious tradition in which nature is the locus of the sacred. In the

Figure 6.13 **Kanthaka and Yashodara grieving over the Great Renunciation**

Japanese Shintō religion, nature is the place par excellence where one can sense the awe and mystery that are the deepest evidence of the presence of the gods. Throughout *Budda*, the action unfolds against a backdrop of spectacular mountain and jungle landscapes, drawn in photorealistic detail (Figure 6.15). The world of nature portrayed here is beautiful, creative, and good, and serves to mute the often horrific stories of human greed, ignorance, and suffering. Nature's splendor provides a feeling of hope, and the possibility of transcending the sordid side of human life and going to a higher level that is one with this pristine natural world. Tezuka's focus on nature as a source of spiritual inspiration is found in the most critical scene of the Buddha's story, his enlightenment under the *Bo* tree (the tree under which Buddha received enlightenment; from the Sanskrit *bodhi*). In Buddhist scripture, this is the moment when the Buddha attains *nirvana* (the cessation of craving through intuitive insight into the suffering, impermanence, and selfless character of all existence). In *Budda*, this scene comes off quite differently. Two crickets alight on Shiddaruta's left thigh. One is male and the other female. They begin chirping. One thing naturally leads to another

Figure 6.14 **The storm outside prince Ruri's palace during his attack on Budda**

and they make love before Shiddaruta's very eyes (Figure 6.16). For Shiddaruta, this is a moment of spiritual breakthrough. The crickets, he realizes, are his brothers and sisters, living, loving, and dying just as human beings do. There is a key difference, however. The crickets live their lives *mushin* (selflessly), free from the distracting thoughts and cravings that ordinarily fill the human mind. Budda muses, wondering how he can live a natural and spontaneous life, as these insects do. Later, when he achieves complete realization, Budda sees that since human

Figure 6.15 **The beautiful natural world within which the drama of Budda's life unfolds**

beings exist in this natural world just as "the trees, the grass, the mountains, and the rivers [do], there is definitely a purpose to human life!"[22]

A Buddha Drama for Young Boys and Their "Spiritual" Concerns

Perhaps the most dramatic shift in Tezuka's retelling of the Buddha's story lies in the changes he makes to appeal to his young, male audi-

Figure 6.16 **Crickets falling in love on Buddha's thigh**

ence. Tezuka not only divides the narrative into easily consumable episodes that provide adventure and thrills, but also reworks it around the central theme of losing one's mother. What is the story of the Buddha about, after all? Generally speaking, it is a story about facing up to the facts of human life—that life is suffering and that the Buddha has found

Figure 6.17 Queen Māya dying after giving birth to the infant Shiddaruta

a way to overcome suffering through renunciation and meditation. In *Budda*, however, one particular form of suffering stands out: maternal loss. What marks the first tragedy in the Buddha's life? The death of his mother Māya at his birth (Figure 6.17). This loss, plus the loss of his first love, Migeera, are the defining moments that lead to Budda's flight from the palace in search of spiritual freedom.

Several other major characters in *Budda* lose or are separated from their mothers at an early age as well. Chapura abandons his mother in order to pursue his dream of becoming a general of the Kosara kingdom. He does succeed in becoming Buda Shōgun's heir, but then suffers enormous guilt when his mother rushes to his side to tend him after he is wounded by the treacherous Handaka. The climax of this scene is reached when Chapura is killed along with his mother as he tries to save her from Buda Shōgun, who intends to kill her to hush up the slave status of his heir. Ironically, mother and son are reunited in death when they are skewered together by a spear. Tatta, a companion of Chapura in volume 1 and a close friend of Budda throughout the rest of the story, also loses

Figure 6.18 **Ananda's mother is executed**

his mother, who is killed when Buda Shōgun's army burns his city to the ground.

Budda's most famous and infamous disciples also experience maternal loss. Ananda, Budda's closest follower, lands on the wrong side of the law early in life, turning to violence and crime in response to the childhood trauma of seeing his mother brutally executed by soldiers (Figure 6.18). Daibudatta, Budda's evil disciple and most dangerous opponent, loses not one but two mothers. His birth mother is forced to abandon him after he kills some schoolmates who have bullied him beyond endurance. Banished from his village, Daibudatta eventually finds a new home with a family of wolves, only to lose his wolf mother as well when she dies soon after in a drought (Figure 6.19). The two major lay characters in the story, Prince Ruri and Prince Ajase, lose their mothers as well. Prince Ruri kills his, burning down her hut after learning that she was a low-born slave of the Shaka. Prince Ajase is separated from his mother after his failed attempt on Budda's life; as punishment he is imprisoned in a tower where she cannot visit him. The slave girl Yuderika eventually takes her place, mothering Ajase until he falls in love with her, but she is then killed by Ajase's father because as a slave she interferes with the father's plans for his son's succession to the throne.

As these examples show, the frequency of maternal loss in *Budda* is striking, with some boys abandoning or killing their mothers in their drive to get ahead, while others lose their mothers to violent men who

Figure 6.19 **Daibudatta's wolf mother dies**

kill them viciously, forcing the boys to go it alone in the cold, harsh "real world" without a mother's love and support. What is one to make of so many cases of maternal loss? Perhaps the best way to view this recurring pattern is in light of some of the social realities that are basic to a young boy's life in modern Japan. Many researchers on Japanese childhood have pointed out that the transition from infancy to adulthood is more demanding psychologically in Japan than in other countries. The famous Japanese psychologist Takeo Doi sees Japanese childhood as marked by feelings of *amae* (passive dependence), a continuation of the infant's experience at the mother's breast. Children in Japan stay very close to their mothers in their early years; they are rarely left alone, usually sleep beside their mother, and traditionally have been carried on their mother's back *(onbu)* when taken outside (though this has changed in recent years as baby strollers have become more common). Children are also weaned from the breast rather late in childhood. As a result, as Ian Buruma states, "emotional security tends to depend almost entirely on the physical presence of the mother."[23] Male children in particular, and especially eldest sons, like all the aforementioned characters in *Budda*, experience in early childhood a paradiselike situation in which they enjoy pure freedom, the indulgence of their every whim, and unconditional love. As Japanese boys reach school age, however, they must go through the trauma of separating from their mothers and submitting to the demands of a formal education with its increasingly harsh requirements to study hard, conform to the group, and struggle for success in a highly competitive examination system. To successfully make this transition and achieve a measure of individual autonomy, Japanese boys must thus come to terms with fears of losing maternal intimacy and yearnings to return to a state of amae.[24]

Given these circumstances, it is natural that the loss-of-mother stories in *Budda* should have a strong appeal to boys or young men who are themselves going through a similar experience. The mothers in *Budda* personify traditional mother figures—warm, supportive, nurturing, and indulgent—while their sons express the feelings of sadness and guilt that a child may experience when faced with the inevitability of breaking away from a life of amae to live as a more autonomous individual. Is *Budda* not about dealing with the powerfully conflicting emotions of yearning for amae versus striving for independence? This is certainly what the young Shiddaruta seems to personify.

In another sense, though, Budda resembles the mothers that populate his story. The mothers in *Budda* willingly play the scapegoat and suffer any punishment in the service of their sons, in giving their sons unconditional love. Similarly, Budda's body is tortured by horrendous acts of asceticism, pummeled by rocks, shot with arrows, and cut with knives throughout the twelve volumes of *Budda*, all in the hope of helping suffering human beings. The climax of Budda's acts of unconditional love comes in the final volume when he saves Prince Ajase, Budda's deadly opponent and the heartless killer of his own father. For two years, Budda tries to heal Prince

Ajase's horrible head swelling, caused by the poison given him by his traitorous ally Daibudatta. Here Budda plays a nursing mother, touching Ajase's wounds day after day until he is cured by the power of love. In Tezuka's narrative, Budda is brought to his second and most important experience of enlightenment when he finally sees Ajase smile. What he realizes, not under the Bo tree but at Prince Ajase's bedside, is that this capacity for love lies not just within himself, but within all beings, including the prince. This is what Budda means in the final volume when he exclaims to the world around him that all humans are *kami* (divine beings who possess the capacity to love with selfless compassion in the face of evil and suffering).[25] Tezuka here is touching in a very general way on the key Mahayana Buddhist ideal of the bodhisattva.

This spiritual ideal is underscored by the wordless story that frames the beginning and the end of *Budda.* This is the Hare Jataka, a popular tale from Buddhist scripture that relates a previous life of the Buddha. In the Hare Jataka, the Buddha to be, reborn as a bunny, offers his own body as flesh for a starving Brahman. This is a tale of selfless compassion in the most basic sense. Its message is one that Tezuka doubtless felt was important to convey to an audience growing up in an increasingly atomized, competitive, and materialistic society.

Notes

1. Ian Reader, "*Manga:* Comic Options—The Japanese Tradition for Illustrated Stories," *Japan Digest* (October 1990), p. 19.

2. Frederik L. Schodt, *Dreamland Japan: Writings on Modern Manga* (Berkeley, CA: Stone Bridge, 1996), pp. 19–22.

3. Ibid., p. 237.

4. "Tezuka Osamu, Father of Postwar Manga Culture," *The East* 31 (September–October 1995), p. 10.

5. Chiei Go, "Kaisetsu," in Osamu Tezuka, *Budda*, vol. 1 (Tokyo: Ushio Shuppansha, 1995).

6. Kazuhiko Murakami, "Kaisetsu," in Tezuka, *Budda*, vol. 3.

7. Nobuyuki Ukita, chief editor, *Komikku Tomu*, private correspondence. *Budda* began its twenty-second printing in 1995.

8. See, for example, Tezuka, *Budda*, vol. 1, pp. 6–7. After showing a map of the country of Kōsara, where the story's plot will unfold, Tezuka has a town merchant in a succeeding panel explain to readers the region's geographical details. See also vol. 2, p. 32, and the final pages of each volume.

9. See, for example, Howard Hatton, "Translating Scripture in the Comic Medium," *The Bible Translator*, 36 (October 1985), pp. 430–437.

10. The motif of the failed hero is a staple in Japanese folklore, history, and drama. See Ivan Morris, *The Nobility of Failure* (New York: Noonday, 1975).

11. See Tezuka's "In Lieu of an Afterword" (The Actual Legend of Gautama Buddha), in Tezuka, *Budda*, vol. 12.

12. Roland Barthes, *Empire of Signs* (New York: Hill and Wang, 1982), p. 77.

13. Schodt, *Dreamland*, p. 26.

14. Eri Izawa, "What Are Manga and Anime?" Unpublished paper, Internet Web site, http://www.mit.edu/people/rei/Anime.html.

15. An "aspect-to-aspect" transition is a series of comic panels that move from one part of a scene or image to another — for example, a frame of someone's full face, then the eyes, then one of the eyes, with a tear beginning to roll down the cheek. Using different aspects or angles extends the drama of a moment out over a full manga page.

16. See Scott McCloud, *Understanding Comics* (Northampton, MA: Kitchen Sink, 1993), p. 77 ff.

17. Tezuka, *Budda*, vol. 9, pp. 139–143.

18. McCloud, *Understanding Comics*, p. 36.

19. Wendy Doniger O'Flaherty, *Other People's Myths* (New York: MacMillan, 1988), p. 50.

20. See Murakami Yoshio, "Bullies in the Classroom," *Japan Quarterly*, 32 (October–December, 1985), pp. 407–411.

21. Ishigami Mitsutoshi, *Tezuka Osamu no Jidai* (Tokyo: Tairiku Shobō, 1989), p. 207.

22. Tezuka, *Budda*, vol. 6, p. 246.

23. Ian Buruma, *Behind the Mask: On Sexual Demons, Sacred Mothers, Transvestites, Gangsters and Other Japanese Cultural Heroes* (New York: Meridian, 1984), p. 20. For more on child rearing, see Takie Sugiyama Lebra, *Japanese Patterns of Behavior* (Honolulu: University of Hawaii Press, 1976), especially chapter 8, "Early Socialization."

24. Ibid., p. 21.

25. Tezuka, *Budda*, vol. 12, pp. 188–194.

7

The Romantic, Passionate Japanese in Anime

A Look at the Hidden Japanese Soul

Eri Izawa

To say that the Japanese are romantic—imaginative, sentimental, individualistic, passionate!—might earn one strange glances in much of the world. The Japanese word *roman* (from the English "romance") symbolizes the emotional, the grand, the epic; the taste of heroism, fantastic adventure, and the melancholy; passionate love, personal struggle, and eternal longing. Yet many Westerners see Japan as a cold, calculating land of antlike workers, brutal efficiency, and overwhelming bureaucracy. Students are seen as oppressed slaves to their studies, pounded down like nails until their imaginations and individuality are crushed, or until they are driven to suicide. World War II gave us the image of the fierce *samurai* warrior in his *kamikaze* plane, fanatic to the point of suicide. Japanese social culture is often seen as blanketed under stifling layers of politeness and formality, characterized by endless bowing.[1] Finally, it is often assumed that Japan cannot produce anything original on its own—that perhaps even culture with a "romantic" flavor is simply borrowed from the West.

Much of the limited *manga* (comic book), animation, and video game material that trickles into the West from Japan, and for which Japan is becoming well known, does little to counter the heartless, flat image that many people hold of Japan. Many of the Japanese animated videos that come into Western countries seem almost obsessed with sex and violence. The best-known Japanese video games, such as Capcom's *Street Fighter* series, also tend to highlight violence.

Certainly these stereotypes are not completely undeserved, and those who accuse Japan of trade wars, racism, or sexism have quite an arsenal of supportive facts at their disposal.[2] It hardly helps that the Japanese do not often share their private thoughts with outsiders, displaying instead the faces they are taught to show each other: brusqueness toward perceived inferiors and equals, and polite submission to social superiors. But there is another way to explore the soul of Japan, and that is to look at what the Japanese themselves read, watch, and play in their own spare time, and what they create for their peers. Anyone familiar with Japan's folklore and traditional arts will not be surprised to find a strong "romantic" element in this material.

Romanticism is hardly new or unusual in Japan, and is found in a variety of media. The Lady Murasaki, who lived at the turn of the millennium, is renowned for writing what may have been the world's first full novel, *The Tale of Genji*, which is rich in poetic emotion and imagery. Though the feudal years pushed the arts into the background of Japanese thought, historic figures like the tragic warlord Yoshitsune were eventually painted with a legendary, Arthurian brush. In the meantime, Japanese folklore remained rich in fairy tales of fantastic creatures, ghosts, and monsters, aided by belief in gods and spirits from Shinto and Buddhism and given depth by Taoism. Even World War II-era Japan, geared up for battle, fell in love with "romantic" music about soldiers' experiences in China. Akira Kurosawa's films have inspired such movies as *The Magnificent Seven* and even *Star Wars*. And up to the present day, Chinese legends and literary classics, such as the *Shui-hu Chuan* (known as *Suikoden* in Japanese and *The Water Margin* in English), have been heavily romanticized by the Japanese and have spawned offshoots from traditional artwork to a computer game.

Today, one of the best places to get a taste of Japanese roman is in what is commonly known as the *anime* media. This includes the manga industry, the anime (animated video and film) industry, and the video game (e.g., Nintendo and Sony PlayStation) industry, all of which are tied together by their reliance on a characteristic, animation-style art. Why, one might ask, look at anime? One reason is its huge popularity, not just in Japan but increasingly overseas as well. Another is the nature of the medium itself; it is an ideal story-telling mechanism, able to combine graphic art, prose, characterization, cinematography techniques (even in the manga), and a variety of literary narrative techniques. The video games and animated films also incorporate music, an added form of romantic expression. Drawn by hand, anime is also separated from reality by a crucial gap of fiction. Drawn characters and worlds can depict fantastic and otherwise impossible scenes, making the stories and images "safe" for exploration without, in theory at least, either disrupting or being disrupted by the real world. The images are also simple enough, unlike some forms of highly detailed traditional art, to allow people to project their own ideas onto the images. Finally, anime can be explored alone, in the privacy of one's mind, free from outside observation. Possessing these traits, the anime-based media provide an ideal path for escapism, and hence a look at what people are seeking at a deep, personal level that the "real world" cannot touch.

As a bonus for non-Japanese, anime are also relatively accessible to those who do not speak or read the Japanese language, as the pictures make following the story fairly easy, and even exciting. The expressiveness of the characters' faces is often proof that "a picture is worth a thousand words." Since many of the faces and settings do not look specifically Japanese, Western audiences can immerse themselves in the anime universe with relative ease.

For real inquiry, however, we must push past the narrow sample of anime material that is available outside Japan and look deeper. Past the pure combat video games lie plot-rich epic fantasy role-playing and social interaction games, only a fraction of which make it into Western countries. On Japanese bookstore shelves and movie and TV screens are many works that may contain slapstick, sex, and violence, but that also reach far beyond these elements. To get an idea of what lies beneath the surface, the less visible and often surprising heart that beats at the core of much of Japanese anime, let us first take a look at three particular examples.

Final Fantasy

One of the best examples of romantic anime is the video game *Final Fantasy VI* (available as *Final Fantasy III* in North America). Hugely popular in Japan, the *Final Fantasy* series shook up the world video game industry in 1997 when it jumped ship from Nintendo to Sony, helping lift Sony's PlayStation past Super Nintendo into the number one spot in video game machine sales. *Final Fantasy* also contains the classic elements of Japanese roman, aspects that echo throughout other anime again and again.

One of *Final Fantasy VI*'s most striking features is its music. Music plays a key role in the game, with each major character having his or her own theme song; in fact, in the game's plot, one of the characters must sing her theme song in an opera! Most of the tunes are melancholy, reflecting the tragic histories of their characters. (One player's mother insisted her son turn down the sound, because she found the music too "depressing."[3]) In barren, snowy wastelands, the music is mysterious and lonely; in a bustling town, it becomes lively and simple; when the heroes' airship flies through the skies after the final victory, the music is proud and triumphant, yet still a little sad.

Visually, too, *Final Fantasy VI* distinguishes itself. As small as the characters are on the screen, they still display surprise, joy, and sadness. The scenery is incredibly vivid, dripping with atmosphere. A town of thieves is dark, rainy, and decrepit. An enemy castle is austere and colorless, built of imposing stone and metal. An ancient ruin is filled with magnificent but bizarre statuary and walkways. Certain scenes leave a permanent impression, such as one where a character hurls herself into the ocean in lonely despair.

The story itself is romantic, set in a fantasy world where magic and technology are intermixed, yet where swords are still the weapon of choice. Mythical monsters and spirits haunt the world, and hidden treasures abound. A group of people, brought together by desperation, join forces to stop the growth of an evil empire; later, when disaster occurs, they band together once more to fight the evil plans of a powerful madman.

The characters are themselves romantic figures; tragedy has haunted their lives, and tragedy sometimes strikes them even within the game. Terra has a mysterious past that has made her into a target in the present; Locke is haunted by memories of his inability to save his girlfriend from death; Cyan had lost his entire family to war; Gau was abandoned by an insane father. The characters struggle through their grief, anger, and uncertainty, torn by fear and conflicting demands. They have to learn to work with one another. At the end of the game, they have won, not only against the enemy, but against their own failings.

The very word "game" tends to imply a shallow pastime, not a long, epic quest filled with grief, passion, and personal growth. Yet such a quest is exactly what *Final Fantasy VI* provides, and it is hardly unique in the anime world.

Fushigi Yūgi

The manga *Fushigi Yūgi* speaks as another prime example of the roman in anime. A girl's comic by Yū Watase, *Fushigi Yūgi*'s main character is

Miaka, a schoolgirl who travels to a magical version of ancient China via a mysterious book. She despises her life in the real world, where she is a *juken* (studying-for-exams) student, trapped in an "examination hell" where her test scores will determine (she thinks) the rest of her life.

The ancient China Miaka visits is a land of enchantment, the Eastern equivalent of Western high fantasy, featuring handsome people in beautiful clothing, spectacular magic, strange monsters, and fascinating legends. Terrible forces are struggling for power, leaving bloodshed in their wake, and Miaka becomes a key player in the contest. With death commonplace, striking even her powerful friends, Miaka discovers what is truly important. Though she falls in love with someone special, caring for and protecting all her friends becomes her first priority. She also learns that there is something else that is just as important as friendship: one's duty to persevere. The death of her friends must not turn her from her mission, because those same friends are trusting her to ensure that they have not died in vain.

Galaxy Express 999

Few authors have focused on the "romance" of space drama as much as Leiji Matsumoto, who is well known for works such as *Captain Harlock* and *Uchūsenkan Yamato* (known as *Starblazers* overseas). One of Matsumoto's best pieces of work is the *Galaxy Express 999* series. The hero in this boys' manga (which has also spawned a TV series and two movies) is young Tetsurō, a destitute earth boy who is suddenly swept up into a high science fiction adventure. The mysterious and beautiful Maetel asks Tetsurō to accompany her on board the legendary spaceship *Galaxy Express 999* to a distant planet where people are given eternal, mechanical bodies for free. Tetsurō willingly agrees, since he desires immortality to help him accomplish his many goals in life.

The setting and imagery of *Galaxy Express 999* is at once fantastic and familiar. The spaceship is modeled after a classic steam locomotive, yet the scenery passing its windows is of strange planets and swirling starscapes. The people Tetsurō meets range the gamut from friendly to treacherous. Each train stop yields a new story—about the pettiness of the shallow-minded, the cowardice of the greedy, the desperation of the destitute, the courage needed to break free of beggary and fight for one's needs, the power of young people who dare to dream. Dreams are lost, found, and sometimes made to come true. Throughout his experience,

Figure 7.1 Leiji Matsumoto's *Galaxy Express 999*. Tetsurō's spaceship-train travels through space, while Tetsurō and Maetel gaze out its window at a passing planet.

Tetsurō discovers, over and over, that immortality is not what he needs; what really matters, he learns, is the ability to dream, and to strive toward turning one's dream into reality.

What do *Galaxy Express 999*, *Fushigi Yūgi*, and *Final Fantasy* have in common, aside from the anime artwork style? They share several things: the magical, fantastic world; the epic story; the focus on the characters' inner struggles, passions, and tragedies. In this, these works are hardly alone; as we shall see below, these themes are everywhere. But where is the romanticism pointing? What is its final message? What are the common threads that bind these creations together? Let us start with a look at the music of anime.

Music

Though not all anime music has an even remotely romantic theme (and manga, obviously, has no music at all), some anime music is distinctly passionate, mysterious, and often melancholy. The original 1981 *Gundam*

TV series music sang of the burning wrath of justice and the grandeur of space. Many of the animated movies and TV series of Leiji Matsumoto feature music that matches the themes of the stories, singing of desperate quests, the passing of the centuries, the vastness of space, and humanity's lost dreams. Even the comedy series *Ranma 1/2*, known for the way it turns serious moments into laughable fiascoes, has songs that express, completely seriously, the preciousness of both happy and sad memories, of walking through a cold rain and reflecting on having failed a loved one, or of the need to stand tall in the face of adversity. Such music encompasses both the personal and the beyond, connecting the individual's heartfelt emotions, whether of heated battle or gentle nostalgia, to a broader, deeper reality such as the sheer enormity of space or the fleeting passage of time.

Images

Of course, the anime world relies primarily on visual images to tell its stories. Some of these provide an exceptional distillation of the romantic element in a single scene or frame. We might see, for example, eternally youthful Locke (*Chōjin Locke*), staring out into a night sky of brilliant stars, alone upon an alien landscape[4]; the young traveler Tetsurō (*Galaxy Express 999*) watching the lights of a mysterious planet fading past his space train's window[5]; the swordswoman Oscar (*The Rose of Versailles*), astride her war-horse with sword raised, commanding her men forward to war in Revolutionary France[6]; post-holocaust warlord Sarasa (*Basara*), engulfed in a gust of cherry blossom petals, weeping for friends killed through own her negligence[7]; cyborg Gally (*Gunnm*) perched on a tall smokestack, overlooking the moonlit maze of a metallic city and contemplating the incompatible mixture of machines and life[8]; the slowly unfolding view of the ancient, proud, vast ruins of a floating castle, as yielded by the clearing clouds (*Laputa: Castle in the Sky*). Though disconnected from the viewer by a vast chasm of time and space, these images somehow remain understandable, capturing in one glance a profound sense of loneliness, grandeur, history and future, and even timelessness.

The Stage and Its Characters

Like many works of European romantic literature, such as *Frankenstein*, many stories from the anime world are touched with the brush of

Figure 7.2 **Yuki Hijiri's *Chōjin Locke.* Eternally youthful Locke, alone upon an alien landscape, stares into a night sky of brilliant stars.**

fantasy. *Final Fantasy*, *Fushigi Yūgi*, and *Galaxy Express 999* are just a small fraction of the works set in fictitious worlds, which should come as no surprise to Western audiences exposed to Japan's fascination with science fiction via TV shows like *Ultraman*, *Robotech*, *Battle of the Planets*, *Voltron*, and *Captain Harlock*. Many other manga and animation stories, however, center on more mundane fields such as baseball, student life, firefighting, medicine, and cooking. Yet even these are often touched by the extraordinary and the supernatural. *Kimagure Orange Road*, at first glance, looks like any other boys' "soap opera" set in modern-day Japan and centered on the relationship between the main character and his two would-be girlfriends—except that the hero has psychic powers. Daigo, an otherwise normal firefighter (*Megumi no Daigo*), has a remarkable sixth sense that enables him to find lives in danger. This presence of the supernatural and beyond within the normal and familiar is a feature frequently encountered in anime.

The essence of the anime world, however, lies in the characters that

Figure 7.3 **Riyoko Ikeda's *The Rose of Versailles*. Swordswoman Oscar commands her men forward to war in Revolutionary France.**

inhabit it, and it is here, perhaps, that the ingredients that attract the Japanese are most apparent. Though the West may see Eastern thinking as quashing individuality, the mental and emotional plight of the individual character in anime is almost never forgotten. In fact, it is often central, and the characters' emotions, even if not on center stage, are often the lights that illuminate the action and give it meaning. *Final Fantasy VI* may be exceptional for its pervasive air of tragedy, but the tendency to highlight the individual struggle is found throughout the anime world.

Even stories about "normal" people are turned into high drama. A young baseball player's struggle to prove himself and to form a functioning team from a collection of schoolmates, most of whom start off as poor at sports, rude, and obnoxious, or with other failings, takes on the proportions of greatness (*Major*). A young golfer, through sheer love of his sport, manages to transform the lives of his friends and competi-

Figure 7.4 **Kishiro Yukito's *Gunnm*. Cyborg Gally, perched on a smoke-stack, overlooks the moonlit maze of a metallic city while contemplating the incompatible mixture of machines and life.**

tors on the golfing greens (*Dan Doh*!!). A high school girl helps a gang member revive his long-twisted dreams of becoming a boxer *(Rokudenashi Blues)*. These thoughts, actions, the very expressions on the characters' faces—joy, sorrow, humiliation, triumph—are magnified by the lens of cartoon art and writing, giving the seemingly minor trials of life a fresh glory, impact, and meaning.

Many characters lead unusual lives in the "lone wolf" mode, burdened with hidden powers, knowledge, or scars that distinguish them from others. A recurring theme in the world of anime is that of the stranger in a strange land. From Osamu Tezuka's *Tetsuwan Atom* (Astro Boy) in the 1960s, to the modern animated production of Masamune Shirow's *Ghost in the Shell*, anime is replete with stories of those both blessed and cursed by the extraordinary. Many characters fight secret battles beneath otherwise normal exteriors. Young students Yūsuke (*Yū Yū Hakusho*) and Ushio (*Ushio to Tora*) fend off ravaging demons of vari-

Figure 7.5 **Osamu Tezuka's *Black Jack.* Maverick surgeon Black Jack, holding a patient who has died, cries out accusingly to God, "Why did you put doctors on this earth?!"**

ous sorts which pop up in their lives, while trying to hide from their friends the knowledge that they are in danger. A more subtle battle smolders quietly within the maverick surgeon Black Jack (*Black Jack*), whose mysterious past has marred his standing in the medical establishment but whose skill with a scalpel is unmatched. Though heartless on the surface—yes, he will perform the life-saving operation, but only for large amounts of money—inside he still cares, often working free of charge to help patients who are weak, good at heart, or victims of evil.

One of the heaviest burdens borne by anime heroes is that of immortality, a subject that the Japanese seem particularly fascinated with. A number of characters possess or achieve immortality, but inevitably find it to be a curse rather than a blessing, with the passing years bringing more pain and frustrated longings than one might expect. The demon high school girl Sōko (from *Ao no Fūin*) and three-eyed Pai (from *3x3*

Eyes) seek nothing more than to become human and live an ordinary life, and even eternally 13-year-old Miyu (*Vampire Princess Miyu*) secretly weeps for her old, human life. Powerful, ever-young Locke is dragged unwillingly time after time into galactic conflict, though he is seemingly more fond of simple farm life. For manga artist Leiji Matsumoto's characters, such as Maetel (*Galaxy Express 999*), immortality is either a plunge into a meaningless existence or a lifetime of bittersweet moments.

Trying desperately to fit in, to understand, to change, to save others, these "different" characters fight fervently for the right to exist as what they are, or were meant to be. In an early story of *Chōjin Locke*, Locke says to a psionic (telepathic) woman warrior who considers herself a mere throwaway tool for someone else's war: "Why don't you live as a human being? . . . [or] will you live on as just a tool . . . ?"[9] In the video game *Dragon Quest*, the young warrior Dai leaves his friends behind and goes off alone to seek clues to his powers, saying, "It seems that people won't be friends with me if they find out I'm not human, . . . so I want to go find the truth by myself. I don't want [you] to hate me."[10] *The Rose of Versailles* finds Oscar, a woman raised as a man, suffering from her secret love for Axel Fersen. "Do all humans endure their desires and hide their love, all alone, like this . . . ?" she wonders.[11] In *Vampire Princess Miyu*, the now-immortal heroine cries deep within herself for her former life as a mortal girl; as she sends a foe to his eternal rest, she asks, "I have no world in which to rest. I wonder . . . which one of us suffers more?"[12] For the immortal characters in anime there often seems to be no rest, only an eternal search for solace.

At this point, it might be appropriate to ask whether all this has any relationship to, or meaning for, the real-world lives of the audience. Or is it all simply escapism? Certainly, the adventures, the exotic landscapes, and the exciting struggles and passions are designed to be fun to read, watch, or play. Anime is definitely commercial entertainment, and big business as well, which some would say practically makes it escapist by definition. Most people need some escape, however, and so rather than discounting anime for providing it, we might better ask: What is it that the consumers of anime are escaping from? What are they escaping to? What is it they seek, or need, that they find in anime?

An easy and perhaps accurate answer to the first question is that anime provides escape from the pressures for conformity and academic and job performance that Japanese seem to suffer more than their share of.

Immersed in one of the worlds of anime, these burdens can be, for the moment at least, left behind. As for what people seek and find in romantic anime, beyond escapism, two elements stand out: lessons about life, and dreams.

Life lesson number one concerns struggle, which may not be fun, but is necessary. The fight is never easy, and the path is often unclear. Sometimes the heart falters and fails, and even triumphs are mixed and bittersweet. The pirate Captain Harlock's battle to save Earth is rewarded by hostility and mistrust (*Captain Harlock*). The high school tennis player Love (*Love*), a girl masquerading as a boy, loses again and again both to her female body, which is physically weaker than a man's body and suffers from severe menstrual cramps, and to her male opponents. Locke's seemingly eternal struggle for peace is set back time and time again by senseless wars and genocides. The game *Lufia II* ends with the deaths of its heroes. Circumstances are cruel; victories come with penalties; and our heroes stumble and fall into fits of despair, anger, and apathy. Sometimes they die. Yet they fight on. Often, the characters find that they must conquer themselves before they can take on the world. It is this dynamic, passionate, continuing struggle of the individual characters that gives these stories life, and not only keeps the audience intrigued but gives them encouragement in their own everyday trials. "Never give up," it tells them, "no matter what happens!"

Lesson number two concerns the interdependence between individuality and teamwork. Obviously, the characters that populate anime are anything but simple cogs in the machine. They wake up to their own unique burdens, tragedies, joys, triumphs, and dreams, in what amounts to almost a glorification of the individual and his or her private struggle. It is also true, though, that one of the most common "morals of the story" bears the superficial title of "teamwork." This message is so common that one almost suspects it to be the work of a national propaganda machine designed specifically to create and maintain a harmonious society. A closer look, however, adds an important insight: that the trumpeted Japanese emphasis on "teamwork" and "duty to others" is, at least in the anime world, a product of friendship, love, and mutual respect, not just some motivational technique employed by large corporations. Even the tragic lone wolf character finds that he fights best when he fights to save others; moreover, he learns that this is his strength and his salvation. This theme is found in *Dragon Quest*, *Ruroni Kenshin*, *Major*, *Fushigi Yūgi, Ushio To Tora*, *Yū Yū Hakusho*, and numerous other anime; indeed, it seems ubiquitous. A real team, according to the world of anime, is a group of friends united by ties of love and a common, worthy purpose. The true warrior is a member of a team, who is made wiser and stronger by those he fights with and for. The message is caring over cruelty, teamwork over selfishness, truth over fleeting lies. Yes, it is that very same famous, universal theme that says "love conquers hatred" and "light dispels the darkness."

Something More . . .

Often, though, there is more: some flash of wisdom or enlightenment that the hero, and through the hero the audience, catches a precious glimpse of. Recall that in *Fushigi Yūgi*, the heroine is the young girl Miaka, a troubled student, perhaps a bit like the average reader of this fantasy manga. Like the reader, Miaka has traveled to a fantasy world through a mysterious book. At last, though, Miaka must return home to the life she once hated, leaving behind the many new friends she has known and loved. Through her unhappiness over this prospect, Miaka suddenly comes to a realization that there is hope for her own life in the real world. There is meaning, and there is help. "Believe in oneself, love others, know that one is loved,"[13] she says. Never stop dreaming, and life, even painful, boring life in the everyday world, might just yield its hidden treasures.

These hidden treasures, a connection to something vast, beautiful, perhaps even infinite, are one of the best-kept secrets of these stories. Somewhere, someday, anime tells us, there may shine a joy that outshines transient pain and pleasure, an eternal love that survives even death. This is the treasure that is worth the struggle, the hidden answer to the hero's (and perhaps the reader's or viewer's) desperate search. The visitor to the world of anime journeys across the boundaries of time and space, through mysterious realms and epic histories, through the lives of characters who laugh and cry and dream, through emotions and experiences too profound for words . . . and then gently back to reality, carrying priceless and encouraging echoes of the message of hope, which promises: "The future will be glorious, if only we remember what is truly important and persevere no matter what." Surely this message strikes a chord in the hearts of the audience, for it is repeated quietly in manga after manga, animated movie after animated movie, and even in video games. How many people have found solace this way, and the will to survive their own small and large sufferings—maybe even to conquer them—along with the hope for something far better? The message now has surpassed notions of mere "romanticism"; it has sailed on into the very edges of the divine!

These, then, are some of the secrets of the Japanese soul which anime reveals, secrets which many in the West rarely see, but with which, undoubtedly, many could sympathize. Within the heart of the "salaryman" or "office lady," the corporate samurai, the housewife, and the high school student cramming for exams, the soul's natural yearning for something profound and beautiful glimmers fitfully. Of course, just like any other people on the planet, the Japanese too often forget these secrets, and the consequences of the loss add fuel to the stereotypes. It is hard to maintain something divine in this world; it is too easy to forget. Anime serves to remind.

Notes

1. Remarks by Ross Perot posted on Reform Party Web site in 1997. References to bowing: "Go to Japan, bow nicely and say, we will take the same trade deal we gave you. Can't be fairer than that, right? Or let's send you over there and that doesn't work, bow again and say we will take the same trade deal you negotiated in Europe."

2. This Web site provides a good example: http://me.udel.edu/ecseed/delnegro/japan.html. It includes a copy of the paper "Japanyes," by Louis Leclerc, and contains quite a collection of warnings about Japan's warlike economic tactics and social drawbacks.

3. Private e-mail correspondence, 1996.

4. Yuki Hijiri, *Chōjin Locke*, vol. 2 (Tokyo: Hit Comics, Shōnen Gahōsha, 1981), pp. 254–255.

5. Leiji Matsumoto, *Galaxy Express 999*, vol. 3 (Tokyo: Big Comics Gold, Shōgakukan, 1997), pp. 152–153.

6. Riyoko Ikeda, *Berusaiyu no Bara* (The Rose of Versailles), vol. 8, *Margaret Comics* (Tokyo: Shūeisha, 1974), p. 73.

7. Yumi Tamura, *Basara*, vol. 1 (Tokyo: Flower Comics, Shōgakukan, 1991), p. 184.

8. Yukito Kishiro, *Gunnm*, vol. 2 (Tokyo: Business Jump, Shūeisha, 1992), pp. 74–75.

9. Hijiri, *Chōjin Locke*, p. 195.

10. Yūji Horii, *Dragon Quest*, vol. 9 (Tokyo: Jump Comics, Shūeisha, 1992), p. 112.

11. Ikeda, *Berusaiyu No Bara*, vol. 4, p. 113.

12. Narumi Kakinouchi, *Vampire Miyu* (Vampire Princess Miyu) (Tokyo: Horror Comics, Akita Shoten, 1989), p. 62.

13. Yū Watase, *Fushigi Yūgi*, vol. 13 (Tokyo: Flower Comics, Shōgakukan, 1995), p. 145.

References

The following manga, video games, and animated movies are referenced in this essay. The year represents the publication date of the relevant material, and does not necessarily indicate the entire time period during which the work was being produced.

Final Fantasy VI (*Final Fantasy III*) (Squaresoft, 1994).

Fujita, Kazuhiro. *Ushio to Tora* (Shōnen Sunday, Shōgakukan, 1996).

Hijiri, Yuki, Chōjin Locke (Hit Comics, Shōnen Gahōsha, 1981).

———. *Dragon Quest* (Jump Comics, Shūeisha, 1992).

Ikeda, Riyoko. *Berusaiyu no Bara* (The Rose of Versailles) (Margaret Comics, Shūeisha, 1974).

Ishiwata, Osamu. *Love* (Shōnen Sunday, Shōgakukan, 1996).

Kakinouchi, Narumi. *Vampire Miyu* (Vampire Princess Miyu) (Horror Comics, Akita Shoten, 1989).

Kishiro, Yukito. *Gunnm* (Business Jump, Shūeisha, 1992).

Lufia II (Taito, 1996).

Matsumoto, Izumi. *Kimagure Orange Road* (Jump Comics, Shūeisha, 1984).

Matsumoto, Leiji. *Captain Harlock* (Champion Graphic Anime Comics, Akita Shoten, 1981).

———. *Ginga Tetsudō 999* (Galaxy Express 999) (Hit Comics, Shōnen Gahōsha, 1981).

Mitsuda, Takuya. *Major* (Shōnen Sunday, Shōgakukan, 1996).

Miyazaki, Hayao. *Tenkū no Shiro Laputa* (Laputa: Castle in the Sky) (Studio Ghibli, 1986).

Morita, Masanori. *Rokudenashi Blues* (Shōnen Jump, Shūeisha, 1996).

Netsuki, Nobuhiro. *Ruroni Kenshin* (Shōnen Jump, Shūeisha, 1996).

Shinohara, Chie. *Ao no Fūin* (Flower Comics, Shōgakukan, 1994).

Soda, Mashito. *Megumi no Daigo* (Shōnen Sunday, Shōgakukan, 1996).

Takada, Yūzo. *3x3 Eyes* (Young Magazine, Kōdansha, 1993).

Takahashi, Rumiko. *Ranma ½* (Shōnen Sunday, Shōgakukan, 1996).

Tamura, Yumi. *Basara* (Flower Comics, Shōgakukan, 1991).

Tezuka, Osamu. *Black Jack* (Shōnen Champion Comics, Akita Shoten, 1976).

Togashi, Yoshihiro. *Yū Yū Hakusho* (Shōnen Jump, Shūeisha, 1993).

Tomino, Yoshiyuki, and Yoshikazu Yasuhiko. *Kidō Senshi Gundam* (Nippon Sunrise, 1980).

Watase, Yū. *Fushigi Yūgi* (Flower Comics, Shōgakukan, 1995).

—— 8 ——

Hadashi no Gen (Barefoot Gen)

Volume 8, pages 17–31

Keiji Nakazawa
Translated by Tim Craig

It may seem odd, even sacrilegious, to present *Hadashi no Gen* as an example of the *roman* in Japanese *manga* and *anime* that Eri Izawa describes in Chapter 7. For *Gen* is Keiji Nakazawa's semiautobiographical account of the atomic bombing of Hiroshima, an event that claimed an estimated 100,000 lives, including those of the author's father, brother, and sister, and that even today is the world's most poignant symbol of the tragedy and folly of nuclear war. *Gen* is indeed a heartbreaking story which takes the reader, through the eyes of schoolboy Gen Nakaoka (Nakazawa's alter ego), through the persecution suffered by those who opposed the war, the devastation caused by the atomic blast, subsequent starvation and social disorder, the slower deaths of those afflicted with radiation sickness, and the lifelong discrimination faced by those who were "contaminated" by bombing.[1] Yet *Hadashi no Gen* is moving not just for the real-life tragedy it portrays so graphically—a portrayal that has hindered the comic's acceptance in the United States[2]—but for the indomitable spirit, the goodheartedness, the dreams, and even the humor of Gen and his friends, a group of street orphans growing up in survival mode in the aftermath of the nuclear destruction.

The main characters of the excerpt presented here are the happy-go-lucky Ryūta (the boy selling the dress), whose past includes time served in prison for shooting gangsters that were preying on his friends; Gen; and Gen's classmate Aihara, whom the war has left bitter and warped, but in whose heart, as we see, life and hope still glimmer.

Notes

1. Frederik L. Schodt, *Manga! Manga! The World of Japanese Comics* (New York: Kodansha International, 1983), p. 238. Schodt's *Manga Manga* also includes an excerpt from *Hadashi no Gen* depicting the dropping of the bomb and the immediate devastation it caused (pp. 239–255).

2. See Chapter 16, "Doraemon Goes Abroad," pp. 305–306.

2. Last chance! Last chance! Weep or laugh, this is it!
3. Take a good look at this!
   These dresses are the latest thing in glamorous America. . . .
   You don't find goods like this just anywhere!
4. And the material! This ain't ordinary cloth. . . .
   It's genuine silk!

1. How 'bout it, Ma'am? Nice, eh? I'll bet you'd like to own this!
2. Hey! Quit pawing the merchandise! You'll get it dirty!
3. All right, here we go! Let's settle it with one bid!
   First come, first served!
4. Okay, how much do I hear?
   500 yen.
5. Give me a break, Ma'am. . . . If this were 500 yen, I'd buy it myself.
6. You must be in a daze from the war and can't see straight!
   You're looking at a quality dress!
7. Just put this on and see what happens! Even the Emperor will turn pale and bow down to you!
   In one stroke you'll be reborn as the most beautiful woman on earth!
8. Okay now, let's hear a better offer!

1. 600 yen.
   Jeez, how pathetic. . . .
2. It's 1950! The year the Hiroshima Carp baseball team was born!
   The year the thousand-yen note with Shōtoku Taishi's picture on it came out! To celebrate, won't someone generously spend a thousand-yen note on this dress?
3. All right. . . . How about 800 yen?
   Let's hear one more bid!
4. Mister, try giving your wife a dress like this to wear. . . . She'll weep with joy and pay you back with full service every day!
5. "Oh, Dear, I'm so happy!"
   "You're so kind! I love you!"
6. Smooch! She'll kiss you so much your face will swell up!
   Ha Ha Ha
   Ha Ha Ha

1. C'mon, Mister, dress your wife in this.
   Walk down the street with her and see what happens!
2. "You're excited! I'm excited!"
   "I call you Darling! You call me Darling!"
3. Mister, you too were robbed of your youth by the war, right? Drafted into the stupid army for a promise and a song. . . .
4. Well, now you can buy this and come back to life!
   Take back your youth!
5. All right, one thousand yen it is!
   I should go for one more bid, but I'd better stop here.
6. I really don't want to sell this, but I've got to close up shop early.
   I can't keep my mind off the Giants-Carp game.
7. I need to hurry up and get to the ball park to root for the Carp!

1. Right now the Carp are ahead three to two!
   Really?!
2. Who's the Giants' pitcher?
   Ōtomo.
3. Ōtomo, eh? That guy's hot. . . . That'll make it tough for the Carp. . . .
4. How's Shiraishi doing?
   He's hit a triple and a single!
5. Shiraishi's great!
   I love Shiraishi! He can hit, run, and play defense!
6. "Shortstop Shiraishi dives to his right! Stabs Kawakami's grounder! Fires to first!"
7. "Out!!! One more out and the Carp win!"
8. Hurray! Banzai!
   Huh?

1. C'mon, Carp! Win!
   Go, Carp!
   So you're a Carp fanatic too?
2. I'm crazy about the Carp myself! When they lose, I can't sleep!
   You too, eh?
3. Thanks to them, I've developed a stomach ulcer!
   No kidding?
4. The Carp aren't like other teams!
   This team was built by the heavy-hearted people of Hiroshima, who saw their city reduced to ashes and lost their dreams and hopes in the nuclear flash. . . .
   Right!
5. When the Carp win, they make us feel happy and bright!
   Yeah!
6. We sure lose a lot, though! The team's got no money. . . . They can't get strong!
   That's right!

1. The poor players! Their salaries come from our donations, and they have to pay for their own travel.
   Yeah.
2. Even so, they all do their best. . . . It's really tough for Manager Ishimoto, too!
   It's so heartbreaking, it makes me cry!
3. We've all got to cheer them on and help them win, no matter what!
   That's right!
4. Mister, I like you! Here, you can have the dress for free!
   R . . . really? You're giving it to me?
5. Sure, take it! It makes me so happy when people say good things about the Carp!
   Thanks a lot!
6. Ryuta! What the hell are you doing?! We're supposed to be running a business!
7. Katsuko and Natsue poured their hearts into making that dress!

1. You're too goddam impulsive!
   Yeah, I guess I got carried away. . . .
2. Stupid idiot! Thanks to you we've lost a thousand yen!
   Don't get so upset! The dress was made out of cheap fake material anyway!
3. C'mon, let's hurry up and get to the ball game!
4. Go Carp! I'm with you!
   Moron!
7. Hey! Gen! On your way home from school?

2. Wh . . . what happened? You're all beat up!
3. I got in a fight with this guy called Aihara, who's in my class at school. . . .
   A fight?
4. Did you win?
   Of course, Ryuta! Gen doesn't lose fights!
5. Yeah, you're right. That Aihara must be an idiot to pick a fight with Gen!
6. I won the fight, but I feel like I lost. . . .
   How come?

1. Aihara! You talk big! What's wrong, can't you stand up any more?
   No way I'm ever losing a fight to someone like you who thinks war's so great! Understand?
2. You win, Nakaoka. . . .
3. Now take the knife and kill me!
4. You idiot! What the hell are you talking about?! I don't get in fights in order to take away a precious life!
5. Don't give me that sentimental crap! I told you I hate half-hearted fights!
6. It's kill or be killed! Fights are the same as war, people kill each other!
7. Hurry up and stab me!
   Kill me!

1. I can't stand looking like a loser! Hurry up and kill me!
2. You idiot! You think I can kill a person, just like that?! Have you lost your mind?!
3. Ha ha ha! . . . So you can't kill me, Nakaoka? You're pathetic!
   Kill me, I tell you! I'm not gonna complain or hate you for it! Do it!
4. Ha ha ha ha! . . .
5. Wow, that Aihara's a pretty tough nut!
6. That's a first for me, getting into a fight with a creepy guy like that!
7. Ha ha ha! You've got some interesting characters in your class!
8. Hey, I almost forgot! If we don't hurry up and get to the Carp game, it'll be over!

1. Gen, why don't you come with us? The Carp are winning!
2. If we beat the Giants, you'll feel a lot better! C'mon!
3. We've got plenty of money. The clothes that Katsuko and Natsue make are so well designed they sell like hotcakes, and the profit just rolls in!
4. It's our treat, Gen! Let's go!
5. Just think, we'll eat noodles and rice cakes and drink sweet potato wine!
6. Sure. Why not?
7. Ha ha ha! Let's do it, said Taro! Let's do it, said Hanako! And they lived happily ever after!
   Ha ha ha!

1. "Hiroshima versus Giants"
2. Ha ha ha! Listen to the crowd!
3. Go, go, Carp! Win, win, Carp!
4. That guy's really making a fool of himself!
   Shut up!

1. "Hiroshima Carp Donations"
3. They haven't collected much money. . . .
4. Well, guess I'll have to make a donation!
5. Ryuta! That money belongs to all of us! It's not yours to throw away!
   Tightwad! Why not help out the Carp?
6. That's the money we're saving to start our dressmaking shop! Don't waste it!
   All right! All right!
7. Just ten yen's okay, isn't it?
   O . . . okay.

1. Ha Ha Ha! We're winning! We're winning!
2. Hey! Carp players! I donated ten yen! If you win, go and have yourselves a big meal!
   You moron! How much can you eat for ten yen?! Quit embarrassing us, Ryuta!
3. Huh?
5. I . . . isn't that Aihara?!
   I didn't know he liked baseball. . . .

9

Gender Roles and Girls' Comics in Japan

The Girls and Guys of *Yūkan Club*

Maia Tsurumi

A karate-kicking girl beats up bad guys and a polo-playing boy is afraid of fisticuffs. These rather unlikely characters are found in the Japanese *manga* (comic book) *Yūkan Club* (Leisure Club). Unlikely, that is, according to what are commonly thought to be gender norms in Japan. "So what?" you might reply. After all, comics aren't part of the real world; they belong to the realm of the fantastic. However, while most of us do not believe that Superman and Astro Boy really roam the skies, comics may have something to say about the world we live in and the roles we are expected to play in that world. The prevalence and popularity of manga in Japan suggest that in that country in particular, comics may indeed be reliable indicators of social values and norms, serving a role similar to that of the popular culture media of television or magazines in many countries.

Manga are a major source of entertainment in Japan, read by people of every age group and class. A 1987 survey found that 69 percent of Japanese high school students read manga,[1] and in 1974 it was reported that Japanese white-collar workers spent 15 percent, and blue-collar workers 28 percent, of their free time reading comics.[2] Manga artists are prominent figures in Japan, many becoming household names. Machiko Hasegawa, the author of *Sazae-san*, a manga and animation series that has run continuously since the war, has a museum in Tokyo devoted to her work. When Japan's "god of comics," Osamu Tezuka, died in 1989, young people wept openly and the television and print media ran numerous specials on his life.[3]

Many Westerners, for whom the word "comics" often connotes *The Far Side* or *Garfield*, may be unaware of the sophistication of the manga genre, and of its power to both reflect and influence social realities in Japan. Fredrick Schodt, whose books *Manga! Manga! The World of Japanese Comics* and *Dreamland Japan* have helped introduce Japanese comics to the English-reading world, writes that manga reveal "legacies from the past, ideals of love, attitudes to work and perfection, and a basic love of fantasy."[4] He adds that manga have as much to say about life as novels or films, a thought echoed by Peter Duus, who writes in his introduction to the English version of the famous business manga *Japan, Inc.* that manga have become, like television, a powerful medium for entertainment, the transmission of knowledge, and the diffusion of values.[5] Other scholars agree that, at the very least, comics contain recognizable symbols of social reality and are a form of expression in which it is legitimate to search for social norms, including gender roles, of the culture within which they are produced.[6]

This chapter looks at *Yūkan Club*, a popular manga series by female manga artist Yukari Ichijō, in order to ascertain what kinds of values or messages, if any, are being communicated to the young Japanese women who read this comic. *Yūkan Club,* primarily geared toward high school-aged girls, ran successfully in the manga magazine *Ribbon Original* from 1982 to 1992. It has since been published in paperback form. I have chosen to look at this series because it is one of my personal favorites and because I wanted to look at what the images of women found within its pages might be saying to and about the reader (including myself). I also examine gender images in *Yūkan Club* from the target reader's perspective, something that previous studies of manga have not always done. Ledden and Fejes's 1987 study of female role patterns in manga magazines, for example, surveyed *men's* comics to see how women were represented.[7] Though this may tell us something about male attitudes toward women, there is no reason to believe that these comics reflect social reality for women or women's views of their place in the world. If we want to know what Japanese society is telling women about women, it is important to look at manga that Japanese *women* read.

I have been reading manga since I was 8 years old, but for a long time I never gave much thought to what the pictures and stories may have been saying to me beyond the telling of a story that required no intellectual effort from me to enjoy. Recently I began to think about the possible significance of the characters and stories found in manga and to wonder how these might influence or support cultural values and behavior. From this came the idea of studying *Yūkan Club* more critically, and comparing the female (and male) characters that appear in this manga with traditional and widely accepted Japanese gender models.

I use as a basis for comparison the models of the behavior of women in Japanese society as put forth by scholars Takie Sugiyama Lebra and Iwao Sumiko.[8] Both Lebra and Iwao present clear stereotypes of the division of the sexes in Japanese society. Lebra states that there is a traditional dichotomy between the masculine and feminine dispositions in Japan. In other words, there are characteristics that are supposedly desirable for women, and characteristics that are desirable for men. Women who exhibit the desirable "female" characteristics are "unworldly," are refined in thought and speech, and desire to be stay-at-home wives and mothers. Men, by contrast, are worldly, are physically brave, and work hard outside the home to provide for their families. The traditional differentiation of male-female roles can be seen in the division of labor, with men having full-time occupations outside the household, while women occupy the domestic sphere full time. According to Iwao, for the most part, women's behavior is still expected to conform to the wife-mother role set forth by society, and many Japanese women fail to learn and think independently. These scholars may be criticized for being somewhat dated, as many would argue that women in Japan are challenging and changing their and society's concept of womanhood, but their ideas about gender are still widely believed in Japanese society at large. There persists an impression that women and men are often miles apart in their daily lives, in spite of some acceptance of gray zones between traditional ideas of what is male and what is female.

Yūkan Club: The Characters

Yūkan Club is centered around a group of six private high school students, three girls and three boys, who live in urban Tokyo. They are the daughters and sons of the fabulously wealthy, the elite, and/or the socially important (with the exception of one girl whose mother is divorced and runs a jewelry business—her store is very exclusive, though). Each episode contains a separate and complete story involving this gang of teenagers, in which they usually face some kind of challenge. Popular themes are mysteries, ghost stories, and the need to aid someone who is faced with a dilemma that cannot be resolved through the usual legal or authoritative adult channels. The collective individual abilities and talents of the group members are generally needed to bring each story to closure.

Seishirō is the son of a famous and successful heart surgeon who is also the administrator of a large hospital. Seishirō is the *Yūkan Club*'s leader, and the mastermind behind all the group's schemes and adventures. Overall he is the best at everything, especially martial arts, academics, and athletics, and is a perfectionist with a wide range of interests. Noriko is the daughter of a renowned Japanese traditional brush painting artist and a tea ceremony master. She is an expert player of *igo* (go, a Japanese board game) and holds her own academically with Seishirō. She is considered the quintessential "Japanese woman"—cultured and refined, although unworldly and hopeless at sports. Miroku is the son of the Tokyo Chief of Police, and his mother comes from the ranks of the nobility. He is not as successful academically as Noriko, but is of about equal status in the group because he is "knowing" or worldly, and is usually in on what Seishirō is up to. His specialty is mechanics and gadgets, and he has connections with the underworld of youth gangs, motorcycle gangs, and gangsters.

The other three members of the group provide most of the comic relief and are the butts of many of the jokes. Karen is the daughter of the aforementioned jewelry store owner and so is of a slightly different class than the other five. She is often portrayed as frivolous and silly. She prides herself on her looks, which she uses as her "talent," and her driving ambition in life is to net herself a good husband. She and the third male in the group, Bidō, are seen as good at heart and can be serious when the need arises even if they are usually superficial. Bidō is a typical *bishōnen* (beautiful boy). He is portrayed differently from the other two male characters—in fact what is applicable to the women in the stories is often applicable to him. Son of the Swedish ambassador to Japan, he is one-quarter Japanese and three-quarters Swedish, although the others refer to him as half Japanese and he interacts socially like a native Japanese. He too prides himself on his looks and uses them to his advantage; he is a playboy who knows by name or sight (if not more intimately) all the elite, beautiful women of Europe. Karen and Bidō are made fun of by both the author and the other *Yūkan Club* characters.

Finally there is Yūri, the daughter of one of the richest men in Japan; her father is Kenbishi of Kenbishi Zaibatsu, a fictional conglomerate of countless other companies with interests all over the world. She is the

Figure 9.1

THE GIRLS

Noriko Hakushika (lower right):
Daughter of a tea master and a famous brush painting artist.
Excels academically and is an expert go player.
Very popular with the boys at her school, but dislikes men.

Yūri Kenbishi (lower middle):
Heiress to a *zaibatsu* (corporate) fortune.
Is academically disinclined, but excels at athletics and martial arts.
Very popular with the girls at her school.

Karen Kizakura (upper left):
Daughter of an upscale jewelry store owner.
Is concerned with clothes, boys, and her looks.
Her driving ambition: to catch a rich husband.

THE BOYS

Bidō Granmarnier (lower left):
Son of the Swedish ambassador to Japan.
A playboy who dislikes physical and mental hardship.
Is often made fun of along with the three female characters.

Seishirō Kikumasamune (upper right):
Son of the chief of staff at a large Tokyo hospital.
A thinker who is talented, a martial arts expert, and the group's leader.
Less popular than the others, sometimes seen as "cold."

Miroku Shōchikubai (upper middle):
Son of the Tokyo Chief of Police.
Likes mechanical things and loves action.
He was friends with Yūri before they both joined the Leisure Club.

stupid one in the group but is amazingly strong. Athletics, martial arts, and eating are her specialties, while academics and elegance are clearly her weak points. She is always at the bottom of the class in terms of grades, and her tastes, behavior, and speech are patterned after her father's uncouth peasant mannerisms. Her speech is not male, but is more gender-neutral than the others', similar to that of a child. All six teenagers in *Yūkan Club* speak *hyōjungo* (standard Japanese), which marks them as distinctly from Tokyo.

An obvious question that arises when critically examining a work such as *Yūkan Club* is whether there is social relevance in the way attributes are assigned to the characters. The first thing I noticed was that a woman, Yūri, was the stupidest one in the stories. Based on this, one might make a superficial generalization about allocation of "type" to male and female characters, but a comic foil is essential, and in *Yūkan Club* it is provided by having someone play the role of the slow-witted twit. Does assigning this role to a female signify something significant about Japanese society's attitudes toward women? The answer to this question might well be yes, but before jumping to such a conclusion it is important to go beyond the mere fact that Yūri is thick and look at what else is occurring in the stories in order to see what other kinds of ideas are being transmitted.

What kind of message is Yūri's character sending? There is more here than a simple negative stereotype of a dense girl. Wild, carefree, and happy with simple pleasures, Yūri, along with Bidō and Karen, is often made fun of; but unlike them, she is always involved in the action. She is strong and courageous as an action heroine, and does her share of beating up the bad guys, along with Seishirō and Miroku. She is a match for, if not better than, almost any man when it comes to strength and athletic prowess. She is popular with the girls at her school, and appears as well to be the most popular character among *Yūkan Club*'s readers, if the number of stories in which she is central and the number of pictorials (including the sketches that appear on the cover, on the margins, and on blank pages between episodes) in which she appears are any measure. Yūri may appear to be merely a masculine version of a woman, but she is definitely *not* lesbian and the reader is constantly reminded that she is in fact a girl by the continual comments made about her unladylike behavior.

Yūri and Miroku sometimes hang out together away from the group with Miroku's motorcycle gang friends, and it is always Yūri, Miroku,

Figure 9.2 **Yūri beats up two shady students from another high school who were molesting a student from her own school, St. President's, while Noriko thinks, "In . . . incredible . . . I had heard rumors about her, but to think that she is that strong. . . ." In the third frame, Yūri tells the thugs that if they raise a hand to students from her school again, the punishment will be much worse next time. At the bottom, two other St. President's students, who had been watching, comment on the unpleasantness of having such a wild, uncouth person as Yūri as a fellow student and how she brings down the reputation of their famous school. Noriko then gets angry and tells them off for saying such things when they did nothing to help.**

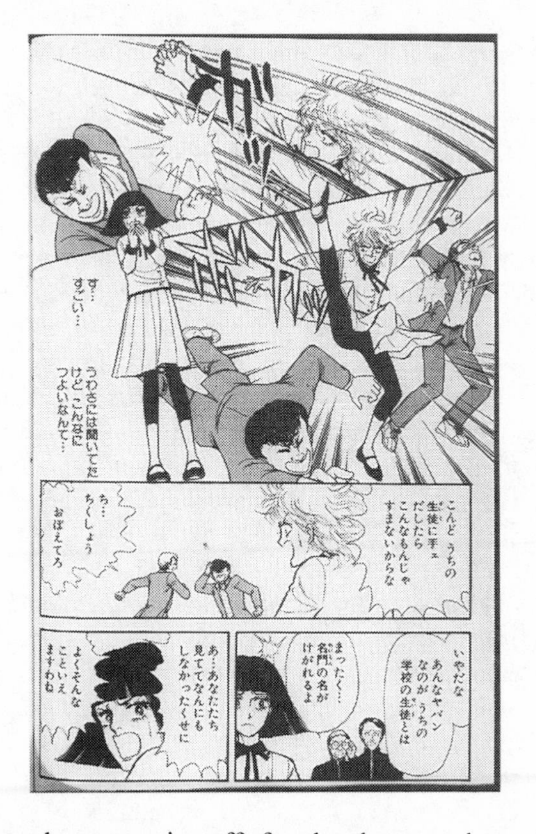

and Seishirō who go running off after the ghost or other evil character. It may be that Yūri is only able to be "one of the boys" because she is portrayed as asexual—she is definitely not interested in men. But is she really gender-neutral? Does her dislike of traditionally feminine things negate her as a female? Perhaps the answer lies in comparing her with Noriko, who is very popular with men but also has no interest in them and in fact is *otokogirai* (dislikes men). Noriko comes across as definitely feminine and is the *Yamato nadeshiko* (archetypal Japanese ideal of a woman). Perhaps we see her as irrefutably feminine because she is so popular with men, regardless of her preferences, while Yūri seems less feminine since she is popular with women. This would suggest that in Japan, society's standards of what is male and what is female are defined by men, a concept many feminists would agree with. To add more confusion to the meaning of Yūri's character, although everyone in the text agrees that she is the stupid one, it is questionable whether she is really all that stupid. Introductory remarks about her state that she is dumb, the other characters all agree that she is, and she is at the bottom of the barrel as far as academics are concerned. However, when one searches for evidence in the stories of her intellectual shortcomings, there is little to be found. On the contrary, in many of the episodes she is the first one to notice such things as cars trying to run people over and rocks starting avalanches. This results in her being responsible for saving many people from harm. Also, when Seishirō is explaining the circumstances of things that were previously unintelligible to everyone else, Yūri usually gets it when everybody else does. In fact, it is difficult to find actual story segments where Yūri is actually slow-witted, although places where she is told she is dim, or others talk about her being dim, are numerous. One possible interpretation of this is that the appearance of being stupid is a character "flaw" which permits her to be better than men at some traditionally masculine things and still be popular and accepted.

Further insight about how women are "supposed to be" can perhaps be gained by looking at Bidō, the other *Yūkan Club* character who is confusing in terms of gender, though certainly not sexually neutral. Bidō's actions are more easily grouped with the two clearly feminine characters, Noriko and Karen. Bidō is physically weak, and is athletic only insofar as he is good at sports that are genteel and supposedly useful for picking up women: tennis, skiing, fencing, and polo. He often complains of physical danger and hardship, and he is likely to stay behind (by his own wishes) with Noriko and Karen to wait while Yūri, Seishirō, and Miroku are involved in the dangerous action. Is Bidō, as a man, allowed to be cowardly and shallow because he is feminine, a character "flaw" that mirrors Yūri's and that similarly makes "nonstandard" gender behavior acceptable? Again, it is hard to discern what kind of message is being transmitted. The homosexual *bishōnen* (beautiful boy)

Figure 9.3 **This scene is from a story in which the situation is such that the boys have to be disguised as women. The woman at the bottom is Miroku's mother saying how much like women they look.**

image is not uncommon in the world of *shōjo manga* (Japanese girls' comics), and it could be that the author is poking fun at this by creating a caricature. Yet the fact that Bidō is heterosexual is made very clear in his dealings with gay characters and his endless quest for female sexual conquests; though he acts feminine in many ways, he is definitely male sexually.

It has been argued that behavioral variations within one sex help to overshadow the differences between the sexes, and thus provide a uniformity or commonality across sexual boundaries.[9] A corollary to this is that similarities between people of opposite sex have the same effect. Looked at either way, the outcome is that society is given a push toward greater gender equality. The masculine-feminine crossing over found in the characters of Bidō and Yūri reinforces this idea. Whatever the author's intention, for the reader the differences among *Yūkan Club*'s same-sex characters, along with the similarities between Yūri and the two more masculine boys and between Bidō and the two more feminine girls, help blur cultural distinctions between men and women. Adding to this effect is the style of drawing in this manga, which makes the female and male characters look physically similar. Though all are distinguishable by their height, hair, and certain facial features (mainly the eyes and eyebrows), they otherwise look quite alike, and the men, when dressed as women, look like women.

Yūkan Club: Heroines and Villainesses

Girls and women in *Yūkan Club* seem to be the ones who get themselves and others into trouble most often. Yūri, Karen, and Noriko all have pivotal roles in story lines in which through their actions they cause some kind of crisis for the group. There are also a number of episodes in which their female schoolmates and various wronged women are in trouble and need rescuing. Most common are cases in which women get into trouble because of a man. In fact, the majority of "bad" female characters are bad because they are weak with regard to the men they love and will commit crimes for the sake of these men. It is presumed that these women would not have caused the problems they did if they were not so weak and easily manipulated by men. This sends another ambiguous message. On one hand, women are made out to be malleable and to lack a strong sense of self. On the other, by portraying these weak-willed women negatively and making them villains, the author seems to be warning her female readers not to be so easily manipulated when it comes to men. The more positive model that the negatively portrayed female villains are juxtaposed with is Karen, who loves men and their attentions, yet remains always emotionally in control. Even though she actively seeks her own gold mine in the form of a rich and, if possible, titled husband, Karen does so on her own terms and never compromises her values, character, or personality in this quest.

If it is not a man lying at the root of the harm done by women in these stories, then it is usually revenge. For example, four episodes deal with female ghosts and their need for retribution. There is a tradition in Japanese stories and pictures for ghosts to take the form of women who need some kind of deed performed before they can rest in peace, and this tradition is reflected in these episodes. Although they play the role of antagonists, these ghosts are not depicted as evil. True, they inflict pain on others, but quite often this is because they and their families have been wronged. Usually they are willing to depart for the afterworld with no further fuss once they have been persuaded of the error of their ways and have had help in settling matters. In the West, the idea of the implacable vengeful woman is well established—"Hell hath no fury like a woman scorned." But this is not the case for wronged female ghosts in Japan. In Japanese folklore, ghosts, even scary ones, are not usually bad, just terribly unhappy. None of *Yūkan Club*'s ghosts are motivated by jealousy, even though the image of the jealous woman is not uncommon in Japan.

However mixed the messages in *Yūkan Club* may be about the general characteristics attributed to women, if one compares the evil women with the good women in these stories (excluding the ghosts and the three main characters), what emerges at first are some rather ugly stereotypes. Evil women tend to be unattractive, uncouth, and career-oriented. Good women are usually attractive, refined, and committed to their families. But when one looks further, one sees that these stereotypes are tempered with uncertainty. Beautiful villainesses are also found, as are homely heroines. Many of the "good" women have their own careers and accomplishments, and both the "good" and the "bad" types are represented by women who are independent, and are physically and psychologically strong.

Yūkan Club: Male Images

A brief look at how the men in *Yūkan Club* are depicted, as compared to the women, shows strong, careerist, goal-oriented males on the surface. As mentioned earlier, Bidō is an exception to this. When they are examined more closely, the fathers of Seishirō, Miroku, and Yūri turn out to be not so strong psychologically—all can be manipulated by their children or wives. Nevertheless, the status of the boys within the club is generally somewhat higher than that of the girls in terms of "cool" and knowingness.

Miroku and Seishirō are hardly ever drawn to look silly, as is done with Yūri, Karen, Bidō, and to a lesser extent Noriko. Miroku and Seishirō are rarely laughed at either, and one wonders whether it is significant that in the episode in which they *are* made fun of, they are dressed as women. The males can all drive, and seem to have more mechanical ability than the females; Miroku even goes so far as to make an exasperated comment to the effect that women do not understand machines.

Seishirō is definitely of premier importance to the resolution of the various problems that occur, and he is number one in whatever he puts his mind to. Nevertheless, in an episode in which he and Yūri end up fighting each other, we see that, although Seishirō is the better fighter, his is a learned skill, while Yūri has more natural ability and potential. Also, although Seishirō manages to defeat Yūri in this episode, he does it only by resorting to trickery, and in the end he gets his dose of humility when he is beaten by his old karate master, who is a Living National Treasure. In another story there is no winner when the group is split in two and he and Noriko are pitted against each other. In spite of Seishirō's obvious talents, he possesses these at the sacrifice of some of his humanity; he is less popular than the other characters and is sometimes viewed by the others as a rather cold person. Despite these qualifiers, the fact remains that Seishirō is male and has superior traits and has been given the leadership role. This in itself seems to reflect some of the dominant thinking in society; one wonders whether a female character in a group dynamic such as this could have been given this role.

In view of all of this, it seems safe to say that a distinct dichotomy between female and male is not seen in *Yūkan Club*. Female and male characters are found who exhibit traits traditionally thought of as belonging to the opposite sex (Yūri and Bidō), and the club members who most closely resemble standard gender archetypes (Seishirō and Noriko) are not necessarily the most popular characters nor the intended role models for the audience. In fact it is Yūri, a character with a more confusing gender, who comes across as the most human and the easiest for many readers to identify with. If these are the teenagers in *Yūkan Club*, is the same thing true of their parents? Perhaps there is a generation gap at work here, not just between the *Yūkan Club* members and their parents, but also between the generation of Japanese women studied by Lebra and Iwao and today's generation, about and for whom *Yūkan Club* is written. With this possibility in mind, let us look at how the mothers and fathers in this manga series are portrayed.

Yūkan Club: The Parents

The mothers of the six members of the Yūkan Club are for the most part minor characters in the series. Bidō's mother is seen only once, briefly, and nothing is known about her life apart from the fact that she is his mother and is as vain as he. Seishirō's mother appears to be a housewife, but no further information is given about her either. Noriko's mother shows up in one story, and it is known that she is an important master of the tea ceremony. Although her father is a respected artist as well, Noriko's household is centered on her mother's career, with her mother's apprentices living in their home. Karen's mother is seen only occasionally, but we know she is a working woman who has her own career and raises her daughter by herself. Karen's burning ambition is to find a rich man and make her mother comfortable, but her mother is ambivalent about this and seems to enjoy her work even though she is often exhausted by it. Miroku's mother is young-looking, and she makes her son call her by her first name because she does not want to be reminded that she is getting old. At first she seems to be the bored wife of a busy career policeman, but one soon learns that she is not the "typical" housewife by any means; her attire is risqué, she drinks and smokes, and she flies around the world for her father's company in search of suitable places to open resorts. Indeed, she is very "hip."

Yūri's mother is a very strong character and is involved in the stories quite a bit (although not as much as Yūri's father). She is the epitome of the idle rich, but has an incredible strength of will and an ability to elicit intense fear in those who dare to defy her. She is devoted to her husband and children—she is willing to sacrifice her life for theirs—but she also has her own interests and personality and is adored by her husband. She can be unreasonable at times, but this is a trait many of the adults in the story exhibit. She is definitely not stupid. All the mothers are beautiful and youthful looking, and while it is true that these are idealized and fantastic portraits, it is equally true that they largely contradict the ideal of the selfless, suffering woman who is a passive victim of fate and circumstance, a picture that is often painted of the Japanese mother.[10] The *Yūkan Club* mothers that we know the most about are vibrant, strong-willed, independent, cherished, and sometimes selfish women, capable mothers and wives who can also hold down a career or pursue other extrafamilial interests.

In contrast, the fathers we are shown are malleable (Seishirō's), frivolous (Bidō's), or downright silly (Yūri's and Miroku's). The fathers of Yūri and Miroku are both afraid of their wives. Interestingly, the "domestic prerogative,"[11] the strong tie between mother and child, is not seen here. Seishirō, Miroku, and Yūri may not always identify with their fathers, but they all appear to have more shared experiences with them than with their mothers. Indeed, it is the fathers in *Yūkan Club*, not the mothers, that seem the more "human" parent in their deviation from the traditional model of the Japanese father, whose (supposed) authoritarian power is summed up in the Japanese proverb about the four frightening things of the world: earthquakes, lightning, fire, and father.

One traditional assumption that is not questioned by the teenagers of *Yūkan Club*, or by their parents, is that the female members will all become wives and mothers themselves. It is clear, though not directly stated, that all the girls, even Yūri and Noriko (who aren't interested in boys), are expected and expect themselves to marry eventually. Thus, despite the rising marriage age of Japanese women, this manga seems to support the prevalent idea that women in Japan should become wives and mothers. However, again we find one thing said and assumed while another is depicted in direct opposition to it. Love interests for the main characters come and go, but one thing or another always manages to ensure that the group never splits, and dissolution of the club is never a threat. Rarely, except in the case of Bidō, are there even any romantic story lines at all. The members' devotion and commitment to the group are evidenced by the desire of Seishirō, Miroku, and Noriko to go to the same university together, even though their individual interests lie elsewhere and their academic abilities could certainly get them admitted to any university they wished to attend.

Conclusion

Any conclusions one might reach about Japanese society based on a critical reading of *Yūkan Club* must rely on an assumption that this manga at least partially reflects reality, if indeed it does not actually help readers construct their ways of looking at the world. This seems a reasonable assumption to make; even allowing for the influence of the author's own particular views, experiences, and creativity, it seems unlikely that a series would be as popular as *Yūkan Club* if it did not resonate to a significant degree with the real-world experiences of its audience. At any rate, the idea that manga reflect and may even influence reality is one that is widely accepted by manga fans and critics and by academic scholars. Given this, what does *Yūkan Club* reveal about, and say to, today's Japan? The six main characters, who are the potential role models for *Yūkan Club* readers, reflect ideals of modern Japanese society insomuch as they are young, suburban, knowledgeable (more "with it" than any adults in the stories), upper-class Tokyoites like the young people who populate many Japanese television shows, books, and manga. Many of the messages these characters convey are the sort of ideals one would typically expect among young people in Japan: the glorifying of an elite young urbanite Tokyo existence and an emphasis on group cooperation to solve problems. When it comes to gender roles, however, the message is less clear. Certainly, the characters in *Yūkan Club* do not fit neatly into the "standard" gender models as described by scholars such as Lebra and Iwao, a fact which suggests that models of women's behavior may no longer hold true (if indeed they ever did). One thing that can be said with confidence is that the attributes of the male and female characters in *Yūkan Club* are not limited to narrow models of masculinity or femininity. If there is any message here for the reader concerning how men and women should be, it is that there are many ways for an individual to feel and behave, and that adherence to traditional gender stereotypes is not a prerequisite for being an accepted, liked, and valuable member of society. Such a message, like the members of the *Yūkan Club*, is young and modern. We may have manga such as this one to thank for helping close the curtain on restrictive gender roles in Japan and ushering in an era in which it is the individual person, more than his or her gender category, that counts.

Notes

1. Peter Duus, "Introduction." In Ishinomori Shōtaro, *Japan Inc.: An Introduction to Japanese Economics* (Berkeley: University of California Press, 1988), p. ixx.

2. Leo Loveday and Satomi Chiba, "At the Crossroads: The Folk Ideology of Femininity in the Japanese Comic," *Communications (Saint Augustine)* 7 (1981), p. 247.

3. Fredrick L. Schodt, *Dreamland Japan: Writings on Modern Manga* (Berkeley, CA: Stone Bridge Press, 1996), p. 233.

4. Fredrick L. Schodt, *Manga! Manga! The World of Japanese Comics* (Tokyo: Kodansha, 1986), p. 16.

5. Duus, "Introduction," p. ix.

6. Loveday and Chiba, "Crossroads," p. 246.

7. Sean Ledden and Fred Fejes, "Female Gender Role Patterns in Japanese Comic Magazines," *Journal of Popular Culture* 21 (Summer 1987), pp. 155–176; also see Loveday and Chiba, "Crossroads," pp. 246–263, and *Mangajin* 1 (October 1990), pp. 20–81.

8. Takie Sugiyama Lebra, "Sex Equality for Japanese Women," *Japan Interpreter* 10 (Winter 1976), pp. 284–295; Sumiko Iwao, *The Japanese Woman: Traditional Image and Changing Reality* (Cambridge, MA: Harvard University Press, 1993).

9. See Lebra, "Sex Equality," p. 291.

10. See, for example, Ian Buruma, *A Japanese Mirror: Heroes and Villains of Japanese Culture* (London: Jonathon Cape, 1985), pp. 18–37, as well as Chapter 6 by Mark MacWilliams and Chapter 3 by Christine Yano in this volume.

11. Lebra, "Sex Equality," p. 286.

10

From *Sazae-san* to *Crayon Shin-chan*

Family *Anime*, Social Change, and Nostalgia in Japan

William Lee

While a cult following for certain avant-garde Japanese *manga* (comics) has now developed in the West, and some recent fantasy and science fiction manga that have made the successful transition to *anime* (animation) are currently airing on television around the world, the bulk of the manga and anime produced in Japan are still intended primarily for, and have their greatest success in, the domestic Japanese market.[1] Indeed, in one sense of the term "popular"—the sense of that which appeals to a wide audience or attracts a large number of consumers—it is these mainstream products for the Japanese market that have the greatest claim to the label "popular culture." This chapter looks at three popular manga, all of which have become highly successful television anime with appeal to family audiences: *Sazae-san*, *Chibi Maruko-chan*, and *Crayon Shin-chan*. Although these mainstream works may lack the critical edge associated with popular culture on the margins of society, this does not necessarily disqualify them from serious analysis. On the contrary, I would argue, their very popularity demands that they be taken seriously and the reasons for their popularity carefully examined. I shall take it as a given that the success of the three works I have chosen could not have been achieved without their speaking to and reflecting widespread trends and values in Japanese society. Since all three concern family life and address family audiences, I shall concentrate on their contrasting images of the family. More specifically, I shall show how these three manga/

anime present three different views of the family, reflective of changes in family structure and values in Japan over the last thirty or forty years.

Sazae-san, the oldest of the three, began as a comic strip in a daily newspaper in May 1946. It first ran in the *Fukunichi* newspaper, but from December 1949 until the last installment in February 1974 it appeared in the major daily, *Asahi Shimbun*.[2] *Sazae-san*'s creator and artist was a young woman named Machiko Hasegawa. It is perhaps not surprising, therefore, that the main character of this series was also a young woman, Sazae Isono. That a comic strip drawn by a female artist and focusing on a female character appeared and found success at this time, however, was no doubt due, in part at least, to the spirit of liberation that characterized the immediate postwar years. Among women, this spirit found confirmation in the new constitution, which included an equal rights clause and gave women for the first time the right to vote. Direct references to the issue of women's rights can be found in several of the early strips. In one, for example, Sazae-san attends a public discussion on equal rights, at which she declares that men too must strive for women's liberation. At this point a member of the audience stands up to voice approval for Sazae-san's point. Another member then shouts out that men should be fighting for men's rights. Little did this second speaker realize that the first, though sporting short hair and dressed like a man, was actually a woman.[3] Another episode finds two "liberated women" engaged in a discussion about politics. Sazae's younger brother and a friend of his overhear this conversation and remark that women recently have become "affected" and "unfeminine." The joke here, however, is on the men, for in the last frame we see two middle-aged men, that is, those who traditionally should be interested in politics, discussing the prices of pickles and potatoes while returning from a shopping trip.[4, 5]

While the episodes cited above show that *Sazae-san* successfully exploited the early postwar issue of women's place in society, it would be going too far to read the comic strip as a call for women's rights or to suggest that the reason for its popularity lay solely in the image it projected of the modern, liberated woman. Women's liberation was just one of the hot topics of the Occupation years. More important for most Japanese at this time was the struggle for survival. In this sense, too, *Sazae-san* can be seen as reflective of contemporary society. The concern with finding enough to eat in a period of food shortages, for example, is reflected in the name of the title character herself as well as those of other members of her family. All these names contain puns on the names of seafood. A *sazae*, for example, is a kind of shellfish, while Katsuo, the name of Sazae-san's younger brother, also means bonito, and Wakame, the name of her younger sister, means a kind of edible seaweed.

Looking back at the early *Sazae-san,* it is indeed surprising to realize just how many of the strips are devoted to such topics as ration lines, bartering with farmers for food, and the problem of burglars. One strip, for example, depicts Sazae-san and Katsuo on a trip to the countryside to barter for food. Along the way Katsuo's attention is caught by a magician who turns a handkerchief into an apple. "Watch, I can do that too," declares Sazae-san, who then proceeds to show her brother the trick of turning a kimono into a bag of rice (by trading with a farmer).[6] In one of the many strips dealing with burglars, Sazae-san and her mother arrive home to find a burglar caught in the "new-style burglar trap" Sazae-san has devised: a ladder, placed over a hidden pit, on which the two women then carry the thief off to the police station.[7]

It is in episodes like these, I would suggest, that we see the real appeal of *Sazae-san* for the early postwar audience. Not only would the audience have recognized in such episodes their own common problems, but also the strip's humor no doubt helped make those problems seem less serious and thus easier to face. If the people were looking for heroes or models for inspiration, then surely the strip provided one in the form of the title character, Sazae-san, whose age and sex spoke of the promise of a new age and whose relentless optimism in the face of hardships held out the hope that things would somehow turn out all right.

Things did in fact turn out better. Food shortages and ration lines became a thing of the past as the bleak postwar years gave way to the high economic growth rates of the late 1950s and 1960s. In the process, though she still maintained her optimism and her sometimes unconventional ways, Sazae-san herself lost some of her freedom and became more domesticated. It was perhaps inevitable in such a long-running strip that sooner or later Sazae-san would marry and settle down, and this she soon did. After a short-lived career working for a magazine publisher, by the third year of the comic strip's run Sazae-san had married and given birth to a child. Since the names of all the members of this family alluded to the names of seafood, her husband was given the name Masuo, which includes the word *masu* (trout), while her infant son was named Tara-chan (little codfish).

Sazae-san's married life has been somewhat unusual in that she did not move in with her husband's family, as was the traditional custom, but instead, her husband moved in with the Isono family. This arrangement, which is itself not without historical precedent, could be seen as another effort to advance the cause of women's rights or at least as a compromise between the liberated spirit of the early prewar years and Sazae-san's coming of age. However, that Sazae-san and her young family came to live with her parents was also dictated in part at least by the comic's popularity—for, although Sazae-san was the title character, many of the strips focused on other members of her family. Having Sazae-san move in with her husband's family would thus have necessitated not only the creation of a whole new cast of characters, but also the elimination or downplaying of her own family members, whom the readership had by this time come to know and love. Hasegawa at first attempted to solve this problem by having the newlyweds rent a house near the Isono household. This was not an altogether satisfactory arrangement, however, and soon she had the young family forced to move out of their home by a landlord who wanted to sell the house. Thus it came about that Sazae-san and her family moved in with her parents and brother and sister.

Despite this somewhat unusual family situation, family life in the Isono home did not differ significantly from the norm in Japan's male-dominated society. Sazae-san's husband and her father were *sarariman* (salaried company employees), who went off to work each day while Sazae-san and her mother were left to look after the house and Sazae-san's younger siblings. The image of the family projected in the comic strip thus became a very conservative one: three generations, roles clearly determined by gender, living harmoniously together under one roof. While this represents somewhat of a change from the early strip featuring the free-spirited, single Sazae-san, it certainly did not result in any diminishing of the work's popularity, as the length of its run attests. This same family, moreover, was carried over to television, where *Sazae-san* was to go on to even greater fame and popularity.

Since Hasegawa stopped drawing the comic strip *Sazae-san* in 1974 in order to move on to other topics, it is the weekly television anime of the same name that is best known today. Indeed, people under 30 may never have even seen a *Sazae-san* comic strip. On the other hand, that millions of contemporary Japanese know and watch the television program is beyond any doubt. Since its debut in 1969 the program has regularly achieved viewer ratings of over 25 percent and consistently placed in the weekly top ten, often even grabbing the number one spot. To cite just one example, from January 23 to February 26, 1995, the program held the top rank in the Kantō (greater Tokyo) region for five consecutive weeks, with ratings ranging between 29.4 percent and 31.0 percent. During the same period, in the Kansai (Kyoto-Osaka-Kobe) region the program was ranked second to sixth, with ratings ranging from 24.9 percent to 27.5 percent.[8] In millions of homes around the country, settling down to watch *Sazae-san* while eating dinner has become a Sunday evening ritual. In 1996 the TV show was in its twenty-eighth year, which is exactly how long the daily comic strip ran. It seems unlikely, however, that the Fuji Television network will soon pull the program off the air. Both the network and the program's sponsor, Toshiba, obviously know the value of a hit program, and as long as *Sazae-san* continues to earn top ratings, the show will no doubt go on.

But why? What is it about this program that draws millions of viewers every week? One answer that quickly comes to mind is that the family and the events portrayed are so ordinary. Like millions of other Japanese families, the Isonos live in the suburbs. Every morning the men go off to their downtown white-collar jobs while Katsuo and Wakame go to school. Sazae-san, meanwhile, stays home to look after Tara-chan and help her mother in the house. Occasionally she will leave Tara-chan with her mother and go shopping, usually with her best friend, another young mother in the neighborhood. In the afternoon Katsuo and Wakame come home from school, and the children and their mothers have an afternoon snack. The children then play or do their homework, and Sazae-san and her mother set about preparing dinner. In the evening the men come home, often after stopping off for a drink on the way, and the whole family are reunited around the dinner table.

This, then, is a typical day in the life of the Isono family, and the routine will be familiar to anyone who has seen the program a few times. The actual format of the show, however, is somewhat different. Each half-hour program is made up of three short episodes, each one, as in the earlier comic strip, typically focusing on one family member. In the course of an episode we may see the men at their jobs or in a bar after work, the children at school, or Sazae-san and her mother busy at home or out in the neighborhood. No matter what the episode or whom the primary focus may be on, however, the rest of the family inevitably gets involved. Often, for example, an unusual adventure one family member has had during the day will be discussed at the dinner table after the men get home from work. Sometimes the episode may highlight a particular problem one of the characters has, in which case the dinnertime gathering gives the other members of the family a chance to give advice. In this way, viewers of *Sazae-san* have over the years shared with members of the Isono family hundreds of minor adventures, problems, embarrassing moments, and, occasionally, triumphs. This may be one reason for the appeal of the program, for none of these events are really exceptional—they are the kinds of experiences many viewers no doubt have had or could have. Moreover, since the show includes and features in turn the stories of three different age groups (a middle-aged couple, a young married couple, and young children), the show is able to appeal to a wide audience. Yet I believe that these are not the only reasons for *Sazae-san*'s continuing success; for while each episode focuses on a single character or event, the stories ultimately remain firmly anchored within the context of the family. What is most striking about the program as a whole, in fact, is not the banality of the individual episodes but the apparently conscious attempt to produce an image of typical and wholesome family life. It is this image of the family, I would suggest, that viewers, especially adult viewers, find so attractive. The question still remains, however: Why?

One way to go about answering this question is to compare this image of the family with the real thing. The three-generation, extended family portrayed in the television program would seem to represent a typical, albeit somewhat traditional, family. But how typical is such a family in today's Japan? As the statistics given in Tables 10.1 and 10.2 show, although the number of households has steadily risen in Japan over the last 35 years, during the same period the average family size has declined from 4.14 persons to only 2.84 persons. In 1995 roughly a quarter of Japan's 43,447,000 households were single-person households, while another quarter was made up of two-person households. On the other hand, families of five or more persons accounted for only about 14 percent of the total. Even more revealing are statistics on the composition of today's families. According to the 1995 census, nuclear families make up 59.1 percent of the total number of households. These plus the 10,768,000 single-person households thus account for almost 84 percent of the total. By way of contrast, households made up of married couples with child(ren) and one or more parents amount to only 4,091,000 or about 9.4 percent of the total.[9]

Table 10.1

Number of Households and Average Size, 1960-1995

Year	Number of households	Average size
1960	22,539,000	4.14
1970	30,297,000	3.21
1980	35,824,999	3.22
1985	37,980,000	3.14
1990	40,670,000	2.99
1995	43,447,000	2.84

Source: Japan Almanac 1997 (Tokyo: Asahi Shimbunsha, 1996).

Table 10.2

Households by Number of Family Members, 1995

No. of members	No. of households	Percent of total
1	10,768,000	24.780
2	10,087,000	23.220
3	8,088,000	18.620
4	8,267,000	19.030
5	3,545,000	8.160
6	1,721,000	3.960
7	743,000	1.710
8	181,000	0.420
9	37,000	0.085
10 or more	11,000	0.025

Source: Japan Statistical Yearbook, 1997 (Tokyo: Statistics Bureau, Management and Coordination Agency, 1996).

Far from being the norm, therefore, large extended families like the one portrayed in *Sazae-san* are now clearly the exception. If this is the case, then what today's families are drawn to and watch each Sunday evening is not an image of themselves, but an idealized and nostalgic image of what families were or should be. Family, in other words, is defined in the program not through reference to contemporary social reality but by the construction of an ideal reality that harkens back to an earlier era. This nostalgic image, moreover, is not confined to the composition of the Isono family alone, but permeates their entire world. Examples of this old-fashioned atmosphere can be seen in the parents' preference for traditional dress, Tara-chan's unusually polite way of talking to the older family members, and the regular appearance of Saburō, the delivery boy from the local grocery store, who comes personally to take orders. Probably the most telling evidence that this is not a contemporary family, however, lies in the fact that the Isonos are seldom shown watching television and do not own a car. This apparently deliberate attempt to suppress the present in the television series stands in sharp contrast to the topicality of many of Hasegawa's earlier comic strips. We have already seen how those from the Occupation years made explicit reference to contemporary social conditions and issues. In a similar way, strips from later years provide snapshot-like views of postwar Japanese history. Many strips from 1964, for example, touch on the topic of the Tokyo Olympics of that year and how enthusiasm for the games boosted interest in television watching.[10]

In contrast to Hasegawa's attempts to be topical and make the comic-strip world of the Isonos up to date, the producers of the television anime have deliberately suppressed such topicality in order to create an image of family life frozen in some vaguely defined, idyllic past. The appeal of this picture of the past for older viewers no doubt lies in the program's ability to evoke memories of earlier days or childhood. For the present generation of children, on the other hand, the program can be said to function as a guide for what family life "should be." In either case the present is denied in order to provide viewers with the chance to experience an ideal family life. This being said, it would perhaps be fair to conclude that the success of the television version of *Sazae-san* can be attributed to the way this image of the ideal family makes up for the deficiencies, be they real or imagined, in contemporary viewers' own family lives. I do not think it is enough, however, to say simply that the program affords viewers an opportunity for escape into nostalgia or fantasy, for I believe its ideological function is more subtle than that. Not only does the program provide a definition of family, it also implicitly defines what it means to be Japanese. One example of how this is done is through reference to seasonal traditions. While the program rigorously avoids allusion to current social issues, it does frequently deal with seasonal topics. Episodes dealing with national holidays and other seasonal events and activities, for example, are carefully timed so as to be broadcast at just the right time in the current calendar. As the seasons pass we thus see the Isono family celebrating New Year's, enjoying the cherry blossoms in the spring, or participating in a summer festival. In this way viewers are not only reminded of the meaning of these holidays and events, but also shown how to celebrate them. It need hardly be said, moreover, that in all these activities the Isono family's behavior is traditional. Again, comparison with the comic strip is instructive. In one strip from early 1964, for example, the father is shown calling the other family members to join him in the ritual of throwing beans at *setsubun* (the day before the beginning of spring, according to the traditional calendar), which usually falls on February 2 or 3. At this time it is the custom to throw beans to drive away any lingering evil spirits, while calling out "*Oni wa soto, fuku wa uchi*" (Out with the devil, in with good fortune). Often a member of the family will don a devil's mask and attempt to get into the house, thus providing other family members with a target for their bean throwing. In the comic strip, however, the father's enthusiasm for the ritual is first dampened by Wakame, who declares that devils do not exist, and then by Katsuo, who suggests that his father is weak-minded if he believes that such actions will really bring about good fortune. In the last frame the mother is seen scolding the children for having spoiled their father's fun.[11]

The television treatment of the setsubun topic is radically different, for now the children are portrayed as great enthusiasts of the ritual. One episode, for example, broadcast in *Sazae-san*'s Tuesday evening rerun slot, begins with Katsuo's teacher explaining the meaning of setsubun to the class.[12] In response to their teacher's questions, however, it is revealed that most of the other pupils' families have stopped celebrating the event. Several of Katsuo's classmates thus ask him to help them perform the ritual, and Katsuo agrees, vowing he will take on the task of "preserving the tradition." A subsequent version, broadcast on Sunday, February 2, 1997 (the day before setsubun), again begins with the teacher explaining the meaning of setsubun custom. This time, however, there is no suggestion whatever that the tradition is in danger of dying out. All Katsuo's classmates are enthusiastic about it, and in the final scene several of them join the Isono family to participate in the bean throwing.

Like family, then, which is defined in the program through the presentation of a now largely antiquated family structure, seasonal activities in *Sazae-san* are shown to be firmly rooted in tradition. In both cases the present is ignored, while the disappearing facets of Japanese life are valorized and celebrated. Implicit in this is the ideological message that it is these vanishing structures and traditions that define the essence of Japan and the Japanese.[13] That it is Japan and not just the Isono family that is being portrayed is rendered somewhat more explicit by the opening of each half-hour program. While there have been several formats for this opening over the years, some of the recent ones feature Sazae-san touring the country. Lest viewers fail to recognize the places she is visiting, place names and scenes of famous tourist sights are flashed on the screen as Sazae-san makes her journey. In this way all Japanese are encouraged to identify with the image of life presented in the program, for even those whose town is not featured on the tour will probably have been to one or more of the places visited by Sazae-san.[14] That the sole function of this type of opening is to invite viewers from all over Japan to identify with the program is clear from the fact that travel is actually of little relevance to the show's content. The Isono family, in fact, seldom travels; having them do so would only place the family geographically and highlight regional differences, which would be inimical to the show's ideological function of constructing a national identity for its viewers. For just as the program's image of family life must be timeless in order to function as an ideal, so too must it be devoid of explicit place references in order to serve as the model for all Japanese. The suggestion, in other words, is that the Isono family can be found anywhere. It would be more precise, however, to say that the family lives nowhere. In the final analysis the Isonos' world is an imaginary construct, a utopia, which, as the etymology of the term "utopia" reminds us, is really "no place."

While *Sazae-san* has had perennial success and usually ranks as the number one anime on Japanese television, it has faced competition and even occasionally been upstaged by other family-oriented TV anime. One of these shows is *Chibi Maruko-chan* (Little Miss Maruko), which first appeared as a manga by Momoko Sakura in the girl's manga magazine *Ribon* (Ribbon) in 1986 before hitting the television airwaves in 1990. Actually this anime does not so much compete with *Sazae-san* as complement it; it also is produced by Fuji Television and is aired just before *Sazae-san*, the two shows thus providing the network with a Sunday evening one-two punch. In its early years the show often captured a higher weekly viewer rating than *Sazae-san*. In 1991, in fact, it broke the all-time record for a television anime with a rating of 39.9 percent in the Kantō region.[15] More recently it has settled down to a ranking in the middle of the overall top ten with ratings in the low to mid 20 percent bracket. During the same five-week period in early 1995 when *Sazae-san* held the number one spot, for example, *Chibi Maruko-chan* ranked fifth to seventh, with ratings ranging from 23.2 percent to 25.6 percent in the Kantō area.

The title character of *Chibi Maruko-chan* is a third-grade student. Many of the episodes deal with her experiences at school or with her classmates, and to this extent the program could perhaps be considered a children's anime rather than a family anime. Many episodes do take place entirely within the family, however, and in any case we get a clear enough view of Maruko's family and their family life to allow comparison with *Sazae-san*.

Like Sazae-san's family, Maruko's family is made up of three generations. The family includes, besides Maruko herself, her older sister, her parents, and her grandparents. Unlike the ideal family presented in *Sazae-san*, however, this one is more realistic. Maruko's mother, for example, who is seen most often in the kitchen, is shown as an overworked and underappreciated housewife, while her father, when he is at home, spends most of his time sitting in front of the television set and drinking beer or tea. Maruko's sister, meanwhile, usually considers herself too cool to have much to do with either her parents or her little sister. As for the grandparents, the grandmother is portrayed as a bit senile and does not often have much of a role, but the grandfather, who seems to be enjoying his second childhood and has a soft spot in his heart for his little granddaughter, plays a big part in many episodes. Finally, there is Maruko herself. While she can be cute, she is also not above nagging her mother when she wants something or manipulating her doting grandfather into granting her wishes (see Figure 10.1).[16]

Given the nature of the characters, it should not be surprising to learn that life in Maruko's family is less wholesome and more strained than it is in the Isono household. The characters often have their own selfish agendas which lead to trouble. Even the doting grandfather can be a cause of family strife, as his favors to Maruko are usually objected to by her mother, who worries that Maruko will become spoiled. In order to show how much this picture of family life differs from that of *Sazae-san*, I shall briefly describe an episode broadcast in January 1997 that deals with the family's New Year's celebrations. As was shown earlier, in *Sazae-san* traditional holiday themes are used to reinforce an ideal of the Japanese way of life; in *Chibi Maruko-chan*, on the other hand, holidays can be an occasion for family trouble.

In this particular episode Maruko is sent to the store by her mother to buy some fish for the New Year's meal. Since her mother has nothing smaller, she gives Maruko a ¥10,000 bill. At the store Maruko becomes

Figure 10.1 **Maruko-chan and her sister receive some money from their grandfather after having been refused by their mother**

Top left:
Sister: Mom, can we have ¥80 each, please.
Maruko: Please!
Mother: No!
Second row, right:
Sister: Stingy.
Maruko: Grandpa!
Grandfather: Hey, hey.
Second row, left:
Grandfather: It's all right. I'll give you some spending money. Keep it a secret from your mother.
Mother: What's the secret? I can hear them.
Third row:
Grandfather: Here you go.
Maruko: Thanks.
Text:
The ¥100 coin I received from grandfather's wrinkled hand was very warm.
Fourth row, right:
Text: In my hand it continued to feel warm.
Grandfather: Here you go.
Sister: Thanks.
Fourth row, left:
Voice of mother: Grandpa! You mustn't just give the children money whenever they ask for it.

fascinated with the *ise-ebi* (a species of lobster), which cost ¥3,000 each. Despite the store owner's advice that she should first call home to see whether it is all right, Maruko purchases one of the lobsters. Her mother, not surprisingly, is outraged at Maruko's extravagance and demands that she take the lobster back. Maruko's father and grandfather, on the other hand, are excited about the prospect of eating the lobster, and the father suggests that they may as well keep it. The mother still objects, however, and before long an argument develops in which the father accuses his wife of being stingy. Soon things become so heated that there is even talk of divorce. Finally the father declares that having lobster for their New Year's meal is such a good idea that he will go out and buy another one. By this time even Maruko and her grandfather are insisting that they can do without lobster. They are unable to dissuade the father, however, who is determined to have his way. He thus leaves the house in a huff and heads for the fish store. Fortunately for family harmony, when he gets to the store he finds that all the lobsters have been sold.

In this episode, then, it is only a matter of luck that the family is saved from complete breakdown. While *Chibi Maruko-chan* does not always feature such an intense level of domestic strife, the episode is typical of the program in that it does not shy away from portraying the weaknesses of individual characters or a family life that is less than ideal. Indeed, when seen alongside *Sazae-san*, the mother's frugality, the father's stubbornness, the grandfather's childlike doting, and the grandmother's senility all add up to a satire on the ideal of innocent family life presented in the older anime. While both programs concern extended families, insofar as *Chibi Maruko-chan*'s satire hints at the breakdown of that traditional family structure, it can be considered a closer reflection of contemporary family life.

One of the reasons for *Chibi Maruko-chan*'s more realistic portrayal of family life no doubt stems from the fact that the manga upon which the anime is based is highly autobiographical. Maruko's family name in both the manga and the anime is Sakura, the same as the author's, and as the manga makes clear, most of the episodes are drawn from the author's own childhood experiences. The television program has taken over from the original manga this flavor of childhood reminiscences, and this has important consequences for the nature of the anime. Since the author, who was born in 1965, was still a young woman when she began to publish the manga, and since the anime has adhered to the same atmosphere of childhood, *Chibi Maruko-chan* thus portrays life in a period that is obviously more recent than the idyllic past of *Sazae-san*. Still, there is an unmistakable air of nostalgia about the program, and surely this is one of the reasons the program is popular with adults as well as children. Although I have no evidence to back this up, I would hazard a guess that among adult viewers the show appeals most to those who grew up in the 1970s, for this was the period of the author's own childhood and the period that seems to correspond best to social life as presented in the anime. As long as the program continues to target this particular audience group, however, it is destined to become, like *Sazae-san*, more and more out of touch with contemporary social reality—if the program survives, that is. Yet, given the appeal of nostalgia for Japanese viewers, as evidenced in the success of *Sazae-san*, there is no reason to suppose that it will not continue for many more years to come.

One family-oriented anime that does not exploit this preference for nostalgia is *Crayon Shin-chan*. The manga of the same name, upon which the anime is based, is written by Yoshito Usui and began to appear in the manga magazine *Action Comics* in 1991. Unlike both *Sazae-san* and *Chibi Maruko-chan*, this manga/anime deals with a nuclear family. Until recently the family consisted only of the title character, Shin-chan, and his parents. In 1996, however, a fourth family member was introduced, when Shin-chan's mother gave birth to a baby girl, Himawari. As the statistics examined earlier testify, the size and makeup of Shin-chan's family correspond more closely to the norm in today's Japan. In this sense *Crayon Shin-chan* can be said to be more up to date than either *Sazae-san* or *Chibi Maruko-chan*. It is not only size and composition that make this a more modern family, however, for in their day-to-day, *mai-hōmu* (my-home), *mai-kaa* (my-car) lifestyle the family is clearly revealed to be contemporary.[17]

Much of the humor of both the manga and the anime lies in portraying the difficulties modern parents face in raising children. Sometimes, for example, Shin-chan can be a hindrance to the parents' attempt to enjoy their private life as a couple (Figure 10.2).[18] Of course it does not help much if the child is one like Shin-chan, whose vulgarity often brings shame to his parents (Figure 10.3).[19]

It need hardly be said that this vulgarity stands in sharp contrast to the purity of family life in *Sazae-san*, and even *Chibi Maruko-chan*'s view of childhood appears innocent by comparison. There is more to

Figure 10.2 **Shin-chan interrupts his parents' lovemaking**

Top right:
Father: Shinnosuke is back in bed. Now. . . .
Top left:
Shin-chan: Mommy, toilet.
Bottom right:
Parents: He's seen us.
Bottom left:
Shin-chan: That's not fair. I wanna wrestle too.
Mother: "That's right, we're wrestling."
Father: Shit.
Text: The desperate wrestling match continued late into the night.

Crayon Shin-chan than vulgarity, however, for the program often includes some rather biting satire. Shin-chan, in fact, has an uncanny penchant for exposing the foibles and pretensions of his vain and materialistic parents and other adults, just as the program as a whole reveals the contradictions and difficulties of modern life in general. Among the topics dealt with in various manga and anime episodes, for example, have been the mother's craze for catalog shopping, her sensitivity about the size of her bust, the father's daydreams of having an affair with an office girl, the rivalry between grandfathers to show their affection for their grandchildren, the desperate attempts of Shin-chan's kindergarten teachers to appear sexy and attract an ideal husband, and the difficulties of enjoying a "my-car" lifestyle when one is stuck in a traffic jam. While much of the humor comes from exaggerating these incidents or problems, in every

Figure 10.3 **Shin-chan discovers the wonders of video cameras while visiting an electronic appliance store with his parents**

Top right:
Shin-chan: "Oh."
Top middle:
Shin-chan: "Ha, ha."
Top left:
Father: "And I just told him not to run off."
Mother: "It's because you didn't hold on to him."
Bottom right:
Mother: "What's that?"
Bottom left:
Shin-chan: "Can you see it?"
Father: "Grrr."
Mother: "You idiot!"

case they appear more typical of contemporary life than what one finds in either *Sazae-san* or *Chibi Maruko-chan*. Unlike these older anime, in other words, *Crayon Shin-chan* can be said to exploit rather than ignore the present. Since the focus is on a young nuclear family, its appeal for television audiences can perhaps best be attributed to the opportunity the program provides for the young families of today to laugh at themselves.

In conclusion, then, it can be said that the three family manga/anime examined present three different versions of the Japanese family, each corresponding to a different period of postwar history. In the case of *Sazae-san*, although its anime version has been in a certain sense dehistoricized, the atmosphere evoked nevertheless corresponds roughly to life in the 1960s. In *Chibi Maruko-chan*, on the other hand, the temporal setting has been moved ahead by focusing on a period identifiable as the 1970s. Finally there is *Crayon Shin-chan*, everything about which indicates that the setting is the 1990s. Seen in this way, an interesting correlation is revealed between the temporal setting and popularity of the three programs. *Sazae-san*, as already mentioned, has been the perennial number one anime on Japanese television, while *Chibi Maruko-chan*, after shooting into the limelight in its early days, has settled into second place in that category. *Crayon Shin-chan*, on the other hand, usually ranks third at best. During the same five-week period in early 1995 examined earlier, for example, *Crayon Shin-chan* placed sixth to twelfth in the overall weekly rankings, with ratings of from 20.7 percent to 23.9 percent. To be sure, this is still a phenomenally high viewing rate in comparison to many other television programs. That the show's popularity regularly falls short of that enjoyed by anime that present nostalgic images of the Japanese family, however, suggests that viewers as a whole are drawn more to the ideal than to the real, and that one of the most important functions of popular culture in Japan is not to reflect or examine contemporary society but to provide cultural consumers with a chance to escape the present by identifying with a nostalgic and less troubling past.

Notes

1. Examples of recent English-language anthologies of avant-garde Japanese manga are *Sake Jock* (Seattle: Fantagraphic, 1995) ; and Kevin Quigley, ed., *Comics Underground Japan* (New York: Blast Books, 1996). Japanese television anime, meanwhile, have been seen in local versions in many countries around the world ever since Osamu Tezuka's *Tetsuwan Atom* (Atom Boy) first went international soon after its Japanese debut in 1963. Among science fiction anime currently enjoying an international reputation are *Sailor Moon* and *Dragon Ball Z*.

2. Unlike the now more common "story manga," episodes of which are published in weekly or monthly manga magazines and which can run to several hundred pages in length, *Sazae-san* resembles the American newspaper comic strip in that each comic is confined to four frames and is self-contained. The entire corpus of some 6,000 strips has been republished in book form twice. The first edition, in sixty-eight volumes, was published by Hasegawa's own publishing company, Shimaisha. This has now been republished in forty-five volumes by Asahi Shinbunsha.

3. Machiko Hasegawa, *Sazae-san*, vol. 1 (Tokyo: Asahi Shinbunsha, 1994–1996), p. 70.

4. Ibid., p. 109.

5. The Hasegawa Machiko Museum Foundation declined to grant permission to reprint illustrative *Sazae-san* strips in this book.

6. Hasegawa, *Sazae-san* 1, pp. 92–93.

7. Ibid., p. 38.

8. "Za Kiroku" (Records), *Za Terebijon* (Television), nos. 7–11, 1995.

9. Statistics Bureau, Management and Coordination Agency, *Japan Statistical Yearbook, 1997* (Tokyo, 1996), p. 56

10. For example, see Hasegawa, *Sazae-san*, vol. 29, p. 38.

11. Ibid., p. 131.

12. *Sazae-san*, Fuji Television, January 28, 1997.

13. This attempt to define the essentially Japanese through the nation's threatened and vanishing traditions is not limited to *Sazae-san* but can be observed in many other examples of popular culture. For a penetrating examination of this phenomenon, see Marilyn Ivy's stimulating book, *Discourses of the Vanishing: Modernity, Phantasm, Japan* (Chicago: University of Chicago Press, 1995).

14. As Andrew Painter has pointed out, a similar technique for appealing to an audience from all over Japan can be seen in the morning news show, *Zūmu-in Asa* (Morning Zoom-in, on Nippon Television), which every day begins with a whirlwind tour of Japan made possible through brief relay feeds from the network's affiliated stations around the country. See Andrew Painter, "Japanese Daytime Television, Popular Culture, and Ideology," *Journal of Japan Studies* 19:2 (1993), pp. 298–300.

15. Mark Schilling, "What's Hot on Japanese TV," *Mangajin* 15 (1992), 12–15.

16. Momoko Sakura, *Chibi Maruko-chan*, vol. 1 (Tokyo: Shūeisha, 1987), pp. 8–9.

17. Mai-hōmu and mai-kaa represent two of the most common goals of young families in Japan today, namely, possessing a private home and a car.

18. Yoshito Usui, *Crayon Shin-chan*, vol. 1 (Tokyo: Futabasha, 1992), p. 56.

19. Ibid., p. 106.

Part III

Television and Film

11

New Role Models for Men and Women?

Gender in Japanese TV Dramas

Hilaria M. Gössmann

Television dramas are an important and influential form of popular culture in many countries, often providing value that goes beyond mere entertainment. For many viewers, television serves as a kind of "significant other" against which they "develop, maintain, and revise their self-concepts, including perceptions of gender and role-identification."[1]

This is particularly the case in Japan. According to a survey on media consumption by Japanese women, many female viewers watch TV dramas not just for entertainment, but also to learn about life.[2] It can be assumed that to a certain extent this is true for men as well. Thus, the way men and women are depicted in television dramas not only reflects actual or idealized conditions in society; it also contributes to the creation and acceptance of gender roles.

It is generally accepted that popular culture, while basically conservative, is potentially supportive of social change. Concerning the social influence of TV dramas, Elizabeth Lozano and Arvind Singhal have written: "By depicting intimate personal relationships and giving the audience the opportunity to identify with certain characters, melodramatic serials can address certain social issues as no other narrative can. . . . [Dramas can either] reaffirm traditional social structures, or legitimize social change."[3] This chapter discusses the relationship between television drama content and changing gender roles in Japan, beginning with a look at the portrayal of women in TV dramas up to the mid 1970s, and then turning to the changing roles played by women, and men, in Japanese television dramas of the 1990s.[4]

"Reliable Mothers" and "Suffering Women" in TV Dramas through the Mid-1970s

When television broadcasting started in Japan in the 1950s, American TV serials like *Father Knows Best* and *I Love Lucy* were aired and served as models for the first Japanese production of TV dramas.[5] During the 1960s, however, when rapid economic growth caused the majority of Japanese men to be absent from their family homes in the evening because of long working hours, TV series featuring patriarchal families gradually disappeared and the so-called mother-centered dramas became popular.

The pioneer analysis of women's roles in Japanese TV dramas was conducted by sociologist Yasuko Muramatsu in the 1970s. Muramatsu categorized prime-time TV dramas into two genres, the "home drama," focusing on the family, and the "dramatic drama," which deals with situations outside the home, such as work. The typical heroine of a home drama up to that time was a *tanomoshii haha* (reliable mother), who was capable of competently managing any situation.[6] Well-known examples of these mother-centered dramas are *Kimottama Kāsan* (Courageous Mother)[7] and *Arigatō* (Thank You),[8] both created by female producer Fukuko Ishii.

In the "dramatic drama," the heroine, whose life lies outside the domestic sphere, is an unhappy *taeru onna* (suffering woman). Indeed, the very structuring of these TV dramas seems to act as a warning to Japanese women: As long as you remain within the traditional sphere allotted to women, you will be happy and live a rewarding life; but as soon as you step out of this safe haven, the "sanctuary of the home," you will be punished by becoming vulnerable and powerless.[9] This message is obviously a reflection of the segregated worlds of men, "outside," and women, "inside," which until then was the socially approved and most typical pattern of gender roles in Japanese society.[10]

In the mid-1970s, as the viewing public began to find the perfection and harmony of families in TV dramas to be too idealistic and removed from their own experiences, a new kind of family drama emerged which focused on the problems of family life. One of the first hit dramas of this type was *Kishibe no Album* (Photo Album on the Shore),[11] written by the famous script writer Taichi Yamada. In this drama, aired by the private television network TBS in 1977, a 40-year-old married housewife has an extramarital affair because she is no longer able to bear the isolation of her life with a husband who works all the time and children who are almost adults. Although, in the end, she returns to her family, the role she plays is clearly something other than that of a "reliable mother." This then-new tendency to highlight problems or crisis in the family caught on, and remains prevalent in Japanese TV dramas today.

The "Fuyuhiko Syndrome": Demonic Mothers and Mother-Dominated Sons in TV Dramas of the 1990s

In the weekly television serials of the 1990s (which generally run for twelve weeks, with one hour-long episode per week), script writers and producers have effectively taken up various trends and problems of contemporary society to create stories that often become the subject of public debate. *Zutto Anata ga Suki Datta* (I've Always Loved You), aired by TBS in the summer of 1992, is an outstanding example of this genre. The theme of this drama, which obtained spectacularly high viewer ratings,[12] is the inability of a young married man named Fuyuhiko to escape the dominance and control of his mother.

The mother-fixation of men, or their inability to break from their mother's influence, appears to be a common phenomenon in many cultures. However, it seems that there are some characteristics particular to contemporary Japanese society that promote an extreme closeness in mother-child relationships, especially in the case of the mother-son bond. One of these characteristics is the conspicuous absence from the home of the father, who spends most of his time at work.[13] Another is the highly competitive Japanese educational system, which has produced a particularly extreme variety of the devoted mother, the *kyōiku mama* (education mother). The percentage of Japanese men with a *maza-kon* (mother complex) is said to be especially high among the "sons of wealthy families who have gained entrance to the academic elite."[14]

The plot of "I've Always Loved You" is as follows. Through an *omiai* (arranged marriage), the 29-year-old heroine Miwa becomes the wife of Fuyuhiko. From the day of the wedding, she endures an extremely unhappy married life because Fuyuhiko is dominated by his mother. Miwa leaves Fuyuhiko, but comes back when he promises never to let his mother into their apartment again. However, on this and every other occasion, Fuyuhiko falls back into the role of mother-dominated son.

Several times Miwa accidentally runs into her former boyfriend Yōsuke, whom she gradually comes to realize that she still loves.

Miwa is finally forced to recognize that her husband is incapable of communicating with anybody except his mother. Being the absolute opposite of the athletic and manly Yōsuke, Fuyuhiko spends virtually all his time in front of a computer screen, both at work and at home. He hates anything that is alive and does not even allow Miwa to bring flowers into the apartment. However, he is very fond of his collection of preserved butterflies, a thematic leitmotif of the drama. One particularly beautiful blue butterfly appears to be a symbol for Miwa, and it becomes clear that Fuyuhiko has "collected" Miwa in the same way as he has the butterflies. Just as he can enjoy looking at butterflies only when they are displayed in a showcase, he wants Miwa to stay at home to display for him and the world a pretty image of home and wife. Fuyuhiko seems to have no interest in a sexual relationship with his wife. When Miwa asks him why he does not touch her, he answers: *"Mada boku no iu tōri no tsuma ni natte inai"* (You aren't yet the kind of wife I want you to be). During their marriage the couple have sex only once.

Fuyuhiko is also a voyeur who always shadows Miwa when she meets Yōsuke and afterward tells her in detail where she has been. Miwa is frightened by her husband, but her mother-in-law Etsuko is even more threatening. Once, when Miwa arrives at her parents' house after a quarrel with Fuyuhiko, she finds her mother-in-law already sitting in the living room chatting with her parents. Etsuko asks Miwa to forgive Fuyuhiko and stresses that she will scold her son for his behavior. When Miwa leaves Fuyuhiko the first time, she is shadowed by a man in dark clothes, obviously hired by her mother-in-law, who has warned her: *"Zettai ni modotte itadakimasu. Donna shudan o totte mo"* (I will make you go back no matter what it takes). For Miwa, there seems to be no escape from Fuyuhiko and his mother. When Miwa finally decides to divorce her husband, even though she is pregnant, her mother-in-law tries to blackmail her into going back to Fuyuhiko and having the child, threatening that if Miwa leaves, she will force Miwa's father to sell his shop in order to pay back the money he has borrowed from Fuyuhiko's family.

Fuyuhiko, accusing Miwa of having an affair with Yōsuke and refusing to believe that he is the father of the child (which he is), finally agrees to the separation. This is the climactic scene in the drama, as Fuyuhiko tries to free himself not only from Miwa but from his mother as well. When Fuyuhiko tells his mother that he wants to divorce Miwa,

Etsuko slaps her son and says: "The best way for you to live is just as I tell you to! That's been true up to now, right?"

When Fuyuhiko counters that she never lets him decide anything on his own, Etsuko points to his computer and butterfly collection and says in a strict voice: "I've bought you all these things, but I've also taught you that you should be careful with them. With Miwa it's exactly the same. I've arranged this marriage for you, and so it's not for you to decide to leave Miwa."

Screaming that Miwa is different from the computer and butterfly collection, Fuyuhiko goes berserk, dramatically smashing to pieces all the things his mother has given him. Finally, picking up a piece of broken glass from a butterfly showcase, he draws his mother into an embrace, and stabs her. He then calls the police, and announces to Miwa: "Now we are free!"

This turns out to be an illusion, however. Miwa leaves Fuyuhiko to start a new life with Yōsuke, who is willing to raise Fuyuhiko's child together with her. (When Miwa leaves, the blue butterfly on Fuyuhiko's computer screen, which corresponds to the Miwa symbol in his collection, disappears.) Inevitably, after Miwa has left him, Fuyuhiko falls back under the spell of his mother, whose injury was not fatal. Etsuko denies that her son tried to kill her, allowing Fuyuhiko to be released from prison. The last scene of the drama shows us what the future holds for Fuyuhiko: together with his mother, he is on his way to another *omiai* (meeting with a prospective bride). Obviously Fuyuhiko is unable to escape his mother's dominance, no matter how hard he struggles.

This drama presents a fundamental shift in the depiction of men and women in Japanese TV dramas. Fuyuhiko is precisely what is known as a *sankō* (three highs), in Japan: He graduated from the best or "highest" university, Tokyo University; he has a "high" position in a famous bank; plus he is tall (which seems to be less important). Such a man is commonly regarded as the ideal husband in Japan. However, the sankō we encounter in this drama is a weak, childlike man who is dominated by his mother and unable to sustain a happy marriage.[15]

Whereas the evil mother-in-law bullying the wife of her son has long been a common theme in Japanese TV dramas,[16] in "I've Always Loved You" it is the son himself who is the main victim of his domineering mother. In this way, this drama, while extreme in its portrayal, reveals some of the negative consequences of traditional gender roles that force men to concentrate exclusively on study and work while mothers focus

Figure 11.1 **Fuyuhiko is comforted by his domineering mother in "I've Always Loved You"**

on their children. To emphasize the mother's evil effect on the life of her son and daughter-in-law, the drama's producer, Seiichirō Kijima, employs a frequently encountered figure in Japanese culture, the demon woman.[17] Etsuko is depicted as demonic not just through her words and actions but also via the lighting, camera angles, and threatening music that are used to portray her.

The "demonic mother" in this drama is obviously a scapegoat, and her characterization as a woman with demonic power serves to avoid a direct critique of women's inferior position in society. As feminist sociologist Chizuko Ueno points out, such domineering behavior by mothers is likely to arise when women have little choice but to live while relying excessively on men, husband or sons, since "a dependent mother tends to create dependent sons."[18] In this sense, not just the son, but also the dominating mother can be regarded as a victim. Of course, presenting a critical analysis of these kinds of social issues is not the primary concern of commercial television networks, for whom securing advertising sponsors and garnering high viewer ratings is more important. Yet the popularity of dramas which deal with current social issues—and, thanks to that popularity, the growing number of such dramas—is strong evidence that the viewing public values real-life related content in their television fare.

The extraordinary success of "I've Always Loved You" led to the production of a sequel entitled *Dare ni mo Ienai* (I Can't Tell Anybody) by the same producer. Featuring the same actors that played Fuyuhiko, Miwa, and Etsuko in "I've Always Loved You," "I Can't Tell Anybody" is a complicated story centered on a relationship between lawyer Mario, Fuyuhiko's son by his second wife, and Kanako, the daughter of Miwa and Yōsuke. The demon mother in "I Can't Tell Anybody"—played, as was Etsuko, by Yōko Nogiwa, who has built a career out of playing evil mothers over the past decade—this time dominates her daughter Miyuki, Mario's wife. This presents the fixation of mothers on their children as a problem that is not restricted to sons. Happily, at the end of this serial, Miyuki succeeds in freeing herself from her demonic mother's power.

The women in these two dramas, as mothers fixated on their children or as wives sustaining unhappy married lives, are not unlike the traditional "reliable mothers" and "suffering women" that Muramatsu identified as the major character types in Japanese dramas up to the 1970s. The difference is that the demonic mother is a perverted, negative version of the strong, reliable mother, and that women suffer not just in the outside world but within the family as well.

Shifting Gender Roles in Married Couples: Working Wives and Family-Oriented Fathers

To further analyze gender roles in Japanese television dramas of the 1990s, twelve *renzoku* (serial) dramas that depict the lives of married couples were examined (see Table 11.1). These dramas all aired between 1992 and 1995 on commercial networks during prime time. According to the roles fulfilled by the husband and wife at the beginning of each drama, they can be divided into two groups: Type A, in which the wife is a housewife and the husband works outside the home; and Type B, in which both partners work outside the home.

Although since the 1980s the majority of married Japanese women do work outside the home, the majority of TV dramas still depict wives who stay at home. With respect to the starting point of the stories, therefore, the dramas fall short of accurately reflecting contemporary social

Table 11.1

Married couples in Japanese TV serials of the 1990s

TYPE A: At the beginning, the wife is a housewife and the husband works outside the home

Drama title, network, time shown	*Development by end of drama*
No. 1 "I've Always Loved You" *(Zutto anata ga suki datta)* TBS, July–September 1992	*Wife leaves* because her husband is mother-dominated.
No. 2 "Selfish Women" *(Wagamama na onnatachi)* Fuji TV, February–June 1992	*Wife leaves* in order to live alone and work.
No. 3 "Sunflowers on a Hill" *(Oka no ue no himawari)* TBS, April–June 1992	*Wife suffers* because of husband's extra-marital affair.
No. 4 "I Can't Tell Anybody" *(Dare ni mo ienai)* TBS, July–September 1993	*Crisis* because of intrusion of wife's former lover; couple reconciles.
No. 5 "The Section Chief's Unlucky Year" *(Kachōsan no yakudoshi)* TBS, July–October 1993	*Wife starts to work* because of financial problems.
No. 6 "Adult Kiss" *(Otona no kisu)* Nihon TV, October–December 1993	*Wife leaves,* husband cares for child; couple reconciles.
No. 7 "Living for This Love" *(Kono ai ni ikite)* Fuji TV, April–July 1994	*Wife leaves* to live with a new partner and starts working.
No. 8 "Objections of a Woman" *(Onna no iibun)* TBS, October–December 1994	*Wife leaves* and begins working, but returns; couple reconciles.

TYPE B: At the beginning, both the husband and wife are employed

Drama title, network, time shown	*Development by end of drama*
No. 9 "Double Kitchen" *(Daburu kitchin)* TBS, April–June 1993	Husband transferred to Britain; *wife leaves her job to follow him.*
No. 10 "The Eldest Son's Wife" *(Chōnan no yome)* TBS, April–July 1994	Husband transferred to Kansai; *wife stays* with his family to care for them and to *continue working.*
No. 11 "The Wife's Turn" *(Yome no deru maku)* TV Asahi, April–July 1994	After the death of her mother-in-law, the *wife leaves her job* to care for the family of her husband.
No. 12 "Papa's Survival" *(Papa sabaibaru)* TBS, July–September 1995	*Husband refuses a transfer* to Hokkaidō; instead he cares for his daughter while his *wife is working in New York.*

reality. In another way, however, they may be more realistic: in sharp contrast to the dramas of the 1970s, most of the housewives in the 1990s dramas are not content with their present situation. Many suffer because their husbands are usually absent and communication between husband and wife is lacking. This critical view fundamentally contradicts the message of former dramas that the home guarantees happiness for women.

As dramas 1, 2, 6, 7, and 8 in Table 11.1 illustrate, the housewife leaving her husband is a common pattern. In *Otona no Kiss* (No. 6, Adult Kiss), the theme of mother-fixated sons is again dealt with, although no mother or mother-in-law appears in the story. The wife in this drama decides to separate from her husband because she has become aware that she is nothing but a mother for him, and she is no longer willing to fulfill this role. After the wife moves out and starts working, the husband gradually develops into a man who can take care of himself. Thanks to this change, a real partnership between husband and wife actually seems to be possible. It is not only young women who rebel against being stuck in unappreciated housewife roles. In *Onna no Iibun* (No. 8, Objections of a Woman), a middle-aged woman moves out because her husband treats her like a servant. Just as in "Adult Kiss," in this drama the husband changes his attitude and the wife's return becomes possible. These dramas obviously advocate a more family-oriented concept of maleness.

Whereas the wives in earlier dramas often left their husbands because of extramarital affairs, today it is more common for them to leave to search for lives of their own and to pursue careers. Furthermore, there is an increasing number of Type B dramas in which married women have jobs from the very beginning of the story. Still, in these cases, it is the wife who cares for the children and does virtually all the housework, even while working—a double burden. This suggests that the professional career of the wife is of secondary importance to that of the husband, an idea reinforced by the fact that these wives often give up their jobs for such reasons as to accompany a husband who is transferred to Europe (No. 9, "Double Kitchen") and to care for a husband's parents (No. 11, "The Wife's Turn"). The message here seems to be that the professional career of a married woman is acceptable as long as it does not interfere with her family duties. This is similar to the "backlash" against women's progress in the workplace, which American journalist Susan Faludi has described in the case of Hollywood movies and TV series of the 1980s in the United States,[19] and which is also a common pattern in German TV series.[20]

At the end of 1995, a drama titled "Papa's Survival" aired, which reverses the traditional gender roles in marriage. This drama's beginning is an obvious remake of the 1979 Hollywood movie *Kramer vs. Kramer*; in both cases, the husband comes home late one night to tell his wife about a success at work only to find her waiting with a packed suitcase and the news that she is leaving him. In both cases, the wife hands over responsibility for the child and the household to her husband.

The wives' reasons for leaving, however, are quite different. While Mrs. Kramer is frustrated with her role as housewife, the wife in "Papa's Survival" is a career woman whose company is about to transfer her to New York for three years. Since her husband's idea of marriage does not tolerate separation, she asks for a divorce. After the wife leaves, the husband has a very hard time caring for his daughter and combining his duties as father with his job at a company. Gradually, however, he becomes quite fond of fulfilling his new role, and when he himself is ordered to transfer to northern Japan, he refuses because of his daughter, even though this means a likely end to his career with the company. When his wife, back in Japan on a short visit, hears about this, she urges him to accept the transfer and offers to return home so that he can concentrate on his career. Nevertheless, the husband decides to stay with his daughter and wait for his wife's return from New York after the three years are up. He explains his decision this way:

> Until now I've completely devoted myself to my job, but that was wrong. A professional career is not everything. All that time I believed I was fulfilling my duties as a father by working and bringing home money. But now I've come to realize that there is something much more important. Living together with my daughter for these three months finally made me understand this. In the beginning, doing housework was quite hard for me, but now it's fun taking care of my daughter. . . . I'm not giving up my career against my will, and I don't see it as a self-sacrifice.

This change in thinking leads to a reconciliation between husband and wife. When the wife notes that this would mean a reversal of the traditional gender roles, he answers: "Why shouldn't there be a couple like us? This is a decision for me to make as I choose."

The focus of this drama is obviously a fundamental discussion of gender roles. Every episode begins with a computer animation in which the husband and a male friend driving in a car (and real-life husbands watching at home) are confronted with six questions concerning their attitude toward their roles as husband and father. If they score five to six points, they are perfect; if they get less, they are encouraged to make greater effort. At the beginning of the last episode the questions are:

1. Does your child say, "I love you, papa?"
2. Have you ever given priority to the career of your wife?
3. Were you together with your wife when your baby was born?
4. Did you help your wife rear your baby and change its diapers?
5. Do you think you are a good father?
6. Will your family follow you if you are transferred?[21]

As the car ride of the two men in the computer animation symbolizes, this drama can be a journey of self-discovery for men. Further, as the title suggests, the drama is to be regarded as a kind of survival training for fathers. The message: Caring for children can be rewarding for men, too.

While dramas airing between 1992 and 1994 seldom featured fathers looking after their children, quite a few dramas in 1995 and 1996 depicted such single fathers. A good example of this trend is *Ashita wa Daijōbu* (Tomorrow Everything Will Be All Right), which was shown on Fuji Television between January and March 1996. The hero, a 24-year-old working man, loses his wife in an accident and has to care for his 9-month-old baby by himself. Although urged by his company to remarry as soon as possible so that he can concentrate on his work again, he refuses. Forced to face the difficulty of simultaneously raising a child and pursuing a professional career, he decides to devote himself to establishing day care centers within companies. At the drama's end, this effort is rewarded and he is able to take his son along with him to his workplace. In this way, involvement in child care is transferred not only to the male, but also into the public realm. The drama also demonstrates that fundamental changes in working life and society are necessary in order that both men and women may have the chance to combine career and family.

Conclusion

Whereas up to the mid-1970s the portrayal of women in Japanese television dramas was quite stereotyped, with the reliable and strong mother on one side and the young suffering single women on the other, the depiction of female characters has gradually changed and broadened with the emergence of dramas dealing with problems within the family. This may be partially in response to the United Nations Decade for Women (1975–1985) and the strengthened women's movement in Japan. According to Muramatsu, between 1974 and 1984, "the number of women [in TV dramas] satisfied with their lot dropped from 46 percent to 13 percent."[22] As the present study of twelve 1990s dramas revolving around married couples shows, the discontent of housewives has now become a common theme. The cliché of happy housewives, it seems, has been dismantled. These dramas are also a reflection of Japan's rising divorce rate and the fact that women are in most cases the ones who seek the separation.

Many popular dramas of the 1990s take a critical position toward the traditional role of wife and mother, either by portraying them as demonic females domineering their children, even after the children are grown, or by depicting wives who are so unhappy that they decide to leave their husbands. Compared to before, there is much less idealization of the devoted mother-figure and of men that concentrate exclusively on their work. This can be regarded as a decisive step toward conceptualizing new gender roles in TV dramas.

Andrew A. Painter, who conducted research on Japanese television in 1988 and 1989, concluded that "many telerepresentations of gender on Japanese television can be criticized as ideological forms that legitimize, naturalize, and eternalize the subjugation of women in that society." Nevertheless, he admits: "Though dramas like 'Selfish Women'[23] are perhaps not revolutionary, they are indicative of the fact that telerepresentations of gender in Japan are changing, at least in some areas."[24]

Concerning the relation between popular culture and social reality, TV dramas such as "Papa's Survival" and "Tomorrow Everything Will Be All Right" demonstrate that dramas do not always reflect already-existing social conditions. Fathers willing to sacrifice their professional career for the sake of their children or wives are anything but common today in Japan, or in any other country for that matter. But, if it is true, as Lozano and Singhal say, that television dramas "have the potential to entertain *and* to educate,"[25] then such dramas as these may be sowing the seeds of future trends and conceptualizations of gender roles.

In comparison to former decades, there is no doubt that the range of role models for both men and women found in Japanese television dramas has broadened greatly, and that dramas which advocate and help to legitimize social change have increased in number. In this sense, popular culture in the form of Japanese TV dramas, while not radical, can be considered quite progressive.

Notes

1. Barbara J. Newton and Elizabeth B. Buck, "Television as Significant Other: Its Relationship to Self-Descriptors in Five Countries," *Journal of Cross-Cultural Psychology* 16: 3 (1985), p. 295.

2. *Masumedia Bunka to Josei ni Kansuru Chōsa Kenkyū* (Studies of Mass Media Culture and Women) (Tokyo: Tokyo-to Seikatsu Bunka Kyoku, 1986), p. 109.

3. Elizabeth Lozano and Arvind Singhal, "Melodramatic Television Serials: Mythical Narratives for Education," *Communications: The European Journal for Communication* 18 (1993), pp. 117–118.

4. Research for this study was first conducted at the German Institute of Japanese Studies in Tokyo during the years 1992–1995, and is presently being continued in a research project sponsored by the University of Trier. I would like to thank my two co-researchers, Renate Jaschke and Andreas Mrugalla, for their cooperation.

5. For a history of Japanese television dramas and their various genres, see Masunori Sata and Hideo Hirahara, eds., *A History of Japanese Television Drama* (Tokyo: Kaibunsha, 1991); Hiromu Toriyama, *Nihon Terebi Dorama-shi* (History of Japanese Television Drama) (Tokyo: Eijinsha, 1986); *Terebi Dorama Zenshi* (Complete History of Japanese Television Drama) (Tokyo: Tokyo News Tsūshinsha, 1994); and Yomiuri Shinbun Geinōbu, ed., *Terebi Bangumi no 40 Nen* (Forty Years of Television Programs) (Tokyo: NHK Shuppan, 1994).

6. Yasuko Muramatsu, *Terebi Dorama no Joseigaku* (Women's Studies in Television Drama) (Tokyo: Sōtakusha, 1979), p. 94.

7. *Kimottama Kāsan* was aired by TBS between 1968 and 1972. The central character is a widow, played by Masako Kyōzuka, who runs a noodle shop to support her family. See *Terebi Dorama Zenshi*, pp. 172–173, and Sata and Hirahara, *History,* pp. 118–120, for more details on this drama.

8. *Arigatō* was aired by TBS between 1970 and 1975. The daughter of the mother in this drama was played by the famous enka singer Suizenji Kiyoko. See Yomiuri Shinbun Geinōbu, pp. 111–116, for details on this very popular drama, which achieved viewer ratings of up to 56.3 percent.

9. Muramatsu, *Terebi Dorama no Joseigoku*, p. 144.

10. For an analysis of the changing worlds of men and women in Japan and China, see Hilaria Gössmann, Sabine Jakobi, and Kerstin Katharina Vogel, "Crossing Borders between the Public and the Private: How the Worlds of Women and Men are Changing in Japan and China," *Asiatische Studien, Etudes Asiatique*, special ed., *Change, Diversity, Fluidity: Japanese Perspectives* 51:1 (1997), pp.149–185.

11. For details on this drama, which was also published as a novel, see Hideo

Hirahara, *Yamada Taichi no Kazoku Dorama no Saiken: Ai to Kaitai to Saisei to* (Examining the Family Dramas of Taichi Yamada: Love and Dismantling and Rebirth) (Tokyo: Shōgakukan, 1994), pp. 23–45.

12. Starting with 13 percent during the first episode, viewer ratings for *Zutto Anata ga Suki Datta* rose to 34 percent, the highest ever recorded for a Japanese TV drama broadcast at the 10 P.M. time slot. Because of the enormous success of *Zutto*, videotapes of the whole serial were produced for sale and a novel based on the drama was published; see Ryōichi Kimizuka, *Zutto Anata ga Suki Datta* (Tokyo: Wani Books, 1992).

13. See Sumiko Iwao, *The Japanese Woman: Traditional Image and Changing Reality* (New York: Free Press, 1993): "In the absence of husbands to fulfill their needs and desires as wives, mothers who essentially play the role of a single parent often develop very strong attachments to their sons" (p. 150).

14. Ibid., p. 151.

15. Sumiko Iwao's description of mother-dominated sons fits Fuyuhiko perfectly: "Sons may become incapable of making decisions on their own because of the way they were raised. So psychologically dependent have they become on their mothers that they often turn to them for advice even after they are married, much to their wives' consternation. . . . In some cases, these men are so severely fixated on their mothers that they are unable to have a normal sexual relationship with a girlfriend or wife" (pp. 150–151).

16. For a review of friction between mothers-in-law and daughters-in-law in Japanese TV dramas, see Katja Valaskivi, *Wataru Seken wa Oni Bakari* (Nothing But Evil Wherever One Goes): *Mothers-in-Law and Daughters-in-Law in a Japanese Television Family Drama* (Jyväskylä: University of Jyväskylä, 1995) and Andrew A. Painter, "The Telerepresentation of Gender in Japan," in Anne E. Imamura, *Re-Imagining Japanese Women* (Berkeley and Los Angeles: University of California Press, 1996), pp. 46–72; and Andrew A. Painter, "Japanese Daytime Television, Popular Culture and Ideology," in *Contemporary Japan and Popular Culture*, ed. John Whittier Treat (Honolulu: University of Hawaii Press, 1996), pp. 197–234.

17. For a description of demonic females in various genres of Japanese culture, see Ian Buruma, *Behind the Mask: On Sexual Demons, Sacred Mothers, Transvestites, Gangsters and Other Japanese Cultural Heroes* (New York: New American Library, 1984), pp. 47–63; and Meera Viswanathan, "In Pursuit of the Yamanba: The Question of Female Resistance," *The Women's Hand: Gender and Theory in Japanese Women's Writing*, eds. Paul Gordon Schalow and Janet A. Walker (Stanford, CA: Stanford University Press, 1996), pp. 239–261.

18. Chizuko Ueno, *Mazakon Shōnen no Matsuro: Onna to Otoko no Mirai* (The End of Mother-Complex Boys: The Future of Women and Men) (Tokyo: Kawai Shuppan, 1994), p. 66.

19. See chapters 5 and 6 of Susan Faludi, *Backlash: The Undeclared War Against American Women* (New York: Doubleday, 1991), for examples of movies and TV dramas idealizing the role of married housewives.

20. For a comparison of gender roles in Japanese and German TV series see Hilaria Gössmann, "Nichidoku no Renzoku Dorama. Fūfūno Egakikata o Chūshin ni," *Media ga Tsukuru Jendā: Nichidoku no Danjo—Kazoku-zō o Yomitoku*, eds. Hilaria Gössmann and Yasuko Muramatsu (Tokyo: Shinyōsha, 1997).

21. These checklists clearly resemble those published in pamphlets distributed by women's centers in Tokyo.

22. Muramatsu, *Terebi Dorama no Joseigaku*, p. 163.

23. This drama is No. 2 in Table 11.1; see Painter, "The Telerepresentation of Gender in Japan," p. 68, for a short description.

24. Ibid., p. 69.

25. Lozano and Singhal, "Melodramatic Television Serials," p. 122.

12

A New Kind of Royalty

The Imperial Family and the Media in Postwar Japan

Jayson Chun

On November 27, 1958, the headlines of the *Asahi Shimbun* announced the discovery of a real-life Cinderella story that would captivate all of Japan for many years to come: "The Crown Prince Is Engaged!" The Crown Prince's bride-to-be, Michiko Shōda, or "Michi" as she was popularly known, was the first commoner, albeit a wealthy one, to marry a crown prince in Japanese history. According to the media, the engagement was a modern love story which sprang from a chance meeting on a tennis court, in vivid contrast to the arranged Imperial marriages of times past. This made the union all the more appealing to young Japanese.

Public interest in the royal engagement, fanned by intense newspaper and television coverage, reached a fever pitch in the days leading up to the April 1959 wedding. The "Michiko Boom" swept the nation as media hype raised the profile of the Imperial Family and especially that of the central Cinderella-like character, Michiko. During Michiko's first public visit to the Imperial Family, thousands of screaming young women thronged to the car carrying her, hoping for a glimpse of the future Crown Princess. Department stores displayed mannequins closely resembling Michiko, as the dresses, hats, shoes, and tennis outfits in which she was photographed set a national trend. Young men began appearing in the V-neck tennis sweaters favored by the Crown Prince.[1] Businesses throughout the nation scrambled to take advantage of the event and plastered advertisements everywhere congratulating the couple. More important economically, plans to televise the wedding sparked both a nationwide boom in the sale of television sets and the creation of national commercial TV networks.

The royal wedding of 1959 also helped create a "new" postwar Japanese Imperial Family, one whose status came not from prewar-style government coercion but from fame and celebrity in the broader society. Actively promoting this new type of royal celebrity was a symbiotic relationship between the Imperial Household and the mass media, especially television; the Imperial Family exploited the media's need for attention-getting stories, while the media exploited the Imperial Family's need for a means to build popular support. The effect of this alliance is that, today, many Japanese treat Imperial Family members like movie stars. Wherever they make a public appearance, throngs of people gather to catch a glimpse of them. Images of the Imperial Family, especially its female members, grace the covers of weekly magazines and feature prominently in television news coverage. Such media prominence is a far cry from the prewar days of a solemn, sacred Emperor flanked by a rather anonymous wife, and from the wartime days when the government preached the need for citizens to die for the Emperor if necessary. Today, rather than soldiers screaming the Emperor's name while sacrificing their lives on the battlefield, young girls scream the names of Imperial Family members in hopes of attaining an autograph.

The Imperial Family as Mass Media Celebrities

In all monarchies, the images of Imperial Families have been manipulated by governments as a means of influencing the citizenry's views of the throne, and as a means of transmitting values, information, and ideology. The British Royal Family, for instance, was given an image change during the social and political upheavals of World War I. Though they were in reality of Germanic descent, the Royal Family had to face the fact that Germany had become the nation's enemy. In response, the potentially damaging roots of the family were downplayed through the adoption of a new name, the Royal House of Windsor, and a new identity, one which evoked the image of a "normal," homey English family.[2]

Despite this historic government manipulation of Imperial images, the use of mass media in transforming and maintaining these images has not always been so pervasive. While the idea of royalty as media celebrity is hardly shocking to today's Westerners, in Japan the transformation of Imperial Family members into media celebrities was a startling development, given the history of the traditionally revered Imperial System.

Following the overthrow of the Shōgun in 1868, the Japanese government used the Emperor as a central institution to create a sense of Japanese nationalism; the idea of absolute loyalty to a divine Emperor was relentlessly drilled into the minds of Japanese citizens through education, Imperial tours, and the force of law if necessary. The government portrayed the Emperor as a living god, descendant of the sun goddess. The constitution officially declared him to be a sacred and inviolable figure and the source of all government power. During the 1930s, protecting the Emperor and carrying out his will provided the rationale for ultranationalists to steer the country on an expansionist course. During Japan's war of aggression in Asia and the Pacific from 1937 through 1945, the government employed this Emperor-centered nationalist ideology to promote its militaristic agenda by encouraging citizens to fight to the death for the Emperor.[3]

With Japan's defeat came subsequent occupation by U.S. and Allied troops and a decision by Occupation reformers not to try the Emperor as a war criminal, but rather to transform him from divine Emperor to a human symbol of Japan and an agent of postwar reform. On New Year's Day in 1946, Emperor Hirohito, as part of the disestablishment of State Shinto, renounced his divinity. In the following year, the new American-influenced (and American-imposed) constitution redefined the Emperor as a mortal symbol of the state who derived his position from the will of the people. This made it impossible for the Imperial System to continue to operate as it had before the war. Not only had the legal status of the Emperor changed and legal constraints against criticizing the Imperial System ended, but the war had done much to taint the Imperial System in the eyes of many Japanese.

Given the weakened legal foundation of the Imperial System, accusations of war responsibility, and growing public indifference—in a 1957 poll, only 51 percent of respondents agreed that "Japan without the Emperor is inconceivable"[4]—the Imperial Family and its handlers had to find a new means of attracting popular support. The growth of a mass consumer society during the 1950s provided an opportunity. With the onset of rapid economic growth, many Japanese were turning toward lives of consumption and materialism in which the media, and particularly television, occupied a central position. It was in this context of rapid social change and passive popular acceptance of the throne that, through the skillful use of the new media, the Imperial Family underwent a transformation from revered royalty to media celebrities.

This transformation of the Imperial image was due at least in part to deliberate manipulation by the *Kunaichō* (Imperial Household Agency), the government agency in charge of "handling" the Imperial Family. Both before and after the war, the Kunaichō controlled media access to the family, its mission being to portray the Imperial Family as favorably as possible and to preserve an aura of power and legitimacy. The Kunaichō worked closely with the Japanese press, keeping a small group of correspondents on a tight rein in a small clubhouse on palace grounds. These newsmen largely reproduced official press communiqués prepared by the Kunaichō in their respective newspapers. Should anyone write something untoward about the Imperial Family, there was always the threat of violence from right-wing nationalist groups to keep them in line.[5] It was the Kunaichō that, with the cooperation of the media, helped spread ideas about the Emperor to the Japanese people.

Following the war, the Kunaichō quickly grasped the importance of boosting the spirits of the defeated nation and of building public support for a throne tainted by the lingering onus of war responsibility. The agency saw great potential in having the Emperor mingle with the populace and, as part of the recasting of his image, sent the Emperor on tours of the country. These tours brought the Emperor closer to the people, while media coverage of his activities helped to alter his image, transforming him from a cold, distant ruler associated with the militarist governments that had brought Japan to war to a symbol of a new and peaceful Japan.

Even prior to the Imperial wedding of 1959, public appearances of Imperial Family members caused great excitement and even hysteria among the Japanese. In 1954, seventeen persons were crushed to death in a rush to see the Emperor. The Emperor's popularity even seemed to take on an Elvis-like quality; in one 1958 incident, teenage girls swarmed his car, waving autograph books and banging on the windows to get his attention.[6] The Crown Prince had a similar effect on Japanese subjects. As stated by his former American tutor, Elizabeth Vining, the Prince's entrance into a room resulted in sudden tremors, turned heads, quick gasps, held breath, and a wave of excitement.[7]

Given the secretive nature of the Kunaichō, it is difficult to discern how much of the Emperor's new image was the conscious "creation" of the Imperial Household Agency and how much is owed to other factors. It is certain, however, that this transformation from authoritarian ruler to kindly father figure and its reliance upon the mass media embody two of the most pervasive changes within postwar Japan. In this sense it is fitting that Japan's postwar era began with a combination of both these features: the radio broadcast of the Emperor's voice announcing Japan's surrender. This was the first time the Japanese had heard the Emperor's voice, but far from the last; in the coming years, media coverage of the Emperor would become commonplace. The royal wedding of 1959 would mark the maturation of a new kind of Imperial System, one neither authoritarian nor symbolic, but based largely on the public's need for popular entertainment. The wedding also revealed a new and strong interdependence between the Imperial Family and the mass media. The Imperial Family used the mass media as a means to shape its public image, while the mass media used the Imperial Family to sell more media products, and, in the case of the electronics industry, more television sets.

An Imperial Courtship

The 1959 Imperial wedding and the courtship leading up to it were deeply intertwined with the Kunaichō and the mass media from the very beginning. The process of selecting a bride for the Crown Prince began in 1952, seven years before the marriage took place. In accordance with Japanese law, the choice of Emperor and the marriage of male Imperial Family members are subject to discussion by the Imperial House Council, a body of ten people who are to represent the nation and help choose mates for male members of the Imperial Family. The Imperial House Council is composed of two representatives from the Imperial Family, the Speakers and Deputy Speakers of the Upper and Lower Houses of the Diet, the Prime Minister, the Director of the Imperial Household Agency, the Chief Justice of the Supreme Court, and one additional judge. The Kunaichō, in its continued efforts to bring the Imperial Family closer to the people, decided to compile a list of acceptable candidates—ones that the Imperial House Council would not oppose—and let the Crown Prince choose for himself. A conscious effort was made to broaden the list of candidates beyond the traditional five aristocratic families and distant relatives of the Imperial Family. However, the first list of candidates drawn up by the Kunaichō included only old aristocratic families. Newspapers, on the other hand, seizing on the popularity of the search, used broader criteria to try to predict who the bride would be. The *Asahi*

Shimbun put together a list of sixty favorites from a possible 60,000 families, keeping pictures of all candidates on file and cramming their vital statistics into 150 200-page notebooks.[8]

Early in the search, journalists recognized Michiko Shōda as the most likely candidate, despite her commoner background. A renowned beauty, her family, although "common," was extremely prestigious. Her father, president of the Nisshin Flour Manufacturing Company (better known in the West as the company that makes Cup O'Noodles), was an influential businessman and a friend of Prince Akihito's tutor. Michiko's uncle served as president of Osaka University while another of her uncles and the husband of her aunt were professors at Tokyo University, the most prestigious university in Japan. Her mother came from a high-ranking family of samurai ancestry. In short, even though she was a commoner, she had superior qualifications to be the Crown Princess.

The famous first meeting of the Crown Prince and Michiko Shōda occurred on the tennis courts of the posh resort town of Karuizawa in August 1957. The two met twice again, later that fall. As a suitable bride could not be found among the aristocratic families, the official list of candidates had begun to grow. By March 1958, Michiko Shōda's name was on it. When the newspapers discovered Michiko and the Crown Prince together on several subsequent occasions, reporters began to call on the Shōdas and publish stories on the couple's activities. Dr. Koizumi, the Prince's tutor, requested that the Japanese press stop printing reports until a formal decision was made by the Imperial House Council, lest it complicate marriage negotiations between the Council and the candidates family. Not yet willing to break with traditional Japanese journalistic practice, the press complied. Thereafter, the Japanese newspapers and radios refrained from reporting or speculating on the story, waiting patiently for an official announcement and collecting data in private.

After overcoming opposition from traditional conservatives, the Kunaichō finally agreed to the choice of Michiko Shōda. The initial proposal made to the Shōda family, however, was met with a polite but firm refusal. In the meantime, in September 1958, Michiko left Japan, traveling to Brussels as the Japanese delegate to an international conference of school alumni. Vining claims this was a tactic of the Shōda family, an ancient resort of distressed parents and a panicked reaction to the prospect of their daughter marrying into the Imperial Family.[9] This time abroad allowed Michiko to consider the consequences of a marriage to the Crown Prince and provided Dr. Koizumi with the time necessary to persuade Mr. Shōda to allow Michiko to marry. Michiko, however, remained uncertain, and even sent the Crown Prince a letter of rejection. Despite this rejection, the Crown Prince was determined and would not give up.

Upon returning to Japan in October, Michiko found herself the object of intense media scrutiny. Although the newspapers agreed to refrain from publishing information regarding Michiko, they wanted to prepare material for the day that the marriage announcement would be made. Michiko's public profile increased when *Shūkan Myōjo*, a small Japanese weekly magazine, broke the news embargo and published a picture of Michiko in its November 3 issue, announcing her to be the prime candidate.[10] Michiko's home fell under constant media scrutiny, forcing her into hiding. She left her home only twice in three weeks and on one occasion was chased by newsmen into a convent at her university. The Crown Prince proceeded to phone her daily, and finally, confined to her home by the media siege, Michiko gave her consent to marriage over the telephone.

Following her consent, the director of the Council was dispatched to the Shōda home to formally request Michiko's hand. A few days later, on November 27, 1959, the wedding announcement was made. Even though the use of television sets in the nation was limited, Michiko's appearance before the television cameras caused a sensation. She sat in front of the cameras, full of poise and a quiet, feminine charm. When asked about the Crown Prince, she replied, "He is a very pure and sincere person."[11] The *Asahi Shimbun* devoted seven pages to the announcement.

Following the wedding announcement, Michiko continued to be an object of intense media interest. If Emperor Hirohito's and Crown Prince Akihito's cloistered upbringing seemed to cut them off from the ranks of the people, then Michiko was the star who could bridge the gap between the Imperial Family and the populace. As one who had risen from the ranks of the commoner, Michiko was the perfect candidate for the new role of Imperial celebrity. The bride-to-be soon found herself the center of a "Michiko Boom."

Many Japanese identified with Michiko as they might with a screen figure, and her popularity often reached ridiculous extremes, especially when compared to the prewar veneration of the Emperor and the Imperial Family. Weekly magazines ran Michiko look-alike contests and contests for people with the same birth date as Michiko. "Princess Calendars" and Michi picture stands became popular purchases. Songwriters wrote songs with lyrics such as "Tennis Twosome" to reflect the Imperial couple's tennis court meeting, while newborn baby girls were named Michiko and thousands of young couples arranged to marry on the same day as the Crown Prince and his now-famous bride-to-be. The media provided the public with minute details of Michiko's eating habits, divulging such intimate information as her tendency not to eat the rice in her sushi and her love of Japanese oranges.[12] They published endless photos of Michiko on the tennis court, Michiko sitting at home, Michiko strolling with her mother, Michiko in her kimono at her college goodbye party. Even the American press paid close attention to the "down-to-earth" details of Michiko and Akihito. *Time* magazine went as far as to provide Michiko's physical dimensions; at the time, Michiko was a petite five feet two inches tall, weighed 115 pounds, and had a figure measuring 34-24-26.[13]

The effect of such intimate coverage was that people felt they knew Michiko like a close friend, a feeling that enhanced her popularity among many segments of the population. Her acceptance into the Imperial Family, despite her common upbringing, gave the Imperial Family a more "egalitarian" image. The Japanese people viewed Michiko as "one of their own," and expressed their pride and feelings of closeness with the Imperial Family through statements such as "We feel like our own daughter has become a bride."[14] Through the engagement of Crown Prince Akihito to commoner Michiko Shōda, the carefully crafted "closeness" between the Imperial Family and the populace was solidified. With this engagement and the media spectacle that was to follow, the Kunaichō made the final sacrifice of the Imperial Family's divine image in favor of media fame.

A Media Spectacle

Television stations in Tokyo broadcast the Imperial wedding procession and other wedding-related news from six o'clock in the morning until ten o'clock at night on the day of the wedding. The average respondent in a survey conducted following the wedding watched television for ten hours and thirty-five minutes that day, about three times the duration of normal viewing.[15] The media hype surrounding the real-life romantic television drama was such that one scholar referred to the wedding as

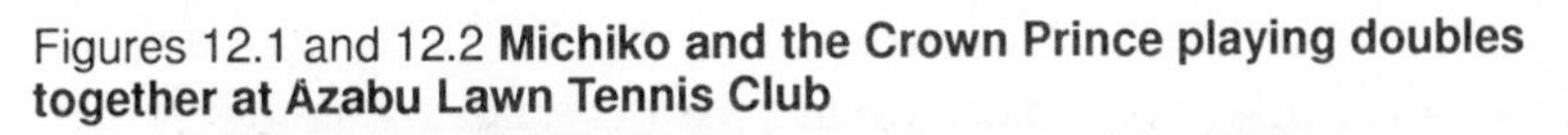

Figures 12.1 and 12.2 **Michiko and the Crown Prince playing doubles together at Azabu Lawn Tennis Club**

Japan's first "electronic pageant," a made-for-television electronic national ceremony.[16]

The effects of live coverage of the Imperial wedding were dramatic. Although government officials expected over a million people to appear on the streets to watch the wedding procession, only half that number actually showed up; most Japanese preferred to watch the proceedings on television. A survey of 598 households living along the procession route revealed that only 17.1 percent actually went out to see the procession; the rest chose to stay at home to view the television coverage, citing road congestion and a more direct experience of the procession as the reasons for this choice.[17] Even along the procession route, police installed more than a hundred television sets in an effort to provide all spectators with a clear view of the procession and to ease the pressure in the streets.

Japanese accounts today, when they mention the Imperial wedding, usually talk about its effect on the growth of the television industry. The event sparked a nationwide boom in sales of television sets, with TV manufacturers capitalizing upon the hype leading up to the wedding and encouraging consumers to watch the wedding on television. Over two million television sets were sold in a single year, a boom attributed both to the 1958 drop in the price of black-and-white TV sets and the mania surrounding the Imperial wedding.[18] The percentage of households owning television sets more than doubled, increasing from 5.1 percent to 11.0 percent,[19] and the number of subscribers to NHK (the Japan Broadcasting Corporation) jumped from one million in May 1958 to two million in April 1959. Whereas it had taken five years after the establishment of Japan's first television station for NHK viewer contracts to pass the one million mark, with the aid of wedding fever it took only eleven months for contracts to reach two million.[20] The wedding also led to the creation of nationwide commercial television networks. Prior to the wedding, all commercial broadcasts were independent and available only in local areas. To cover the marriage, the two commercial stations located in Tokyo broadcast along a network to all the nation's twenty-eight commercial broadcasting companies. Following the wedding, full-fledged networks were formed around the two Tokyo stations.[21] Thus it was that while television benefited the Imperial Family, the Imperial Family benefited the television industry just as much.

As never before, television allowed close-up images of the Imperial Family to be broadcast into the homes of any family with a TV set. This opened up a new world to the Japanese people. In the words of one observer, "Through the link supplied by television, virtually the entire country was able to feel a sense of being part of the festive occasion at the Imperial Palace in Tokyo. Ordinary Japanese, looking at their televi-

Figure 12.3 **Michiko and the Crown Prince at the front entrance of the Kunaichō on the day of the wedding**

sion sets today saw for the first time one of the most sacred sights in their country, the Kashikodokoro Shrine in the Imperial Palace grounds.[22]

For many, the extensive television coverage of the wedding created an electronically induced sense of closeness between viewer and Imperial Family. Many became emotionally involved in the wedding broadcast, and almost half the television viewers in a survey rated the close-up of the Prince and Princess as the most impressive scene from the live broadcast. While about half the respondents watched the wedding broadcast out of curiosity and a desire to see the splendor and grandeur surrounding the Imperial Family, 22.6 percent of the viewers watched because they wished to congratulate the Prince and the new Princess.[23] The power of television provided them with a sense of being able to do so.

Popular Perceptions: Why All the Excitement?

The televising of the Imperial wedding and the intimacy of media coverage, whether or not a planned tactic on the part of the Kunaichō, so-

Figure 12.4 **Michiko riding in the wedding procession**

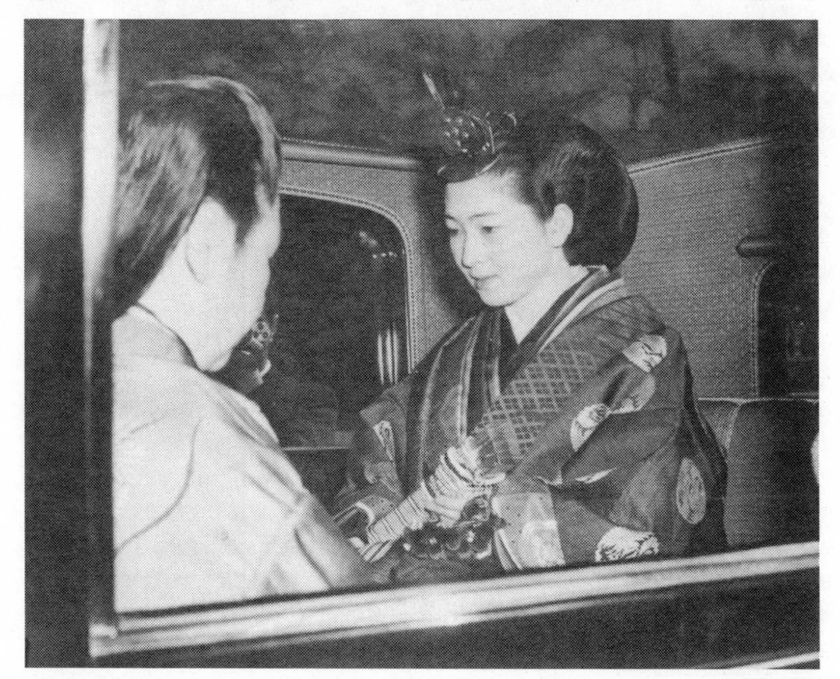

lidified the recasting of the image of the once distant Imperial Family as a more "average" family, representative of Japan. But the appeal of the Imperial wedding did not derive solely from the media's intimate portrayal of the Imperial Family. The wedding also embodied, in an entertaining and pleasing manner, many of the complex issues and values that lay at the heart of postwar Japanese society. One contemporary observer noted that "The Crown Prince has become the symbol of the new constitution, in a sense, of postwar democracy."[24] As such a symbol, the wedding and the couple it united conveyed diverse messages, satisfying both those who supported the dominant ideology of the time and those who held hope for certain kinds of social reform.

The Imperial Family's new, more "average" image resulted in a number of contradictions. Despite the family's ability to represent a "new Japan," one which had broken with its militaristic past and embraced the new ideas of democracy and equality, the very existence of the Imperial Family reaffirmed a hierarchy of birth within society. While the marriage of Crown Prince Akihito and Michiko Shōda was portrayed through the media as a marriage of love, the very process by which

Michiko was selected revealed a support of arranged marriages. While the selection of an educated commoner as the future Empress suggested new ideas concerning the place of women in Japanese society, Michiko's role within the marriage and society also acted to reaffirm the subordination of women to men in Japan.

A Symbol of Democracy

One dominant theme in public discussion surrounding the Imperial marriage was the Imperial couple as a symbol of a "new Japan," a democratic nation breaking with its militaristic past. This image served to show the rest of the world, especially the West, that Japan had become a nation that could be trusted. The American media in particular focused on the marriage as a break with Japan's ancient traditions; *Time* called it "the Imperial Family's greatest leap toward democracy since Hirohito threw off the myth of Imperial divinity in 1946."[25] An editorial in the *New York Times* described the wedding as a symbol of a rehabilitated, peaceful Japan that had "emerged from feudalism and from that modern barbarianism" which had led to war.[26] In Great Britain, *The Times* took pride in the fact that Prince Akihito "was said to have been very impressed by what he saw in England when he attended the Queen's coronation in 1953, and particularly by the affection in which the Crown was held by the British people," noting that the Prince had striven to emulate that ideal upon his return to Japan.[27]

Within Japan, many felt that the marriage of Prince Akihito and Michiko had brought the Imperial Family closer to the people. Michiko received hundreds of fan letters containing the plea, "Please be a splendid bridge between the Imperial Household and the People."[28] A number of Japanese authors wrote of the democratizing effects of this marriage. Wrote Samajirō Takigawa, "When the Emperor, in his 1949 New Year's declaration, denied the divinity of the Imperial line, that somehow didn't feel real. In comparison, the recent announcement [of the Crown Prince's engagement to commoner Michiko] provided a bigger shock."[29] Takigawa further noted that the choosing of the Crown Princess from the rank of complete commoner was not only unprecedented in 2,000 years of Japanese history, but was rare in world history as well.

Others, however, pointed out contradictions in the idea of a new egalitarian, "one-of-us" royalty. Michiko, after all, had led an elite lifestyle, one unattainable to most Japanese. Wrote Masako Shirasu, another Japanese writer:

> I am a little troubled by the idea that the refined social world of the leisured upper class represents the "real" Japan to the couple. Karuizawa should not symbolize the sentiment of the people and society as the two know it. If the Crown Princess, who represents the first tie between the masses and the Imperial Family, remains among the higher class of society, then the marriage will be meaningless.[30]

Shirasu noted further that, historically, "new blood" in the Imperial Family had come from one of the more powerful families of the day. In this sense this marriage was no different; with Akihito marrying the daughter of a corporate magnate, this union represented not ties between the Emperor and the common people, but rather ties between the Emperor and the upper class elite.[31] A further contradiction was that, as symbols of the state, Imperial Family members were denied basic constitutional liberties. They existed under the constant eye of the Kunaichō, which regulated all their official functions and many aspects of their private lives. They had no voting rights, could not easily visit or invite friends for company, were not free to speak publicly about political affairs, and had no private income nor any valuable assets.[32] In short, they lived under extensive government control, contrary to the democratic ideals of postwar Japan.

In Support of Love

One reason that Michiko and Akihito's wedding struck such a chord with many young people was that it seemed to be a statement in favor of marriage based on love, as opposed to the more traditional practice of "arranged" marriages. During the Meiji period (1867–1912), the Japanese government promoted the ideal of a monogamous marriage leading to a hierarchical family as the proper social ideal for the nation. According to this ideal, marriage established a bond between two families, not only between two individuals.[33] Under Japanese law, the head of the household had the legal authority to determine whom family members could marry. A young man could not marry without parental consent until he was 30 years old. For young women, parental consent was required until the age of 25.

This family system underwent change even before World War II, thanks to shifting economic and social conditions and foreign contact. However, it was the postwar influence of the Occupation that dramatically accelerated the rate of both legal and social change. The postwar reformers, in an attempt to democratize the family, legitimized the concept of love marriages through reform of the constitution, especially Article 24, which guaranteed unmarried individuals the right to choose their own spouses and gave legal authority to the nuclear family, rather than to the extended family as was the case under the old, prewar civil code.

It would be a mistake to exaggerate the differences between "arranged" marriages and "love" marriages, as the informal boundary between them was sometimes hardly noticeable and they often overlapped. Still, despite the legal reforms of the Occupation, it was far from clear whether Japanese society would accept love marriages based mainly on the personal desires of the couple involved, and in the years following the Occupation a debate raged in Japan over which was the more appropriate marriage pattern. In many cases, parental and social pressure forced young people to accept arranged marriage. Also, in the relatively segregated postwar Japanese society, young men and women still had little opportunity to come into contact with each other. With this gap between reality and expectations, many young people were forced to live vicariously through the highly publicized romance between the Crown Prince and his beautiful and intelligent bride. To many young Japanese, their romance was the embodiment of a romantic drama. One newspaper reported the following excited reactions to the couple among Japanese female college students: "Romance! How wonderful!"; "The age of the two and also the fact that they are in a love marriage are going to greatly influence us from now on"; "I should have gone to Seishin Women's College (Michiko's alma mater)!"; "Prince Yoshinomiya is still available so we still have hope."[34] It is no wonder that alongside the headline announcing the engagement of the Crown Prince was the header, "He chose the bride himself!" The popular assumption that the Crown Prince's marriage was based on love helped to advance the idea of love marriage, which many young people cherished as an ideal. Vining, the Prince's former tutor, wrote: "Only a girl of Michiko Shōda's caliber, who could capture the imagination and win the immediate respect and affection of the Japanese people as she did, could have swept away the entrenched attitudes of the centuries. For it *was* a love match."[35]

Despite the approval of many young people, much of Japanese society felt displeasure at the possibility that the Imperial engagement might be based upon love. The Kunaichō used this social disapproval to discourage Michiko from being seen in public with the Prince:

> The Kunaichō hates the word "love." . . . They don't like the idea of a love marriage. In the Diet, a member of a conservative party declared, "The Crown Prince is too liberal." The effect was immediate. The two had been planning to play tennis with friends at Karuizawa, when the Kunaichō called the Shōda residence saying "There has been unfavorable criticism [of your appearing in public with the Crown Prince]. What are you going to do?"
>
> Michiko answered neither "yes" nor "no." The Kunaichō continued, "Dr. Koizumi also suggests that it might be best to cancel [the tennis]." In the end, everyone showed up at the tennis court except Michiko.[36]

Despite the Kunaichō's efforts to downplay the choice of Michiko as one based on love, the couple continued to represent to the press and public changes in Japanese society:

> The view, common among young people today, that marriages must be based on love has found strong support in the Crown Prince's marriage—a fact which has caused many a rueful face among parents in the more conservative families.[37]

Japanese youth admired the Imperial couple, as they represented the ideal of romantic love: They had presumably met on their own, without the intervention of their parents, and were an ideal match. A Japanese judge saw this as instrumental in modernizing the throne: "Because [the engagement] is in accordance with the principle of Article 24 of the Constitution—'based on the consent of both sexes'—a fresh breeze has blown through the Imperial House with its many antiquated customs."[38]

As in its representation of democracy, however, the Imperial courtship contained contradictions about the true freedom of the couple's choice. The Crown Prince, as a member of the Imperial Family, was not legally free to marry whom he wished. Prince Akihito's choice of Michiko was not an entirely independent decision, as all potential marriage partners, including Michiko, were first required to attain the approval of the Imperial House Council. From the list of potential marriage partners, the Crown Prince was then permitted to make his "choice." Moreover, even after the Crown Prince made clear his desire to wed Michiko, the Council had to approve his choice by law. In fact, the Council attempted to maintain the fiction that they had chosen Michiko, declaring that they alone were responsible for the final choice of Imperial bride. In the Western press, there was speculation that this was a cover to save face and justify the time (one year) and expense (nearly one million dollars) involved in the Imperial Council's own fruitless search for a bride.[39] Regardless of whether or not the Prince had actually chosen his bride, this act, at least on the surface, required the approval of others, representing a direct contradiction of the freedom of choice outlined in the constitutional reforms.

In addition to being restricted in his choice of a partner, Prince Akihito was not free to date Michiko. The two could meet only on the tennis courts, in the company of their acquaintances, or through telephone conversations. The *Asahi Shimbun* article, "Crown Prince Fidgety over Phone Calls," describes the difficulty the couple had in attaining privacy. Under constant media scrutiny, Michiko could not leave home, requiring the couple to communicate via telephone. Since the Crown Prince was never alone, his friends, in order to give him privacy, would play a record in the background to mask the couple's private telephone conversations.[40] The message conveyed by this and other media coverage of the couple was that, although marriages based on love were possible, young people were restricted in their ability to find and nourish such love.

A Modern Japanese Woman

Just as media coverage of the Imperial couple brought the debate over "love" marriages to the public forum, it also functioned to reveal many of society's assumptions regarding women. *Time* viewed Michiko as a symbol of the emancipation of Japanese women. In the magazine's March 1959 special feature on Japanese women, Michiko was held up as a symbol of liberation:

> For Japan's 46,780,000 women, Michiko-san's unprecedented break with ancient tradition is the most dramatic illustration of a change that has come to all of them. . . . In the eyes of many Japanese women she is the most successful symbol of their emancipation.[41]

Many Japanese saw in Michiko the ideal woman, one who fit perfectly the criteria proposed by the Crown Prince's American tutor that the "woman who would become Crown Princess should be good looking, mentally tough, and have a good sense of humor."[42]

A prominent image of Michiko was that of a "breath of fresh air," who would "humanize" and provide warmth to the traditionally cold Imperial Family. One woman wrote:

> In our ordinary families, we can count on our mother's indulgence and warm love. . . . When sick in bed, we can open our eyes, see our mother sitting by our side knitting, and feel relieved, as if we have been removed from anxiety and transported to a safe place. It may be rude to say this, but I imagine that the Crown Prince has never experienced this kind of feeling. I hope that Michiko, through the affection of her home cooking, witty conversation, and so on, will give the Crown Prince a purposeful and well-spent life. It is my hope that Michiko will open each door with great strength and, like the spring wind, with a warm, fresh, and bright feeling, blow into the Imperial Family—not just that, but into the entire nation—a breath of youth.[43]

At the same time, however, Michiko's image was mixed with messages that served to subjugate Japanese women. According to Kunaichō requirements, she had to fulfill certain criteria in order to be acceptable as Crown Princess. She could not be taller than the Prince, nor have any work experience. She needed perfect eyesight and no hint of a previous boyfriend. These requirements reveal the less democratic expectations of women during this age: those of the virginal girl unsullied by work.

Despite her intelligence and education, Michiko was, in many ways, to serve as no more than an ornament for the Crown Prince. As a graduate from Michiko's all-girl alma mater Sacred Heart put it, "the aim was to shape us into spotless and expensive pieces of jewelry and Michiko got the same treatment as the rest." As a "piece of jewelry," Michiko was not to advance by her own achievements, but rather by marrying into a high family. Because the Imperial Household Law stipulated that only men could ever become Emperor, went one viewpoint, Michiko was participating in a sexist institution geared to perpetuating the supremacy of men over women.[44] Some worried that, rather than Michiko's changing the Imperial Family, the Family would change Michiko:

> We women think that Michiko is a wonderful girl and that the Crown Prince has discriminating tastes, but the Imperial Family will push down her good points: intelligence, strength and humor. The atmosphere around her will oppress her. No matter how much Michiko wants to inject a new breeze into the Imperial household, it probably won't work.[45]

To many a Japanese girl, Michiko was one of them. She had achieved what every young girl was socialized to believe: that if a woman studied hard enough, and possessed enough of the right qualities, she could achieve the ultimate goal of all Japanese women: marrying into a high-class family. Young girls lived vicariously through Michiko's exploits, hoping that someday they too could achieve what she had achieved. In some ways, this was a sad commentary on the limited options for self-fulfillment available to women outside marriage.

The 1959 media coverage of Michiko marked the beginning of what would continue to be a highly publicized life. Young women grew up with Michiko. They shared her joy in marrying into the Imperial Family and in the birth of her three children. They felt the sorrow she experienced as a result of bullying from other members of the Imperial household, her miscarriage, and her bouts with nervous breakdowns. Because so many followed Michiko's life so closely, interest in the Imperial Family, whether positive or negative, grew stronger. Of perhaps greater concern to some, media coverage also had the effect of weakening the male-dominated structure of the family. It is the female members of the family who provide the glamour and create public interest, and so the Kunaichō has increasingly focused on news accounts of Imperial Family women to maintain public attention. This began with the 1959 wedding coverage and continues today with the extensive attention given Empress Michiko and the commoner wives of her two sons. Thus has a gradual "feminization" of the Imperial System taken place, with a male-centered institution coming to rely on its female members to maintain its popularity.

The Price of Fame

One Japanese writer of the era, commenting on the hype surrounding the Imperial wedding, wrote of the emergence of a new *Taishū Tennōsei* (Imperial System for the Masses) with the formerly absolutist Imperial System changing to suit the conditions and needs of a new media-centered society.[46] Although the Imperial Family's history and role as symbol of the state prevent it from actually being just another ordinary Japanese family, television and popular media coverage of the 1959 wedding plus subsequent and continuing media coverage of family members and happenings have transformed the once sacred Imperial Family into a celebrity symbol of the "ordinary" Japanese family, one with which many Japanese can identify.

Over the years, the Imperial Family has begun to bear a close resemblance to *tarento,* a breed of celebrity that is ubiquitous on Japanese television today. Tarento derive their name from the English word "talent," and although these individuals may or may not possess much talent in the ordinary sense of the word, they are famous primarily due to the frequency with which they appear on television. What all tarento have in common is that they are part of the media culture that entertains the nation and helps sell products. Like tarento, the Imperial Family is famous not for special skills or talents, but simply for being the Imperial Family, a family that is constantly in the media spotlight. This media publicity has been important to the Imperial Family, which in the 1950s struggled to find a new identity and to fit into a democratic and changing society. The implications of this new role have been far reaching.

The modern popularity of Imperial Family members does not necessarily, as the Kunaichō hoped it would, translate into public support for a strengthening of the Imperial system, but merely ensures the family's place in the spotlight. In reality, the road toward fame has caused the Imperial Family to lose its aura of sacredness. Imperial Family members have become more and more like commercial spokespersons, either for the magazines their faces adorn or for the consumer-oriented Japanese way of life. From the very beginning, this commercialization has acted to undermine the power of the Imperial Family. Even before the war, a Westerner noted, during the Shōwa Emperor's wedding procession, the power of the camera:

> The presence of photographers along the route of the [wedding] procession . . . and the sale of cheap prints, picture postcards etc., of the Imperial countenance exposed to the vulgar gaze, shocks my sense of the proper. . . . This I regard as a danger—a danger that the respect and reverence due to the Throne may decline.[47]

During the 1960s, the effects of mass media coverage continued to grow:

> Even magazines most favorable to the Imperial cause now seek to exploit the human interest angle in their portrayal of the Imperial Family in order to cater to the mass demand for vicarious glamor and romance. Treatment of the Imperial personage with awe and veneration no longer carries a popular appeal.[48]

By 1975, the transformation was complete. One Japanese writer noted the commercialization of the Imperial System through the obsession with details of its members' lives:

> Crown Princess Michiko is a star in women's weekly magazines. In the first page of every issue of these weekly magazines, readers find her snapshot (in color) in a more or less informal pose, and the running comments are usually about her clothes, jewelry, and makeup. She *is* a private citizen. Royal families can no longer be the sacred—"above the cloud."[49]

Still, as seen in Michiko and Akihito's joint role as catalyst, or at least lightning rod, for debate on advances in democracy, marriage, and women's roles in society, the Imperial Family as celebrity does carry considerable potential for positive social change. What matters is how the Japanese use and interpret these symbols. A *New York Times* reporter, trying to grasp the meaning of the Crown Prince's marriage to Michiko, wrote:

> Does it mean a resurgent respect for the Emperor system? Or were the crowds hailing, subconsciously, what many consider the beginning of the end of the Imperial institution? Or were the people just taking an opportunity to have a "ball" over a long weekend? Whatever the answer may be . . . the fact is that virtually all of Japan celebrated the event.[50]

In this manner, it is the Japanese people themselves who will ultimately determine the meaning and role of these new Imperial celebrities.

Notes

1. Robert Trumbull, "Festive Air Transforms Tokyo as Marriage of Akihito Nears," *New York Times*, April 6, 1959, 11.
2. John Pearson, *The Selling of the Royal Family: The Mystique of the British Monarchy* (New York: Simon and Schuster, 1986), p. 32.
3. Daikichi Irokawa, *The Culture of the Meiji Period*, trans. Marius B. Jansen (Princeton, NJ: Princeton University Press, 1985), p. 282.
4. Takeshi Ishida, "Popular Attitudes toward the Japanese Emperor," *Asian Survey* 11:2 (April 1962), p. 35.
5. Edward Behr, *Hirohito: Behind the Myth* (New York: Random House, 1989), pp. 381, 398.
6. "Seven Court Chamberlains," *Time* (February 25, 1960), p. 49.
7. Elizabeth Grey Vining, *Return to Japan* (New York: J. B. Lippincott, 1960), p. 29.
8. "The Prince and the Commoner," *Japan Quarterly*, April-June 1959, p. 146; "I Do Love Him," *Newsweek* (December 8, 1958), p. 34.
9. Vining, *Return*, p. 223.
10. Shōwashi Kenkyūkai, *Shōwashi Jiten (1923–1983)* (Tokyo: Kōdansha, 1984), p. 520.

11. Kenkyūkai, p. 520. In Japanese, her reply was, "Totemo seiketsu de shinjitsuna okata."

12. "Michiko-san no Episōdo," *Asahi Shimbun* (November 27, 1959), p. 6.

13. "Crown Prince and Commoner," *Time* (December 1, 1958), p. 20.

14. Masako Shirasu, "Koizumi Shinzō-shi e no Tegami," *Bungei Shunjū* (February 1959), p. 83.

15. Akira Takahashi, "TV and the Imperial Wedding," *CBC Report* (June 1959). In *Japanese Research on Mass Communication: Selected Abstracts*, ed. Hidetoshi Kato (Honolulu: University of Hawaii Press, 1974), p. 15.

16. Takashi Fujitani, "Electronic Pageantry and Japan's 'Symbolic Emperor,'" *Journal of Asian Studies* 51:4 (November 1992), p. 825.

17. Takahashi, "TV."

18. Hidetoshi Kato, "Japan." In *Television: An International History*, ed. Anthony Smith (Oxford University Press, 1995), p. 292.

19. Shunsuke Tsurumi, *A Cultural History of Postwar Japan, 1945–1980* (London: KPI, 1987), p. 63.

20. Katsumasa Harada, ed., *Shōwa no Sesō* (Tokyo: Shōgakukan, 1983), pp. 222–223.

21. Bruce Stronach, "Japanese Television." In *Handbook of Japanese Popular Culture*, ed. Richard Gid Powers and Hidetoshi Kato (Westport, CN: Greenwood, 1989), pp. 136–137; Marilyn Ivy, "Formations of Mass Culture." In *Postwar Japan as History*, ed. Andrew Gordon (Berkeley: University of California Press, 1993), p. 248.

22. "Prince Akihito Weds Commoner in Tokyo Ceremony," *New York Times*, April 10, 1959, p. 7.

23. Takahashi, "TV."

24. Ken'ichi Matsushita, "Taishū Tennōseiron," *Chūō Kōron* (April 1959), p. 36.

25. "The Falling Curtain," *Time* (December 8, 1958), p. 26.

26. "After Twenty-Six Centuries," *New York Times* (April 10, 1959), p. 28.

27. "The Japanese Throne Today: Crown Prince and Commoner," *Times* (London) (November 28, 1958), p. 13 ff.

28. Matsushita, "Taishū," p. 34.

29. Takigawa Masajiro, "Kōtaishi Kōnin-shi," *Bungei Shunjū* (January 1959), p. 144.

30. Shirasu, "Koizumi Shinzō-shi," p. 83.

31. Shumon Miura, "Imperial Marriage," *Japan Echo* 20:2 (Summer 1993), p. 74.

32. Shigeko Togo, "Owada Masako, Crown Princess with a New Air," *Japan Quarterly* (April–June 1993), pp. 210–212.

33. Ray E. Baber, *Youth Looks at Marriage and Family: A Study of Changing Japanese Attitudes* (Tokyo: International Christian University, 1958), p. 49.

34. Matsushita, "Taishū," pp. 31–32.

35. Vining, *Return*, pp. 217–218.

36. "Atsui Kabe Kunaichō," *Asahi Shimbun* (April 11, 1959), p. 10.

37. "The Prince and the Commoner," p. 148.

38. Judge Tanaka, "Shinpū Fukikomu Kōtaishihi," *Asahi Shimbun* (November 30, 1959), p. 6.

39. "The Falling Curtain," p. 26; "Tokyo Romance Denied," *New York Times* (February 8, 1959), p. 23.

40. "Kanojo no Denwa ni Denka Sowasowa," *Asahi Shimbun* (November 28, 1958), p. 51; "The Girl from Outside," *Time* (March 23, 1959), p. 24.

41. "The Girl from Outside."

42. Shinzō Koizumi, "Kono Koro no Kōtaishi Denka," *Bungei Shujū* (January 1959), p. 131.

43. Nobuko Nakashima, "Dōsedai Kara no Hatsugen," *Asahi Shimbun* (April 10, 1959), p. 14.

44. Miura, "Imperial Marriage," p. 73.

45. Ineko Arima, "Okisaki Kyōiku wa Gyaku Kōsu," *Asahi Shimbun* (April 10, 1959), p. 14.

46. Ken'ichi Matsushita, "Taishū Tennōseiron." *Chūo Kōron* (April 1959), pp. 30–47.

47. Richard Arthur Brasbazon Ponsonby-Fane, *The Imperial House of Japan* (Kyoto: Ponsonby Memorial Society, 1959), pp. 364–365.

48. Kazuo Kawai, *Japan's American Interlude* (Chicago: University of Chicago Press, 1960), p. 89.

49. Hidetoshi Kato, *Essays in Comparative Popular Culture: Coffee, Comics, and Communication*. (Honolulu: Papers of the East-West Communication Institute, 1975), pp. 1–7.

50. "TV and Cheers," *New York Times* (April 12, 1959), sec. IV, p. 8.

13

Into the Heartland with Tora-san

Mark Schilling

What is the longest film series ever made? The answer, according to The *Guinness Book of Records,* is the *Otoko wa Tsurai Yo* (It's Tough Being a Man) or Tora-san (as it is commonly known) series, which started in August 1969 and ended with the death of series star Kiyoshi Atsumi in August 1996.[1]

The *Guinness* entry is a bit misleading: Other series have been around longer than Tora-san's twenty-seven years—Godzilla since 1954 and James Bond since 1962—but no other series has put more movies into the theaters: forty-eight installments about the misadventures of Torajirō Kuruma, the lovelorn wandering peddler from Shibamata, Katsushika Ward. Before the films, in 1968, there was a Tora-san TV drama series that ran for twenty-six episodes.

What is perhaps more remarkable than its sheer longevity is that its core creative team, including lead actor Kiyoshi Atsumi and director Yōji Yamada, remained nearly unchanged for nearly three decades.[2] This creative continuity was essential to the series' continued success. Godzilla is an ever-escalating special-effects show and, Sean Connery to the contrary, James Bond is more of an attitude than a particular actor. Atsumi was Tora-san the way Charlie Chaplin was the Tramp. Others may imitate, but no one could ever replace the original. Yamada, who scripted every episode, placed his individual stamp on the series so thoroughly that another director's touch would have been immediately noticeable and jarring, like watching a Hitchcock movie and seeing Brian DePalma step out of the shadows for the director's cameo.

The series lacked the usual elements of formula success: sex, action, special effects, and stud superstars. Tora-san was a squat, square-faced, middle-aged man who never finished junior high school, couldn't hold a steady job, and never got the girl. How could low-budget movies about this pathetic figure compete with the best Hollywood had to offer?

But Tora-san competed in every New Year's season until 1988, as well as nearly every August, and won consistently. The films regularly earned more than ¥1 billion in distributor revenues—hit status for a Japanese release. According to Shōchiku Co. Ltd., the studio that made, distributed, and exhibited the series, the forty-eighth installment, *Torajirō Kurenai no Hana* (Torajirō to the Rescue), earned ¥1.16 billion for Shōchiku in 1996—more than *Jumanji*, *12 Monkeys,* and *Goldeneye*, all of which finished in the box office top ten for foreign films that same year. Kiyoshi Atsumi, who was in his mid-sixties at the time, could still beat Robin Williams, Bruce Willis, Brad Pitt, and Pierce Brosnan handily at the Japanese box office.

The series' basic formula remained the same from episode to episode. First there is usually a dream sequence, with Tora-san as a samurai, Heian aristocrat, or other romantic figure from history or legend. The story is often simple wish fulfillment: Tora-san saves the fair lady and discovers that she is really Sakura (played by Chieko Baisho), his long-lost sister.

This sequence gets some of its laughs by gently but effectively mocking the conventions of Japanese period melodrama. If you think what is about to come is corn, it seems to say, here is the *real* thing for you. It also shows us Tora-san's true feelings, which are not always positive, about his family, friends, and neighbors in Shibamata and his image of the man he would like to be (which is reminiscent of similar images in *The Secret Life of Walter Mitty*).

When Tora-san awakens and realizes that he is back in the real world—a grassy embankment, a country inn, a boat on the river—the titles appear on the screen. Though the generic title of the series, *Otoko wa Tsurai Yo,* never changed, the subtitle did—and could be unabashedly poetic. In No. 29 it was *Torajirō Ajisai no Koi* (Torajirō's Hydrangea Love, 1982) and in No. 40, *Torajirō Sarada Kinenbi* (Torajirō's Salad Anniversary, 1988), a play on the title of a best-selling *tanka* (31-syllable verse) collection by Machi Tawara.

Unfortunately, this poetry was often not reflected in the official English titles. *Torajirō Kamome-uta*, for instance, was rendered as *Foster Daddy, Tora-san;* more descriptive, perhaps, but not as amusingly high-flown as the original, literally "Torajirō's Seagull Song." *Tora-san Ajisai no Koi* became *Hearts and Flowers for Tora-san,* while *Torajirō Sarada*

Kinenbi was translated as *Tora-san's Salad Date Memorial.* The flatness or oddness of so many of the English titles may be one reason the series has been less than successful abroad.

Next, while the catchy theme song, sung with great comic brio by Atsumi, swells up in the background, the film offers a bit of silent slapstick. In No. 45, *Torajirō no Seishun* (Tora-san Makes Excuses, 1992), a policeman orders Tora-san and Ponshu (played by Keiroku Seki), his fellow *tekiya* (street-stall peddler) to pack up and move on because they are selling without a license. Tora-san protests angrily and Ponshu tries to slip the officer a bribe, but to no avail: they must go. As they are walking together across a bridge, the policeman, Ponshu, and Tora-san turn to gaze admiringly at a pretty tour guide passing in the opposite direction. The policeman bumps into Ponshu, Ponshu into Tora-san—and the goods they are carrying, including hundreds of brightly colored superballs, go flying.

Like most good slapstick, this scene is more than the sum of its gags. We are shown that, beneath their social roles, these three men are really alike in their desires, foolishness, and humanity. The balls floating down the river at fadeout offer a final comment on the futility of human endeavor that is at once comically contemporary and classically Japanese (the balls bounce off the bridge with high-tech vigor, but once in the water they evoke the paper "spirit boats" the Japanese set afloat during the Bon holiday, or All Souls' Day).

Once these preliminaries have put the audience in a relaxed, receptive mood and reassured them that they are back in familiar territory, the main story begins. An often-heard criticism of the Tora-san films is that the plots are all the same. Yamada was more subtle than that; he may have repeated himself, including scenes and lines that audiences came to expect (and that ensured the series' continuation), but he also gave us the feeling that the times were changing and the characters, including Tora-san, were growing. "It's a very difficult problem," Yamada acknowledged. "Audiences watch the [Tora-san] movies almost as though they are *jidaigeki* [period dramas], but we are living in the present. I think that fact should be reflected in the film."[3]

Though to casual viewers the Tora-san films may have seemed frozen in time, with everyone eternally locked into the same attitudes, like characters in a Dickens' novel, the series did keep evolving. This process was unavoidable, given that the core cast remained largely unchanged for the series' entire run. Long-time fans had a sense—almost unique in the history of cinema—of watching entire lives unfold, in real time, on the screen. Tora-san's sister Sakura and her husband Hiroshi (played by Akira Maeda) matured from a young couple with a newborn into middle-aged parents with a salaryman son. Obachan (Chieko Misaki) and Oichan (Masami Shimojo), who ran the family *dango* (rice-flour dumpling) shop in Shibamata, passed over the border from middle age into old age.

Only Tora-san was supposed to remain forever in his forties (his official birth date was September 10, 1945), but even he was not invulnerable to the passage of time. Episode No. 45, *Tora-san Makes Excuses,* offered clear intimations of Tora-san's mortality. By putting Tora-san on crutches and having his Shibamata neighbors spread rumors of his imminent demise, Yamada was acknowledging that his hero was no longer young and preparing his audiences for Tora-san's eventual departure from the screen.

Yamada also claimed that "even if Tora-san has white hair and a bent back, he will still fall in love." Here we come to the heart of the series' formula: The Tora-san movies were less comedies than love stories. In each installment Tora-san met a new woman—called a madonna in the series' parlance. He fell for her and pursued her, but in the last reel they went their separate ways. There was at least one of these encounters in every episode, with a total of thirty-seven different madonnas. Ruriko Asoka set the record for most madonna appearances, with four, in Nos. 11, 15, 25 and 48. Kumiko Gotō was the official madonna for four episodes, Nos. 42-45, playing the part of the girlfriend of Mitsuo, Tora-san's nephew.

Tora-san is usually portrayed as a hapless, hopeless lover. He may make his new madonna laugh with his jokes and warm her heart with his kindnesses (though these often lead to comic disasters), but his shyness keeps him from expressing his feelings or responding to her advances. Meanwhile, an earnest, sober-sided man of solid professional status—for example, a doctor in No. 2, *Zoku Otoko wa Tsurai Yo* (Tora-san's Cherished Mother, 1969); a University of Tokyo professor in No. 10, *Torajirō Yumemakura* (Tora-san's Dream Come True, 1972); and a tanker captain in No. 24, *Torajirō Haru no Yume* (Tora-san's Dream of Spring, 1979)—appears and wins the madonna's hand. With his lack of a diploma and a steady, white-collar job, Tora-san does not stand a chance. "He's really a sad character, a lonely character," said Yamada.

He is also, as the films make clear, a victim of the sexual conventions

Figure 13.1 **Kiyoshi Atsumi (Tora-san), surrounded by Jun Fubuki, "madonna" Kumiko Gotō, and Hidetaka Yoshioka, in Episode No. 45, *Tora-san Makes Excuses***

imposed by a rigidly hierarchical, credential-worshipping society. In Hollywood the boy from the wrong side of the tracks can win the girl who lives in the house on the hill; in Tora-san's world, it doesn't happen. He does, however, have the romantic upper hand in some movies. In *Tora-san's Dream Come True,* a middle-aged Shibamata beautician (Kaoru Yachigusa) actually proposes marriage. Tora-san, who has been pursuing her frantically throughout the film, collapses into embarrassed silence. In *Tora-san Confesses,* the widowed proprietress of a provincial pub (Hideko Yoshida), who had rejected Tora-san many years before, tells him frankly that she now regrets her decision. His response is to take the next bus out of town.

Tora-san may fail at love, but he remains the incurable romantic. Rather than settle for what is available, he continues to pursue his ideal woman, who is often above him in education or status or far apart from him in age. Ran It) in *Foster Daddy, Tora-san* and Keiko Takeshita in

No. 41, *Torajirō Kokoro no Tabiji* (Tora-san Goes to Vienna, 1989) are young enough to be his daughters. When his ideal comes down off her pedestal and pursues him, he quickly loses interest. He wants the thrill of the first encounter, the passionate dreams of courtship, not the reality of a serious and possibly permanent relationship.

"That's been his pattern for years," Mitsuo tells Izumi in *Tora-san Makes Excuses.* "It drives Mom to distraction."

The pattern also flies in the face of Western film-making convention; even the Tramp, to whom Tora-san has often been compared, always got the girl in the end. But the Tramp was a man of no particular profession, family, or city, who could find happiness with Virginia Cherrill in *City Lights* (1931) and turn up at the beginning of *Modern Times* (1936) unattached, ready to search for love anew. Tora-san, however, is a character in a continuing story, who inhabits a specific milieu. If he were to be united with the love of his life at the conclusion of one episode, he would still have to be united with her at the beginning of the next—or explain why not. But wedding bells would have rung in the end of the series before that happened.

Tora-san's milieu is Shibamata, Katsushika Ward, in the *shitamachi* (old downtown) section of Tokyo. Once the center of the *chomin* (townspeople) culture in the Edo period (1603–1867), the shitamachi is now a cultural backwater that even massive bubble-era investment has not quite succeeded in making trendy. Tora-san is an *Edokko* (Edo boy) with all the typical attributes. He may have a short fuse, an empty wallet, a quick tongue, and a happy-go-lucky approach to life, but he is also religiously faithful to the Edokko ethic of *giri ninjō* (duty and human feelings). In other words, he will do what he thinks is right by those to whom he feels an obligation, even if it means a considerable sacrifice of time, energy, and money (not that he ever has much of the last). In *Foster Daddy, Tora-san,* while wandering about Hokkaido, he meets Sumire, the daughter of a fellow *tekiya*. When he learns that his colleague, her father, has died, Tora-san immediately goes to his grave to pray for the repose of his soul (these grave visits are a frequent feature of the series). When he learns that Sumire wants to go to Tokyo to finish high school and find a job, he takes her back to Shibamata, gives her his room in the dango shop, helps her register at a night school, and even stands watch outside the classroom to make sure that all goes well.

It could be argued that Tora-san has ulterior motives—that he wouldn't have gone to the trouble if Sumire weren't pretty and available. But the idea that Tora-san might be coolly calculating her seduction from the start is absurd. He is the Edokko as divine fool. "His head is completely empty," said Yamada. "In one film, he tells a student that 'the inside of your head is like the wires on the back of a TV—all tangled up. But if you hit my head it would ring clear as a bell.'" Tora-san's heart, however, is in the right place.

Tora-san was more than an inhabitant of the shitamachi in spirit; he set down his battered suitcase—the same one he used for the entire series—in a very real part of town. A three-minute walk from Shibamata Station is the *sandō* (street leading to a temple), the temple, and the dango shop that were used for exterior shots (interiors were shot at Shōchiku's Ōfuna Studio). There are other series locations scattered around the area—a nursery school where an early madonna once taught; a Japanese-style restaurant (formerly a wedding hall) where the nuptials of another madonna were once held; and a 624-square-meter city-built Tora-san museum, complete with a replica of the Tora-ya dango shop, which opened in November 1997. These places have become shrines to the thousands of Tora-san fans who visit every year.

Not surprisingly, the shops that border the fictional Tora-ya have prospered over the years; they may be built in the traditional style—no ferroconcrete or plate glass—but they have a sleek, well-fed look, despite their plain wooden exteriors. It is not quite a neighborhood anymore where a self-proclaimed *fūten* (delinquent) would feel at home.

One of the ironies of the series is that, though he is Shibamata born and bred, Tora-san is not always the most welcome of visitors, often for good cause. He comes back from a long stretch on the road and, barely a minute after he hands over his *omiyage* (gift), he is quarreling with Oichan or Obachan or Tako Shachō (Hisao Dazai), who runs the nearby print shop where Hiroshi works. Usually the reasons are trivial—Tora-san overhears a wisecrack that is not meant for his ears (or one that is), and flies at the offender; or he finds an unexpected visitor occupying his upstairs room. In *Tora-san's Dream of Spring* it was a long, lanky salesman named Michael Jordan (Herb Edelmann), whom series publicists dubbed the "American Tora-san." Whatever the reason, he quickly packs his suitcase and is out the door, off on another trip to the far reaches of Japan (once, in No. 41, he made it as far as Vienna).

Why was Tora-san so touchy? One answer is his Edokko pride; he loves to swagger about, playing the great lover and benefactor and man of the world. He may always wear the same checked beige suit, but he throws his coat over his shoulders with an insouciance reminiscent of Frank Sinatra in one of his "urban sophisticate" roles. When someone punctures that pride—and tells him that he is really a shiftless, bumble-brained ne'er-do-well *tekiya* (the usual offender is Tako Shachō)—he does a very fast burn.

Another answer is that he is an illegitimate child—the product of a union between his father and a Kyoto geisha. Sakura is really his half-sister and Oichan is his half-uncle. Sakura loves him no less because of this fact—she embodies all the traditional virtues of Japanese womanhood, including a soft spot for errant male relations—but Tora-san is sensitive about the circumstance of his birth. It is not a secret—he even makes jokes about it—but it is a never-healing wound.

Still another answer is that, if he did not storm out the door, he would never make the journeys that are another of the series' trademarks. By the end of the series, Tora-san had been to every prefecture of Japan and one foreign country. Nearly all the places he chose as destinations were natural beauty spots. Because of his trade, he frequently found himself hawking his wares to a colorfully dressed crowd on its way to a festival or temple.

This cinematic tourism did not feel forced—Tora-san belonged in these places, with these people. Atsumi, who grew up in the shitamachi and hung around Edokko tekiya like Tora-san (his stories about them gave Yamada the idea for the character), had the rhythm, timing, and attitude down perfectly. Tora-san was salesman as charmer, with a smooth, funny line of patter.

The movies ended at about the same time of year the audience was seeing them in the theater. Always there was Tora-san, selling his old books or balloons or "health rings" to strangers at New Year's or Obon while Sakura and her family (and most of the audience) were celebrating the holiday at home. It was always a bit sad to see Tora-san, alone again but bravely bearing up—or was that relief we saw in him, at being free of yet another entangling romantic commitment?

A main appeal of the series was the very sameness that critics attacked it for; Japanese who rarely went to the movies (the vast majority) would go to a Tora-san film because they knew exactly what they were getting. For them, it was like watching the latest episode of a favorite television series. Also, seeing a Tora-san film became a holiday custom for many Japanese, like *hatsumōde* (first temple visit of the year). In fact, advertisements for the series urged audiences to get their *hatsuwarai* (first laugh of the year) at the latest installment.

Familiarity, custom, and clever advertising are not enough to explain why the series survived so long, however. Seeing a Tora-san movie in Tokyo, after all, was not like watching another episode of *Sazae-san*, an animated family sitcom that has been on television even longer than the Tora-san series was in the theaters. Many moviegoers had to travel an hour or more from their homes and pay the world's highest ticket prices at the door. True, they were getting a deal—the series always played with a second feature—but they still wanted something more than what they could get on the tube.

"People are honest," says Yamada. "If a film is well made, they will go to see it." He obviously believes his own films fall into this category. A director since 1961, Yamada has made several nonseries films that have garnered major Japanese awards, including the 1977 *Kōfuku no Kiroii Hankachi* (The Yellow Handkerchief of Happiness), the 1991 *Musuko* (My Sons) and the 1993 *Gakkō* (A Class to Remember). But far from regarding the series as hack work that made money for his other, more artistic projects, Yamada has long felt that it was his true life work. "I guess I am unique in making only Tora-san movies," he said with a smile, "but I am glad I could do it."

Yamada did make the effort; even the series' more routine installments offer a comic gem or two: a sparkling patch of dialogue or a funny piece of business that deserves the epithet "classic." The Japanese film industry seemed to agree; it honored him and the series cast with major awards over the years. Yamada won the Japan Academy Award for Best Director in 1977, and Atsumi was presented with a Special Prize for his series work at the fourth Japan Academy Awards ceremony in 1980.

In creating the character of Tora-san, Yamada was inspired by a classic Japanese art form: *rakugo* (comic storytelling). One well-known rakugo routine features a character called Kuma-san (Bear), who is a Tora-san in embryo. "I liked Kuma-san, so I blended his character with that of Atsumi," said Yamada. Some of Tora-san's best monologues—such as the ones he delivered at the family table to an enthralled audience—had a distinct rakugo flavor.

But though Yamada believed the Tora-san films "must make people laugh," he also felt that "surface laughs" were not enough: the series had to address deeper issues as well. This attempt to add "depth" sometimes resulted in standard Japanese movie sentimentalism: Tora-san as a pathetic, drunken figure in a police box or Sakura as the anxiously clinging sister.

Yamada often presented his more serious concerns in an appealingly comic guise, however. In *Foster Daddy, Tora-san,* we laugh at Tora-san's bumbling attempts to ingratiate himself with the night school teacher, but we also learn about the students who slip through the cracks of Japan's vaunted educational system. (Yamada's *Gakkō*, which has since spawned two sequels, is about such students.) The films manage to work on several levels at once, without forcing the audience to choose one over another.

But the most important reason for the series' continued success was the character of Tora-san himself. Like all great comedians, Atsumi made his character more than a gesture, an attitude, or a gag. Over the years, Tora-san grew new dimensions and took on a life of his own. (Atsumi often dressed in Tora-san garb for his rare public appearances. Also, though he frequently acted in nonseries TV shows and films early in his career, by the end he had reduced such appearances to the occasional cameo and was almost exclusively identified by movie fans with his Tora-san persona.) We knew that, in Atsumi's words, "Tora-san is a guy who doesn't exist in Japan anymore," but we could still imagine meeting him someday, perhaps seeing him selling his wares at a festival in a small Kyushu town or strolling along a Hokkaido beach.

All such fantasies came to an end with Atsumi's death from lung cancer at the age of 68 on August 4, 1996, but fans were reluctant to let him and his best-known character go. On August 8, only four days after his death, Atsumi was posthumously given the People's Honor Award by the Japanese government—only the twelfth Japanese to receive this distinction since the founding of the award in 1977—for what Chief Cabinet Secretary Seiroku Kajiyama described as his ability to provide "happiness and enjoyment to citizens of this country through his acting." When Shōchiku held a farewell ceremony for Atsumi at its Ōfuna studio in Kanagawa Prefecture, 35,000 fans showed up from all over the country. Meanwhile, special screenings of his Tora-san films drew packed crowds, and video stores across the country ordered 40,000 copies of Tora-san movies in the first three weeks after his death.

In the months that followed, Tora-san fever showed no signs of abating. In November 1996 the city of Yubari in Hokkaido held a Tora-san look-alike contest, with fifty contestants in Tora-san getup competing for a ¥100,000 first prize. In December, Shōchiku released a complete set of forty-eight Tora-san videos and a set of twenty-three later films that together sold a thumping 270,000 units in their first month in the stores. In January 1997 Tokyo post offices began selling a set of forty-eight Tora-san postcards, each decorated with a poster of a different Tora-san movie, for ¥3,500. A limited edition of 720,000 sets sold briskly to eager fans.

Though Shōchiku was the prime beneficiary of the posthumous Tora-san boom, it had to fill the gaping hole in its 1997 New Year's lineup. The company rushed into production *Niji o Tsukamu Otoko* (The Man Who Caught the Rainbow), a film scripted and directed by Yōji Yamada that was intended as a tribute to Atsumi and the Tora-san series. The main character, a provincial movie theater manager played by Toshiyuki Nishida, shared Tora-san's romantic disposition, ineptness with the ladies, and gift of gab, though he was more given to discoursing eloquently on the glories of classic films than to telling amusingly rock-headed anecdotes. The film also featured several familiar faces from the Tora-san series, including former madonna Yūko Tanaka as the manager's inamorata and, played by a double, Tora-san himself in a cameo. Though the film did not do nearly as well as the Tora-san series at the box office, Shōchiku made a second installment for the 1998 New Year's season.

To commemorate the first anniversary of Atsumi's death, Shōchiku released in August 1997 a special edition of the series' twenty-fifth installment, *Torajirō Haibisukasu no Hana* (Tora-san's Tropical Holiday), which fans had voted their favorite in a company-sponsored poll. The film had a revamped soundtrack and five minutes of additional footage directed by Yamada that showed Hidetaka Yoshioka as Mitsuo reminiscing about his uncle in a rural train station when, thanks to the magic of computer graphics, he spots him on the opposite platform.

Tora-san, of course, did not cross the tracks to chat, but millions of fans no doubt wish that he still could have. His films depict a nostalgic ideal; their Japan is not the country of conniving businessmen, lying politicians, and corrupt bureaucrats, but a warm heartland where even a wandering tekiya without the right diploma or business card can feel at home. Though not high art on the order of an Ozu masterpiece, they can entertain us, cheer us, and tell us a great deal about the best of the Japanese spirit.

Notes

1. A previous version of this chapter was published in *Japan Quarterly* 40:2 (April–June 1993), pp. 199–206.

2. Yamada did not direct installments No. 3, *Fūten no Torajirō* (Tora-san: His Tender Love, 1970), and No. 4, *Shin Otoko wa Tsurai Yo* (Tora-san's Grand Scheme, 1970), but he wrote the scripts.

3. All Yamada quotes are from an interview with the author, conducted in Tokyo in 1991.

Part IV

Japanese Popular Culture Abroad

14

Sailor Moon

Japanese Superheroes for Global Girls

Anne Allison

When Serena Tsukino, a boy-crazy 14-year-old whose main talents lie in the areas of eating, shopping, and sleeping, launches into the 45-second "morphing" sequence that transforms her into brave, pretty, evil-fighting superhero Sailor Moon, she is reenacting the transformation from human to superhero that turned Clark Kent into Superman and that lies at the heart of all superhero tales. Sailor Moon, however, is different from the pantheon of superheroes in whose tradition she follows. First, she's a *girl*, in a genre (and from a country) traditionally dominated by male heroes. Second, Sailor Moon is a *Japanese* superhero whose success in conquering evil and audiences at home has been matched by a high level of popularity overseas.

Created by female *manga* (comics) artist Naoko Takeuchi, and serialized in the girl's magazine *Nakayoshi*, *Sailor Moon*, or *Bishōjo Senshi Sailor Moon* (Pretty Warrior Sailor Moon), as she is known in Japan, has been wildly popular in the channels of mass children's culture in Japan since 1992. A true multimedia product—in addition to the manga there are a weekly television cartoon show, feature-length videos, computer and video games, toy dolls and "morphing" toys, books based on the manga and videos, and icons imprinted on everything from clothes to notebooks—Sailor Moon is popular for both the female and the superhero parts of her character. As such, she is something of a hybrid, embodying conventions both of boys' culture—fighting, warriorship, superheroes—and *shōjo* (girls') culture—romance, friendship, and appearance.

As the descriptor attached to her name implies—*bishōjo* (beautiful young girl) *senshi* (warrior)—Sailor Moon represents both a different kind of girl—one who fights and is herself a hero rather than in need of one—and a different kind of warrior—a beautiful female. Her marketers have found these differences to be successful; *Sailor Moon* has been the top-ranking television show for its production company, Tōei, outranking all its programming for boys (including the Japanese version of *The Mighty Morphin Power Rangers*). Further, by the mid-1990s *Sailor Moon* had been successfully exported to eighteen countries worldwide.

According to Mokoto Yamashina, president of Bandai, the toy company that markets Sailor Moon dolls and toys, the idea behind the Sailor Moon phenomenon was to create a new kind of female hero for a new kind of 1990s Japanese girl. Others suggest a more pragmatic impulse behind Sailor Moon and the other bishōjo heroes that have increasingly populated Japanese manga and *anime* (animation) since the 1980s: Given the huge and proven popularity of the warrior tradition among boys, the hope was to expand the consumer market to include girls. Potential market expansion is also, of course, what drives the efforts of Japanese industry to export popular culture, including superheroes, abroad—a business venture that grew so rapidly in the 1990s that the *New York Times* has called Japan the new "superpower among superheroes."[1]

This chapter begins with a look at the most successful Japanese superhero transplant, *The Mighty Morphin Power Rangers*, which can be seen in eighty countries and lays claim to being the most heavily watched children's program on earth. We then turn to *Sailor Moon*, examining a trio of transformations that Sailor Moon illustrates, and that are critical to the successful international circulation of Japanese superheroes, and Sailor Moon in particular, as popular culture. First is the transformation between ordinary human and trans-human hero that characterizes and anchors the plots of all superhero stories. What is the nature of this transformation and what is its appeal, particularly (but not exclusively) to children?

Second, given that superheroes combine a this-worldly and an otherworldly persona, both of which are rooted in conventions, values, and lifestyles found in the world inhabited by their audience, what happens when a superhero produced in one cultural context is transported to another country and context? Can a Superman created in the United States, as an individualist who fights for truth, justice, and the American way, make sense in a foreign environment? How about Sailor Moon, or any other superhero produced for and within Japan's domestic market? Is there something particularly "Japanese" about Japanese superheroes? Do tales of Japanese superheroism translate well to foreign audiences, or must they be reshaped to accommodate different values and "consumer needs" when exported to the global marketplace?

Third, apart from such exceptions as *Wonder Woman*, *She-ra*, and *Xena, Warrior Princess*, the role of superhero has traditionally been reserved for males, and targeted a predominantly male audience. (Even the female superhero of *Wonder Woman* was designed by creator Dr. William Marston as a *femme fatale* who would engender a feeling of "enslavement" in male readers. [2]) Sailor Moon represents a shift in this orientation. Though warrior girls are still a novelty in countries such as the United States, they have become a well-established subgenre in Japan. This raises the question of the relationship between genre and gender: How tied is the genre of superhero to a model of masculinity? How do the story, hero, and audience change when the hero is a female?[3]

Superheroes, Western and Japanese

The myth of the superhero—a character with superhuman powers who can pass as human and fights evil—recurs in folklore, fairy tales, cultural legends, and religions around the world. The best-known Western superhero is Superman, the hybrid man-alien who uses his extraterrestrial powers to fight crime and injustice on earth. Although its creators, writer Jerry Siegel and illustrator Joe Shuster, touted *Superman* as revolutionary—"a science fiction story in cartoons" about "the most astounding fiction character of all time"—publishers simply found *Superman* alien, and rejected him for years. When the story was eventually picked up by D.C. Comics and headlined in *Action Comics* in June 1938, it was Superman's distinctive blend of "unique abilities, flashy costume, and secret identity" that made him an instant hit, particularly among a growing fandom of adolescent boys.[4] That he was good—unlike Siegel and Shuster's original version, in which Superman was a malevolent power on the order of Hitler, whose real presence was then stalking the American consciousness—has been equally critical to Superman's success as a heroic icon. As the incarnation of good boy, chivalrous man, and patriotic American, Superman upholds a very particular social order which he (and his fans) believe to be moral and right.

The two-sidedness of Superman's character—everyday citizen cloaked as bumbling Clark Kent and exceptional hero embodied as the amazing Superman—is also central to his phenomenal success. Put another way, Superman and other superheroes are hybrids: alien/human, robot/cop, warrior/woman, grasshopper/boy. The effect is fantastic, but the phantom reflects very real desires (for strength, power, and control) and defends the very conventional norms (law, order, and justice) that operate in the human world to which the superhero, and his or her fans, belong.

As in the United States, the popularization of "modern" superheroes in Japan was fostered by the rise of mass culture, and in particular the medium of comic artistry. Although heroic figures were occasionally featured in serialized comics in the prewar years—one was a heroic flying mummy in the comic book *Ōgon Batto* (Golden Bat)—superheroes didn't really take off until the 1950s.[5] One of the first to materialize in this period of postwar destruction and national rebuilding was *Tetsuwan Atom* (Mighty Atom, known as "Astro Boy" in the United States). Created by Osamu Tezuka, the artist who revolutionized comics in postwar Japan, this was the story of an atomic-powered boy-robot who is built by a scientist as a replacement for his own son, who has died in a traffic accident. In the guise of the upbeat Atom, robotic technology was made into a friendly "alien" in these stories, one that fuses comfortably with the human qualities of hard work, cooperation, and determination displayed by the boy-robot. As a replacement for a "lost son," Tetsuwan Atom served as a new type of hero through which a generation of war-weary Japanese could begin to re-envision their country: as one built on technology, energized through hard work and good will, and devoted to a new world order of machines and peace.

Inspired by *Superman*, which was then being marketed via the movie and television screen in the United States, superheroes began to appear in serialized television shows in Japan. The first such show was *Starman* in 1957, which was followed by a series of superhero shows including *Jiraiya* (Land Mine Man), *Rainbowman*, *Ganbaron* (Fight Hard Man), *Machine Man*, *Spectreman*, *Ultraman*, and *Gekkō Kamen* (Moonlight Mask).[6] Although this generation of Japanese superheroes was modeled heavily on Hollywood fashions (reflecting the superiority with which American popular culture was then regarded), there were also additions recognized as distinctly "Japanese." First, superheroes became skilled in martial arts; though also provided the more "standard" repertoire of exceptional powers, superheroes became identified as experts in *judō, karate,* and *aikidō*, displaying their skills during battle and posing in martial art stances as part of their morphing rituals. Second, armies of *kaijū* (monsters), fashioned to be highly unrealistic and fantastically beastlike, were introduced as the standard enemy against whose evil the superheroes were forced to fight.[7] With these characteristics, superhero comics, TV shows, and movies became increasingly popular at the end of the 1950s and into the 1960s, and they continue today as a major form of children's mass entertainment, particularly for boys.

In 1975, a new show titled *Go Ranger* (Five Rangers) was introduced by Tōei with what was then considered a distinctive change. Instead of one superhero, it featured a group of five teenagers, a *sentai* (task force) who fought together both physically as a team of individuals and robotically by combining their individual robot weaponry into a collective five-part superrobot.[8] As is common for Japanese superhero programs, *Go Ranger* was on the air for nine months, then was taken off and rebroadcast months later with slight changes. In the twenty-plus years the show has aired off and on in Japan, it has gone through multiple incarnations, one of the more recent being *ŌRangers* (The Oh Rangers) in 1995. In the 1980s, Haim Saban, head of the U.S.-based Saban Entertainment Group, viewed a segment of *Kyōryū Sentai Jū Ranger* (Dinosaur Attack Force Beast Rangers) while traveling abroad and became interested in importing the Ranger series to the United States.[9] Despite the fact that other products of Japanese popular culture had been successfully marketed in America, notably *Godzilla* in the 1950s and 1960s and children's shows such as *Speed Racer* in the 1960s and 1970s, the networks were uninterested, finding the show too parochially Japanese, with stylistic conventions they thought would be unappealing to the differently cultured American kids audience. Specifically it was the fantasy format of the show—a live action show with actors who start off as normal-looking and normal-acting teenagers and then morph into a team of costumed and masked rangers to fight alien, unrealistic beasts led by Rita Repulsa—that the networks found to be "cheezy," "silly," "immature," and "foreign."[10]

Rejected for its "alienness" as *Superman* had been decades earlier, the Rangers series was eventually picked up in 1993 by Margaret Loesch of Fox who, being a fan of Japanese animation since childhood, viewed the show as vibrantly different rather than alien. Renamed *The Mighty Morphin Power Rangers* and retooled as a hybrid production—splicing Japanese footage from the postmorph scenes when the masked Rangers are fighting monsters with newly created premorph scenes featuring American teenagers set in a U.S. high school—the show was an instant hit. Climbing to the top of the children's program rankings within a mere five weeks of being aired, *Power Rangers* launched a boom in "morphin play" that was limited to neither the 3- to 8-year-old audience the show targeted nor to those who actually watched the show on TV. "Morphin time" became the slogan for a new kind of fantasy activity played by children and adolescents who act out the transformative identities of the warrior or superhero. This has translated into a multi-million dollar industry for those who own the rights to the *Power Rangers*—Saban Entertainment in connection with Tōei, Fox Network, and toy maker Bandai (which in 1994 earned $400 million on *Power Ranger* merchandise, putting it in position to aim at overtaking U.S. toy giants Mattel and Hasbro)—and has generated a range of *Power Ranger* products, from movies, comic books, and toys to T-shirts and bedsheets.

The popularity of *The Mighty Morphin Power Rangers* in the United States, which soon exceeded that of the original in Japan, has not only remained strong since its first airing, but has also been duplicated on the global stage; in 1996 it was broadcast in eighty countries and rated the most heavily watched children's television show in the world. Those who have managed the program's production in the United States say that the U.S. success of the *Power Rangers* is due in large part to the substantial adjustments that were made to "Americanize" the product. According to Bandai president Yamashina, earlier attempts to penetrate the U.S. market with Japanese superheroes such as Ultraman failed because they were "too foreign" for Americans and needed to be "translated" to match American tastes.[11] *The Mighty Morphin Power Rangers* is the translated model; its human (unmorphed) figures have American features, its American lineup puts more focus on the team's female members (two out of six), and the television show abides by American notions of teenager lifestyle. One observer calls the result "a campier, California version of the *Power Rangers*"; Haim Saban sees it as a "cultural bridge between the two countries."[12] U.S. fans of the superhero genre put a different spin on this, calling the *Power Rangers* a mutation from the original Japanese program. Some like this because it draws on different strengths from both the American and Japanese superhero traditions, while others consider it a "butchering" motivated by anti-Japanese racism.[13]

If "hybrid" is the right name for this product, the question that arises is: How critical is this blending to the success of future Japanese pop culture exports? In the wake of the blockbuster results of the *Power Rangers*, these exports are certain to increase.[14] Indeed, in anticipating the importation of *Sailor Moon* to the United States, Peter Dang, vice president of marketing for Bandai America, spoke in exactly these terms. Stressing the need to "find the linkage in the American psyche," Dang pointed out the importance of making *Sailor Moon* "culturally appropriate" for the American market.[15] The merely moderate reception given *Sailor Moon* in its initial months on American television was due, according to a Mattel advertising executive, to precisely the lack of such a linkage. In his mind, *Sailor Moon*'s marketers failed to sufficiently Americanize the program—Japanese words appear on the screen; Japanese sites such as temples, noodle shops, and cram schools are left in; and common activities for Japanese but not Americans occur, such as eating box lunches and using chopsticks. Some American children I have spoken with agree, calling the show "too different," which they explain to mean "too Japanese."

Related to the nature of the product itself is the fact of its origins, which in the case of *Power Rangers* have been overtly downplayed and even largely effaced. In the U.S. version, no credit is given to Tōei and little in the show's marketing reveals that it is an export from Japan. Many of those I spoke with about the *Power Rangers*, particularly children under the age of 10, had no idea that it originated in Japan, making one wonder if this is what is needed to guarantee success in the American market. If so, this is a disguise—a "secret identity"—that is strikingly absent from the strategies of American pop culture exporters such as Disney and Mattel, whose fantasies and products for children spread globally under the clear label "made in America." As critics accusing the United States of "cultural imperialism" have pointed out, Disney makes no effort to alter its cultural message for audiences outside the United States.[16]

On the other hand, elsewhere in the world, and especially in Asian countries like Taiwan, Hong Kong, Thailand, and Singapore, Japanese pop culture is booming, in part because it *does* differ from Western products. Naomi Higuchi, author of *Terebi Hero no Sōzō* (The Creation of Television Heroes), discusses this in terms both of blending and difference, pointing out that Japanese pop culture is a product that incorporates Western techniques and graphics but at the same time offers stories and values that resonate with "Asian" values. Takahiro Ōmori, the director of Asian exports/imports for Japan-based toy giant Sanrio, also notes the growing appreciation for Japanese products in other Asian markets where "twenty years ago, we used to admire anything American."[17] For Ōmori, the reason lies not in cultural packaging but in the quality of the Japanese product, much improved in the 1990s compared to earlier examples. The director of Tōei International attributes his company's success in exporting Japanese children's culture—*Power Rangers* has been followed into overseas markets by *Sailor Moon* and *Dragon Ball Z*, both highly successful in most countries where they are playing—to the fact that the programs offer something of value that transcends any particular culture: "Although [Tōei's superhero shows] may have cultural colors, their essential appeal is universal."[18]

What, precisely, *is* the "universal appeal" that this genre of Japanese popular culture possesses, and that is reaching global audiences on a scale unimaginable to those network executives who rejected *Power Rangers* as appealing only to Japanese? Some consumers applaud the "visceral, physical wit" of Japanese cartoons, whose humor is more direct than the subtlety of a show like *The Simpsons* (a Hong Kong mother speaking of the Japanese show, *Crayon Shin-chan*). Others note the visual appeal that Japanese animators create by using an abundance of cinematic techniques and a color range not limited to the bright "kids" colors favored by Western animators.[19]

As for the specific genre of *sentai* (task force) superheroes, three qualities are mentioned most often. First, the human characters are more "real." They exhibit a fuller range of human emotions and are put into more realistic situations, sometimes with unpleasant outcomes, than allowed by Disney's "perfectly preserved, stiflingly safe fairytale-based storylines."[20] Rangers sometimes die in the Japanese *Ranger* programs, for example, whereas they never do in *The Mighty Morphin Power Rangers*. A Bandai executive noted that the inclusion of a child somewhere in the story line (in addition to the older teenagers assigned the superhero roles), with whom younger viewers can identify, is also considered an attraction.

Second, the enemies are more "alien." Typically configured as beastly and prehistoric creatures, their alienness is exaggerated and less "human-like" than in most American programs. This element, which fans like and nonfans do not like, heightens the fantastic (or, as some put it, the "raw" and "primitive") nature of the stories, and contrasts sharply with the more "realistic" treatment of the superheroes' human side.[21]

Third, these two elements, a hero that is more human and "selflike" plus an enemy that is more "otherly," combine in stories that are fast-paced, dramatic, richly developed (due in large part to the length their serialization allows), and violent. Battle scenes always occur and the enemy is always evil, but the transformation of the superhero involves complex psychological issues for the "self." In one episode of *Ō Rangers*, for example, a Ranger displays incredible feats of not only bravery but also spirituality to defeat the enemy. Because the Rangers' superrobot is malfunctioning, Red Ranger retrieves an earlier robotic model which, due to a glitch, killed the Ranger who used it before him. His fellow Rangers and headmaster (the engineer who built both robots) warn him against reigniting the old robot, but Red Ranger insists, convinced there is no alternative. Despite a brave struggle against the enemy, Red Ranger is killed when the robot falters. Immediately his spirit is taken up by the spirit of his dead comrade, who shows him the beauty of the earth, with the reminder that this is what the Rangers must fight to defend. Refortified, Red Ranger's spirit returns to the robot and starts the machine up again, this time succeeding. The last scene shows the Rangers at the grave of their fallen comrade.

In this episode, the plot hinges on transformation, as it does in all superhero stories. But here it is triggered by the mastery of human skills, and what the Japanese call *ganbaru* (never giving up), rather than being the embodiment of alien powers. That the enemy is subsequently smashed to smithereens is a sign, in this plot, of the boy's mastery of the self. Of course, this dynamic is at work in all superhero stories where destruction of an evil other marks victory for the heroic self. Here, though, the intensity at both ends of the transformation—the spirituality of the hero's rebirth and the totality of the foe's annihilation—portrays the self-other dynamic in ways that dramatically heighten the psychic, if not literal, "truth" of the story. This, it can be argued, is one of the key reasons for *Power Rangers*' powerful appeal.

Critics of the show, on the other hand, tend to focus only on the battle at the end of the transformative cycle, and to view its explosiveness not in symbolic or psychological terms, but rather as a manifestation of excessive violence. That *Power Rangers* seems more violent than other children's shows is, in fact, the single most common observation and complaint made by parents of Ranger fans around the world. A 1995 *New York Times* poll ranked it the show second most disapproved of by U.S. parents, next only to *Beavis and Butthead*. It has been banned in some countries—Norway's ban, later rescinded, was triggered by the murder of one child by another, blamed on the show's promotion of violence—and is widely castigated in America for the martial arts-based morphin stance its lead players assume when activated to fight alien enemies and disintegrate them into thin air. The fear is that the fantasy violence of *Power Rangers* promotes real-life aggression in children.[22]

Consumers, of course, feel differently, as do many involved in the very active debate, engaged in by developmental psychologists, educators, media critics, and parents, over the *Power Rangers* phenomenon. Some believe that the transformative play at the heart of *Power Rangers* is empowering to kids. Media critic Ellen Seiter, for example, contends that the rituals of changing and masking identity are psychically healthy for children, who themselves face the very real transformative process of child development.[23] That the Rangers are always successful in managing a crisis situation and do so by activating skills of self-discipline, cooperation, concentration, and physical strength is also an empowering message to children who can adopt these behaviors in real life as a means of coping with situations they often feel are beyond their control. In a similar vein, a child psychologist has told me that children constantly play out *Power Rangers* in her office, an indication, she believes, of the show's power to both reach and express the psyches of kids. These positions resemble that most commonly voiced in Japan: that the fantasy of transformative play at the heart of much of Japan's popular culture (in manga, anime, pornography) is not confused with reality by its consumers, and that, even when marked by sex and violence (as it often is in Japan), it allows for a healthy psychic release of tensions that build up in a society where performance and conformity are in high demand, and from which fantasy provides a useful, even necessary, escape.[24]

Gallantly Girlish Girls

The presence of females as featured heroes in manga, animation, and live action shows has been much stronger in Japan than in the United States, particularly since the 1980s. The reasons for this are complex and, while hardly due to a greater feminist consciousness in Japanese society, are clearly linked to the increase in female manga artists in recent years as well as to the large consumer audience of girls who read, watch, and even write their own, fantasy stories. How different *are* female superheroes and how do they sell in various markets?

Kazuko Minomiya, who has written extensively about girls' manga, observes that heroines like Sailor Moon offer a more *risōkyō* (utopian) version of the superhero, one whose human life is filled with the everyday pleasantries of shopping, playing video games, and visiting amusement parks, and one that differs from the more arduous and serious lifestyle painted for male warriors.[25] A Mattel executive working in New York, by contrast, views the fashion component of Sailor Moon as the crucial difference, a feature absent from earlier models of American heroines such as She-ra and Wonder Woman, and one whose addition makes for a new and attractive combination of the action orientation of boys and the fashion orientation of girls. Dubbing this "fashion-action," he notes that Mattel and Hasbro adopted such lines in their 1996 toy series, targeting what they perceived to be the new girl (but not boy) of the 1990s, one who wants to be pretty as well as strong.

With this background in mind, let us turn to *Sailor Moon*, which in its animated cartoon form aired weekly in Japan (like the *Rangers*, in a series of incarnations: *Sailor Moon*, *Sailor Moon R*, *Sailor Moon S*, *Sailor Moon Super S*, and *Sailor Stars*) and five days a week in its North American showings. The star of the show is a 14-year-old girl, Usagi Tsukino in Japanese (Serena in English), who, guided by her talking cat, Luna, transforms into the superhero Sailor Moon by activating various sources of moon power, such as a penlike device called "moon prism" and the tiara she wears when "morphed." Based on the manga by Naoko Takeuchi, which is published in book form as well as serialized in the girls' magazine *Nakayoshi*, Sailor Moon is so popular among young girls in Japan that her image appears on everything from socks, T-shirts, and hair clips to lunchboxes, umbrellas, and handbags.

The reason she is so well liked, according to one 9-year-old Japanese girl I spoke with, is not that she is powerful but because she has a good figure (*style ga ii*). This is also the reason given for her popularity among *ojisan* (older men). With her leggy, slender body; long, flowing blond hair; and the miniskirt outfit she wears after morphing, Sailor Moon is a sex icon as well as a superhero, one who feeds and is fed by a general trend in Japan toward the infantilization of female sex objects. The fact that Sailor Moon not only wears a sailor suit but is named for one is striking, given that this is both the standard school uniform style worn by junior and senior high school girls in Japan and also the outfit used by marketers in the sex industry to sell a nymphette effect, a popular theme in pornography, men's comics, and clubs where hostesses dress as schoolgirls. Employing the sailor motif thus satisfies two desires: the desire on the part of young or teenage girls to identify with the Sailor Scouts, and the desire, exhibited primarily by older males, to eroticize the Scouts. (Fans communicating via Internet in the United States have noted that there are also homoerotic themes in the Japanese original, and that these were totally deleted in the American version.)

As a story, the key feature of *Sailor Moon* is Serena's transformation to superhero from not just an average girl, but a girl whose mediocrities are exaggerated and constantly remarked upon by her moon-empowered cat, Luna. In the opening episode, Serena receives a 30 on an exam, in contrast to a new girl at school who earns 100 and is rewarded by her parents with a beautiful necklace. Serena, envious, decides to go to the video arcade to play her favorite video game, Sailor V, named for the superheroine who stars in it. Musing on her faults—she loves to eat, shop, and sleep, and is poor at punctuality, self-discipline, and study—Serena first runs into the new girl, Ami Mizuno, at school. Ami, who is not only a brain but so studious she even attends after-school *juku* (cram school), is as ideal a Japanese type as Serena is not. These polar opposites become friends nonetheless, as Serena invites Ami to the video arcade where, with her smarts, Ami becomes the champion of the Sailor V game despite having never played it before. As Ami runs off to her juku, she and Serena agree to call each other by their first names, thereby starting a friendship that will ground the *Sailor Moon* story to follow.

As the plot unfolds in subsequent episodes, Serena, Ami, and three other teenage girls discover they each have a celestial power which enables them to transform into, respectively, Sailor Moon, Sailor Mars, Sailor Mercury, Sailor Venus, and Sailor Jupiter. Together they form a team of *nakama* (friends) and *senshi* (Scouts) who hang out with, and also irritate, each other, and who transform when necessary in order to either save one of their party or collaborate in fighting the evil force known as the Negaverse. Bent upon destroying the human race, the Negaverse is ruled by Queen Beryl, who sends assistant "negaforces" to the earth where, disguised as humans, they work to uncover the sources of human energy and rechannel them into strengthening the Negaverse. To this end, negaforces search for concentrations of energy: the passion of romance in the Scout who is drawn to two boyfriends; exceptional talent such as the genius of a boy photographer and the expertise of a girl tennis player; and the jealousy, anger, and strife that continually erupt among the Scouts and threaten their harmony as a team. Persons

Figure 14.1 **The Sailor Scouts: (from left to right) Sailor Jupiter, Sailor Venus, Sailor Moon, Sailor Mars, and Sailor Mercury**

in such states of heightened emotion are invaded by a negaforce and transformed, changing their behavior and making them unsociable, self-centered, and aggressive. Once the transformation into evil reaches a certain stage, the negaforce exposes itself as a monster and throws off, or even eliminates, its human host.

By this time, one, if not several, of the Sailor Scouts have become involved. But this involvement, especially in Sailor Moon's case, is hardly the straightforward, linear outcome one would expect from a character who is always a superhero in waiting. Rather, Serena starts out the show in a decidedly unheroic mode, as her cat Luna derisively notes. Invariably Serena is obsessed with realizing some desire that both Luna and the watching negaforces view as a waste of energy: she decides to enter a modeling contest, becomes obsessed with exercising after gaining half a pound, or goes crazy over the boy who runs the video arcade. These obsessions preoccupy and distract her so much that she typically discounts the signs of imminent doom signaled by Luna or one of the more serious Scouts like Sailor Mercury (the transformed Ami) or Sailor Mars (the transformed Rae, a girl who in her human form lives in the Buddhist temple run by her grandfather and constantly comments on Serena's flakiness). Only when a negaforce has visibly emerged and acts of destruction are in progress, imperiling a friend or fellow Scout, does Serena regain her senses and initiate the transformation into serious superhero.

Shouting "Moon Prism Power!" she begins her morphing sequence, which, as for all Japanese superheroes, involves a number of ritualized steps. In a transformation that lasts about forty-five seconds and is accompanied by the morphing theme music, Serena's nails become red; her lashes grow long; jewelry decorates her neck and ears; red baubles appear in her hair and a tiara on her head; boots replace the shoes on her feet; and her body becomes first naked and then reclothed, starting with a sailor bodysuit and followed by a miniskirted sailor outfit with a plunging neckline that shows off her newly developed breasts.

Looking much more like a woman, and a sexy one at that, Sailor Moon becomes newly focused, powerful, and self-assured. She announces in a strong voice to her enemy, "I am Sailor Moon, champion of justice. I will right wrongs and fight evil." Luna, who is often looking on, remarks that she's impressed, but often adds to herself, "I wonder how long she can keep it up this time?" Predictably, Sailor Moon often stumbles, screaming in fear like a child and running away. Yet, she always recovers her superheroism and launches into battle, showing courage, determination, and bodily strength. Sailor Moon also activates other moon powers, for example by throwing her tiara which, with its "moon tiara magic," can knock out most foes (and sells in stores as an accessory for kids to use to pretend-morph themselves).

The Sailor Scouts frequently work together. In fact, in one episode, where Sailor Moon hopes to impress everyone by fighting an enemy single-handedly and winds up needing the help of the other Scouts, the moral of the story, spoken in three or four lines at the end of the show before the credits roll, is that we all must learn to work together rather than trying to resolve situations totally on our own. (This last touch, the announcement of the story's lesson at the end, is an American addition that began with *Power Rangers* in an attempt to counteract the charges of excessive violence.)[26]

Sailor Moon is sometimes assisted by Tuxedo Mask, a boy named Darian in "real" life, who, dressed in a tuxedo and flowing black cape, flies through the air and tends to advise Sailor Moon on what to avoid in an enemy or where to attack rather than taking control himself.[27] Sailor Moon swoons at the sight of Tuxedo Mask, whom she has a crush on and daydreams about marrying, but always acts on his advice, which means turning back to the enemy and eventually dismantling it. Tuxedo Mask has always vanished by the time she is done, but he leaves behind a single red rose—a trace, presumably, of both himself and his affection for Sailor Moon.

That Serena spends considerable time desiring to be desired, in a depiction that is both sympathetic and parodic, is an aspect of *Sailor Moon* that distinguishes this product from the typical male superhero series. Serena longs to be pretty and attractive; primps over her hair and makeup; diets; and mentally imagines herself in a wedding gown, though with the unconventional variation of having two grooms—Tuxedo Mask and the boy attendant at the video arcade. Luna is constantly exasperated by these indulgences and speaks of them as counter to the superheroic side and potential of her owner. Once she is transformed, Serena becomes not only powerful and tough, as well as altruistic and humanitarian—qualities assumed by male superheroes as well—but also a beautiful woman. In the episode about the genius photographer Peter, for example, Serena's crush on the boy is totally unrequited. Once she morphs into Sailor Moon, however, Peter becomes so smitten with the "beautiful princess" that he plans to start photographing "moonscapes." Even Serena's brother Sammy, who makes constant fun of his sister, idolizes Sailor Moon to the point of making a Sailor Moon doll to give to his doll-maker friend, Mika.

A girl's desire to be desirable—a mainstay of girls' shows in Japan and elsewhere, with their themes of romance and body consciousness—is not exactly dismantled in *Sailor Moon*. Nor is it totally endorsed. Rather, the show's creators have merged two features that have traditionally been kept fairly distinct: the masculinity of a fighter and the femininity of a romantic. As her amalgamated name *bishōjo senshi* (pretty soldier) implies, Sailor Moon is a warrior who retains, rather than revokes or transcends, her femaleness. She bridges traditional categories of feminine and masculine—Barbie doll female and tough-guy male—rearranging, if not radically transforming, what are often viewed as opposites. Sailor Moon is certainly marketed as both a new kind of superhero and a new kind of female. As a superhero, she is softer and more "human," one whose foibles are played up rather than down and, though criticized, are never curbed. Being a sweets addict, an oversleeper, and a lazy student does not prevent Serena from turning into a superhero, a fact, her marketers point out, that makes her more endearing and easier to identify with for the all-too-human children who watch the program.

As a female, Sailor Moon offers a model for girl (and boy) viewers that is positive and new; she and her friends, while concerned with fashion and romance—"Valley Girls," one American mother calls them, with some distress—are fundamentally happy, fulfilled, self-reliant, and strong. Bandai president Yamashina puts it this way:

> In Japan and all over the world, women are assuming more and more positions of power in society. They don't want to be discriminated against as soft or gentle; they want to grow up to be tough and powerful. Sailor Moon is a role model for this type of girl.[28]

Sailor Scouts on North American Soil

Female superheroes as a whole, and Sailor Moon in particular, have not achieved the level of success in the United States that they have in Japan, where girl heroes are now as common and popular as boy heroes. (*Sailor Moon*'s successor, which hit Japanese TV screens in 1997, was *Cutie Honey Flash*, featuring "average" teenager Honey Kisaragi, who, in fighting for justice, can morph into any of seven different Cutie Honey fighting heroines, each sexy looking and possessing her own unique evil-defeating or criminal-catching skills. Sound familiar?) Although Sailor Moon merchandise has done well in the United States—Sailor Moon dolls sold out quickly during the 1995 Christmas season—the animated television series was pulled off American airwaves after just a nine-month run in 1995–1996. (It subsequently returned on cable.) Some observers attribute this to the failure of DIC Entertainment and Bandai to aggressively market the product, citing the larger expenditures and fuller attention the companies gave to male superhero exports *Dragon Ball Z* and *Masked Rider* (both heavily advertised and broadcast on Saturday morning, kids' "prime time," and in the case of the live action show *Masked Rider* extensively "Americanized" along *Power Rangers* lines). A Mattel executive explained that underlying these marketing decisions is the idea that, in America, girls will watch male-oriented programming but boys won't watch female-oriented shows; this makes a male superhero a better bet.

A more fundamental reason for *Sailor Moon*'s lukewarm American reception may be that *Sailor Moon* is not, and was not altered to be, sufficiently "culturally appropriate," and that the linkage to the American psyche is therefore weak. University students to whom I showed

Sailor Moon at Duke University found Serena's premorph whining irritating and her postmorph sexiness retrograde, interfering with her potential as a New Age female hero. A number of younger American children, in the 7-to-12 age range the show targets, commented similarly that Sailor Moon seemed too "girlie" to be taken seriously as a superhero. It seems that girliness may be more of a detriment to the popularity of a female hero like Sailor Moon in the United States than in Japan, where numerous female heroes are popular precisely because they are both girlie and heroic.

If the failure of *Sailor Moon* to take off in the United States is indeed due not just to passive marketing but also to a mismatch with American views concerning how women "should be," and if these sentiments can be read as reflecting larger trends in North American culture, one can argue that the preferred model of superheroism (in both the fantasy and "real" realms) remains strongly masculine in the United States and strongly biased against a female hero, particularly one who behaves in a feminine or girlie manner. There is also an implicit message that even if a superhero is a girl, she is expected to act, and even look, like a boy, as the female Power Rangers do after morphing. This contrasts with the case in Japan where, instead of one dominant—male—model for heroism, there are two different hero models operating, one male and one female, though with increasing slippage or fusion between the two. Sailor Moon, with her combination of traditional masculine and feminine characteristics, is one example of such a fusion. Another is the popular manga and anime character Ranma 1/2, a boy who turns into a girl when splashed with cold water and back into a boy when splashed with warm water. (A boy originally, Ranma became the way he is—that is, "1/2"—when he fell into a magical spring while doing ascetic training in China.)

It is important to point out, however, that *Sailor Moon* has not been an unmitigated flop in the United States, and it should be noted that the show has been far more successful and long running in Canada. *Sailor Moon* has generated plenty of American fans, many of whom have spawned the Save Our Scouts (SOS) campaign fighting to bring her back to U.S. airwaves. She is a cult favorite among the growing legion of American fans of Japanese manga and anime generally. For many of the preteen girls I interviewed, Sailor Moon is very appealing precisely because she is a "different" kind of female, and feminine, superhero—a strong character who is "more like them" than boy heroes are. Many of these girls have also pointed out to me the absolute paucity of such female-oriented superstars in children's programs, as well as in popular culture more broadly, in the United States.

A More Human and Progressive Superhero

Sailor Moon is "different" as well when placed within the superhero tradition, and may bear the seeds of a significant shift in the meaning and structure of that long-running genre of popular culture. In his book *Super Heroes: A Modern Mythology*, Richard Reynolds states that the superhero is socially conservative, working to uphold standards of law and order that are consistent with the status quo. Traditionally, these superheroes have been males who transform into other, perfected, versions of the self, to battle otherworldly enemies whom they masterfully defeat. *Sailor Moon*'s mythic model is somewhat different. The self, in both human and superhero form, is far more flawed, and the battles, while pitched against enemies who are unambiguously bad, never definitively conclude and consume far less of the story line than do the interpersonal and everyday activities of the Sailor Scouts. The lines between human and hero, and between everyday life and battle, become blurred, and what is ultimately "saved" by the heroes is less a world of law and order than a society in which human interaction and friendship are treasured and valued.

In one show, for example, Ami has won a scholarship to study in Germany. As a model Japanese student who works hard, does well in school, and is academically ambitious, Ami doesn't think twice about accepting the offer despite the loss this will mean of friends and Scout activities. On the day of departure, however, Ami changes her mind, unable and unwilling to sacrifice her membership in and commitment to the Sailor Scouts for the personal goal of her academic career. In an age when Japanese children are facing intense pressure to perform at school and scholastic achievement has become the singular determinant of future careers, the message of this episode is refreshing, perhaps even radical.

Of course, this message will play differently in countries where values and conditions differ from those of Japan. Yet *Sailor Moon*'s rearrangement of the traditional superhero myth bears hints of not only a new social order, but also the kind of moral struggles, alliances, and identities that may create and accompany it.

Notes

1. Andrew Pollack, "Japan, a Superpower among Superheroes," *New York Times* (September 17, 1995), p. 32.

2. Richard Reynolds, *Super Heroes: A Modern Mythology* (Jackson, MS: University Press of Mississippi, 1992).

3. The author conducted research for this chapter both in Japan—studying academic and popular writings on superheroes, talking with children who watch *Sailor Moon* and *Go Rangers*, and interviewing Bandai executives in charge of marketing Sailor Moon toys—and in the United States—watching *Sailor Moon;* studying its marketing; following Internet fan club discussions of *Sailor Moon;* talking with children who like and dislike the show; and interviewing persons responsible for airing, translating, and marketing *Sailor Moon* in North America.

4. Les Daniels, *D.C. Comics: Sixty Years of the World's Favorite Comic Book Heroes* (Boston: Little, Brown, 1995), p. 21.

5. Frederik Schodt, *Manga! Manga! The World of Japanese Comics* (New York: Kodansha International, 1983), pp. 38–67.

6. Naomi Higuchi, *Terebi Hero no Sōzō* (Tokyo: Chikuma Shobō, 1993), pp. 9–13; *Heroes on Film* (November 1995), No. 2.

7. Higuchi, *Terebi Hero no Sōzō,* pp. 9–44; *Kaiju VOW* (Tokyo: Takarajimasha, 1994), pp. 32–35.

8. For a brief history of sentai shows that received limited circulation in the United States previous to *The Mighty Morphin Power Rangers*, see "A Look at the History of *Sentai*s in America," in *Heroes on Film*, 32–34.

9. Sumiko Kajiyama, "Sailor Moon Jōriku" (The Landing of Sailor Moon), *Asahi Shimbun Weekly Aera* 4:17 (1995), p. 46.

10. *Heroes on Film*, pp. 24–25, 33–34.

11. Jennifer Cody, "Power Rangers Take on the Whole World," *Wall Street Journal* (March 3, 1994), p. B1.

12. Ibid.

13. *Heroes on Film*, pp. 24, 34.

14. Studying the rapidly growing fandom in the United States among older youth (teenagers and young adults, overwhelmingly male) for Japanese anime and manga, Annalee Newitz found the Japaneseness of the product to be explicitly recognized and an important part of the appeal. Based on research conducted with fans on the Internet and at a University of California–Berkeley anime club, Newitz concludes that it is the very differences posed with American pop culture that make Japanese animation so appealing in America. This is despite, or perhaps because of, the fact that "these stories are critical of the fan's national culture as well as threatening to the fan's sense of his own (masculine) power" (Annalee Newitz, "Magical Girls and Atomic Bomb Sperm: Japanese Animation in America," *Film Quarterly* 49: 1 (1995), p. 12.

15. Cody, "Power Rangers," p. 1.

16. Ariel Dorfman and Armand Mattelart, *How to Read Donald Duck: Imperialist Ideology in the Disney Comic* (New York: International General, 1976).

17. Jose Manuel Tesoro, "Asia Says Japan Is Top of the Pops," *Asiaweek* (January 5, 1996), p. 36.

18. Ibid.

19. Trish Ledoux and Doug Ranney, *The Complete Anime Guide* (Issaquah, WA: Tiger Mountain, 1995), p. 3.

20. Ibid., p. 40.

21. *Heroes on Film*, pp. 32–34.

22. The viewing audience for the *Power Rangers* cuts across gender and age boundaries. Nielssen ratings for the summer of 1994 reported 57 percent of 6- to 11-year-old children tuned to television were watching the show, 40 percent of whom were girls. In addition, 29 percent of older children (teenagers and young adults) were also viewers (Michael Meyer and Dody Tsiantar, "Ninja Turtles, Eat Our Dust," *Newsweek* [August 8, 1994], pp. 34–35; Danny Biederman, "Those Mighty Saban Rangers Just Keep On Morphin," *Children's Business* [October 1994], p. 113).

23. Ellen Seiter, "Power Rangers at Preschool: Negotiating Media in Child Care Settings," *Kids' Media Culture*, ed. Marsha Kinder (Durham, NC: Duke University Press, 1999); and Ellen Seiter, personal communication with the author.

24. For a discussion of fantasy play in Japan, see Schodt, *Manga! Manga!* on manga; and my own work on the nightlife and corporate use of hostess clubs: Anne Allison, *Nightwork: Sexuality, Pleasure, and Corporate Masculinity in a Tokyo Hostess Club* (Chicago: University of Chicago Press, 1994); and Anne Allison, *Permitted and Prohibited Desires: Mothers, Comics, and Censorship in Japan* (Boulder, CO: Westview, 1996).

25. Kazuko Minomiya, "Onna no Kotachi no Risōkyō" (Girls' Utopia), *Kōei Cult Club, Bishōjo Hero Senki* (Tokyo: Kōei, 1994), p. 127.

26. *Power Rangers* concludes with one of the Rangers providing commentary such as "Hey, kids! Remember this is just pretend. Don't try this at home!"

27. Darian, it emerges later, is a reincarnated prince who lived centuries ago, at which time he was romantically involved with a princess, now reincarnated as Serena/Sailor Moon.

28. T. R. Reid, "Move Over, Morphins, Sailor Moon is Coming," *Washington Post* (July 22, 1995), p. 16.

15

Beauty Fighter "Sailor Chemist"

Yuka Kawada

The popularity of Japanese *manga*, both in Japan and abroad, has spawned not only a lucrative commercial industry but a huge amateur comics scene as well. In Japan there are said to be 50,000 manga "circles"—groups of amateur artists who create and publish their own works. Comics conventions, at which amateurs display and sell *dōjinshi* ("fanzines"), are held throughout the year; a large manga convention in Japan will have thousands of booths and can attract over 200,000 fans.[1] Amateur manga creation is on the rise overseas as well, with Internet home pages providing the outlet for many budding and accomplished artists.

Canadian high school student Yuka Kawada is a fervent manga reader and an aspiring artist with a foot in each of two worlds; born in Kagawa Prefecture in Japan, Yuka has lived in Canada since moving to Vancouver with her family at the age of 11. Yuka's "Beauty Fighter 'Sailor Chemist,'" a takeoff on *Sailor Moon* which was created as part of a school project, provides both an indication of *Sailor Moon*'s popularity in North America—none of Yuka's classmates had to be told what "Sailor Chemist" was based on—and a glimpse of the kind of talent that will produce the next generation of manga artists.

Note

1. For a detailed description of Japan's amateur manga scene, see Frederik L. Schodt, *Dreamland Japan: Writings on Modern Manga* (Berkeley, CA: Stone Bridge, 1996), pp. 36–43.

BEAUTY FIGHTER
SAILOR CHEMIST

Hey Thallium, have you started your project on 'Potassium' and 'Chromium?'
No, I don't even care about it now.
Argon
Thallium
PIKO
But it's due tomor...
I KNOWWW!! Don't remind me about it!
BOOOOOM
What the...

For those who need help in chemistry...
PIKO
I AM THE PRINCESS FROM THE PLANET OF CHEMISTRY..
FLAP
SAILOR CHEMIST PRINCESS INDERA!!
PERIODIC TABLE

.... aren't you Ms. Dodd?
Chup!
SHUT-UP!!

Let ME teach you about Chromium and Potassium.
Let's just stay calm and hope it's not Ms. Dodd.
Ha Ha Ha Ha Ha
CHEM QUEEN
PIKO

Alkali Metals
Periodic Table
Transitional Metals
19 K Potassium 39.098
24 Cr Chromium 51.996
Potassium was discovered on Oct. 6, 1807, in England by Sir Humphry Dary. Its name came from Potash. It is one of the Alkali metals. It has an atomic number of 19 and mass number of 39.098. Potassium nitrate is vital to plant growth. It is also used in detergents. BLAH BLAH BLAH BLAH...
Chromium was discovered by a French chemist Vaquelin in 1797. Its name came from a Greek word Chroma, which means color. It is considered one of the transitional metals. It has an atomic number of 24 and the mass number of 51.996 and can be used as stainless steel. Chromium melts at 1900°c and boils at 2690°C. BLAH BLAH BLAH...
uh... I think that's enough.. Princess Indera
K
Cr
K Cr
Chromium is a bluish-white metal that does not tarnish, is very resistan to corrosion. and takes a high polish
So the connected piece of solid potash to the poles of a batteries
used to before factare mistaken for It was carbonate often Sodium they came from but very different sources

..oh, I'm sorry, did I teach too much? You know, I really hope that you guys will do GREAT on the project. I'm sure that your teacher is expecting an 'A' from you guys.
an "A"!?
That was a great help Princess Indera♡
Well, then these books should help you guys instead of me.
Remember to read the research paper written by Kira and Yuka!. Good Luck!!
POOOF!

... in other words...
Do your own research.
Chemist
Congratulations everyone! You all got an 'A'!
...and no one knows that that 'Sailor Chemist' was me. Ha!

16

Doraemon Goes Abroad

Saya S. Shiraishi

Doraemon for Everyone

A fine sunny afternoon, and a 10-year-old boy comes home from school. Returning to his room on the second floor of his wooden house in a residential area in Tokyo, he suddenly bursts into tears—there in his room sits Doraemon, a large, bright blue robot cat whose ears are missing but who fully comprehends the trials and emotional crises of tender childhood. Doraemon's round hand immediately searches his front pocket for the fantastic high-tech gadgets that will most effectively help the boy deal with the harsh realities of everyday life.[1]

Thus begins *Doraemon*, the most popular comic and animation series in postwar Japan. Created by Hiroshi Fujimoto, writing under the pen name Fujiko F. Fujio, *Doraemon* first appeared in 1970 in the monthly children's magazine *CoroCoro Comic*. In 1978, TV Asahi began broadcasting an animated version which turned Doraemon, Nobita (the 10-year-old boy and Doraemon's "owner"), and the other main characters into full-fledged stars, known to virtually everyone in Japan. Throughout the 1980s, families with young children tuned in to watch *Doraemon* five evenings a week, catching the fifteen-minute episode shown at 6:45, just before the seven o'clock news. Theater animation followed the TV series, and movie houses featured full-length Doraemon films during the summer and winter school holidays. Videos, records, and cassette tapes were sold, as well as a flood of Doraemon "character merchandise," including toys, dolls, games, stickers, stationery, bags, desks and chairs, children's clothes, hats, shoes, boots, umbrellas, lunchboxes, dishes, snacks, calendars, bicycles, and entertainment facilities in playgrounds and amusement parks. The mass merchandising further stimulated sales of the comics, and by 1996 the forty-six-volume paperback series had sold over 100 million copies.[2]

Doraemon has become a virtual family member for many Japanese, and most children and young adults can quickly produce a sketch of the robot cat upon request. On February 10, 1995, three weeks after the Great Kansai Earthquake, a movie theater in Kobe showed a *Doraemon* movie free of charge to cheer up the children of the devastated city. Four hundred children came to see the robot cat and his friends that afternoon, and their jolly laughter filled the 200-seat theater.[3]

Doraemon is well known outside Japan as well. The television version has aired in Italy, China, Taiwan, Korea, Malaysia, Singapore, Indonesia, Thailand, Russia, Spain, Brazil and other Latin American countries, and the Middle East. *Doraemon* comic books, including pirate editions, are widely read internationally. *Doraemon* appeared in Vietnam in 1993 when a Vietnamese student studying in Bangkok discovered the comics there and liked them so much that he began translating them from Thai into Vietnamese and selling them in his home country. The series' subsequent popularity in Vietnam has forced that country's writers of children's books to rethink their craft and to create more imaginative works for kids instead of the moralizing and dogma-laced works they had previously been producing. In Cambodia, educators and parents have praised *Doraemon* for setting good examples of behavior, manners, love for parents, care for friends, and concern for the environment.[4] *Doraemon* is just the tip of the iceberg; similar stories involving other Japanese *manga* (comics) and animation are found from Asia to North America and Europe. More recently, the World Wide Web has helped accelerate the export of this form of Japan's popular culture, with hundreds of Web sites devoted to Japanese manga and animation series and characters.

The popularity of *Doraemon* and other Japanese "cultural" exports calls into question the often-expressed view that Japan has little influence or impact on the rest of the world other than in the fields of business and economics. At the end of the Cold War some observers were asking whether we were witnessing not just a shift in power but a partial transformation in the nature of power. Joseph Nye, for example, coined the term "soft power" to capture the growing importance of cultural factors in world politics. At the same time, however, Nye argued that Japan is a "one-dimensional" economic power marked by a cultural insularity that robs it of relevance for other societies.[5]

I contend that Japan's supposed insularity is less pronounced than Nye and others assume. This is particularly true in Asia, where the products of Japan's popular culture industries—manga and animation, television dramas, pop music—have achieved a position of high visibility, enthusiastic acceptance, and growing relevance and influence. In *The American Dream and the Popular Novel*, Elizabeth Long points out that best-sellers become best-sellers because they have found "resonance" with large segments of the population.[6] The success and presence of Japan's cultural exports in other countries is strong evidence that Japan's culture *does* have relevance for other societies. Something additional is necessary, however, for best-sellers in one country to become best-sellers overseas; they also need a vehicle with which to cross the political and cultural boundaries. This has been provided by Japan's cultural industries, in particular the "image alliances" formed among the producers of comics, animation, movies, and character merchandise, which see in the expanding markets of other Asian countries opportunities for market and profit growth. This chapter examines the roles that cultural resonance and the "image alliance" play in the spread and popularity of *Doraemon* and other Japanese manga and animation throughout Asia.

Doraemon's Resonance Abroad: A Republic of Children and Robots

There are many things to like about *Doraemon* and thus many reasons to expect that *Doraemon* might be popular not just in Japan but in other countries as well. The humor is first rate, and appeals to adults as well as children. School-age kids can relate to Nobita and his friends because they face the same troubles as real kids do: homework, parents and teachers who scold them, secret loves, mates who can be difficult to get along with. The *Doraemon* characters are extremely human: they possess both strengths and shortcomings, they can be in turn nice or mean, they have dreams and experience disappointments. Here, though, I will focus on two aspects of *Doraemon* that give it a particular relevance and appeal in Japan and other Asian countries: kids' empowerment and technological optimism.

Kids' Empowerment

Doraemon is one of many manga that share the theme of empowerment of children and youth. This characteristic can be traced back to Japan's most influential manga artist, Osamu Tezuka (1928–1989), the pioneer known as the *kami-sama* (god) of manga. Postwar children's manga began with Osamu Tezuka. Tezuka himself began drawing comics at a very young age and for more than forty years after the war produced one splendid and voluminous work after another. He also left behind a legacy of innovation, not only in drawing style but in manga production methods. He established the "production system," in which a team of assistants works with the principal artist; this made speedy quantity production possible, provided job security and on-site apprenticeship training, and laid the foundation for the postwar manga industry. Tezuka's enthusiasm and devotion are legendary, and accounts of his warm personal support for and inspirational influence on young comic artists fill the pages of biographies of the celebrated artists of today—Hiroshi Fujimoto, *Doraemon*'s creator, very much among them. Fujimoto and his long-time partner Motoo Abiko—until the mid-1980s these two artists worked under the common pen name Fujiko Fujio—were enticed into the world of comics by Tezuka's works, lived in Tezuka's old apartment, and were deeply influenced by Tezuka. Nobita's home address, "Tsuki-mi-dai [Moon-View-Heights], Nerima-ku, Tokyo" doubtless refers to Tezuka's residence/animation studio in "Fuji-mi-dai [Fuji-View-Heights], Nerima-ku, Tokyo," where *Tetsuwan Atom* (Mighty Atom) and other Tezuka manga classics were created.

Tezuka's manga were initially categorized as "children's manga" not because they were simple but because they were most eagerly accepted by young people, who embraced them as their medium for comprehension, expression, and communication. As the children grew up, manga accompanied them into adulthood, until "children's manga" have become manga for everyone, young and old. While the comics and their themes have evolved in many directions, the category "children's manga" has endured, and the concept and theme of childhood is continuously invoked. Manga like *Doraemon* constitute a "children's domain," inside which children's issues rule, and adult standards and expectations can be broken or ignored.

The boy in whose room Doraemon suddenly appears is named Nobi Nobita. The word *nobi nobi* expresses the way a young child grows up—free, healthy, and happy, unrestrained in any sense. That is precisely the ideal of "childhood" in contemporary Japan. Nobita's gang of friends includes Jaian (Giant), the neighborhood bully, who, though loud and quick to take out his frustrations on others with his fists, has a good

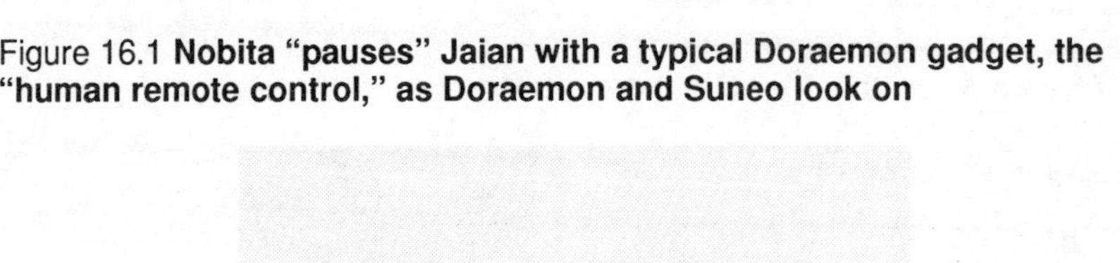

Figure 16.1 **Nobita "pauses" Jaian with a typical Doraemon gadget, the "human remote control," as Doraemon and Suneo look on**

heart; Suneo, the whiny and scheming rich kid who is Jaian's sidekick; and Shizuka, the girl Nobita and the other boys all have a crush on. The three boys, as Japanese pop culture critic Mark Schilling notes, "present a microcosm of Japan's class system, and illustrate the way those classes are perceived, with Suneo representing the arrogant, materialistic, self-centered upper-middle; Nobita the nice, ordinary but much-put-upon middle; and Jaian the impulsive, crude, but salt-of-the-earth lower-middle."[7]

The "children's domain" in Nobita's own household is his room, which is on the second floor of the house and, though connected by stairs, is separate from the first-floor space where Nobita's mother and father spend their time. His mother is a traditional Japanese housewife who stays home tending the family, and his father is a "salaryman" who goes off to work each morning and comes back in the evening to have dinner with his family, and is usually found reading the newspaper or watching TV when at home. This arrangement leaves Nobita's childhood world undisturbed.

Outside his window Nobita can see the blue sky where white clouds float by, and from his room Nobita and his friends use gadgets from Doraemon's fourth dimension pocket to explore and find adventure and

Figure 16.2 **Doraemon, Nobita, Jaian, Suneo, and Shizuka step through the "dokodemo door" into the heart of Africa**

trouble in a variety of outside worlds. For local travel they attach to their heads a "*take*-copter," a small hat with a helicopter blade made of *take* (bamboo) which enables them to fly from place to place.[8] To travel instantly to more distant places, they walk through the "*dokodemo*-door" (anywhere door), which opens to any location its user wishes. They can also travel to the past or future by using the time machine which Doraemon leaves parked inside Nobita's desk drawer. How many adults would love to have such devices at their disposal, to escape from crammed train cars during rush hour "hell," or to return to the past or visit the future?

Doraemon's wonderful gadgets are for children only, however. The child's room and this children's *manga* are privileged spaces in modern society, where kids can hang up a "No Adults Allowed" sign and dream dreams that transcend time and space and the concerns of adults. Fujimoto believes that his own personality has allowed him to create manga that are truly for kids: "You can't draw children's comics from the perspective of adults and try to create what you think the children will like," he says. "You have to create something you really enjoy, that they also happen to enjoy. You have to be at their eye-level, in other words, with their perspective. I guess I have a bit of the child in me that refuses to grow up, because I'm extraordinarily lucky in that what I like to draw, they like, too."[9]

It is not surprising that *Doraemon*, which legitimizes not only the existence of a "children's domain" but the freedom and power of children to rule that domain, has a strong appeal in contemporary Asia. Doraemon and his pocket, handier and more effective than a Sears catalog in producing gadgets perfectly suited to Nobita's personal needs, are a consumer's dream in a region of consumer societies. For Asia's young people, who in real life face pressures to conform and to excel academically, the children's domain offered by Doraemon is a welcome respite. It offers, as Schilling writes, a "breath of freedom and a glimpse of a funnier, friendlier world where all dreams, even foolish ones, can come true."[10]

Technological Optimism

Through the sky to the distant stars
Goes Atom, as far as his jets will take him.
The oh-so-gentle child of science
With one hundred thousand horsepower,
It's Mighty Atom.

Listen carefully and watch out
That's right, Atom, be on your guard.
The pure-hearted child of science
With his seven powers,
There goes Mighty Atom.

On the street corner or at the bottom of the sea
There's Atom again, protecting mankind.
The oh-so-cheerful child of science
Everyone's friend,
Mighty Atom.[11]

Although *Doraemon*'s Nobita has his own room, his own "child's domain," this does not mean that his life is easy. This happy, easygoing, and thoroughly undisciplined child nevertheless faces many daily problems: he is doing poorly in school, is hopeless at sports, is routinely bullied by shrewder or stronger children in the neighborhood, is constantly scolded by his mother for not doing his homework or keeping his room clean, and is never very successful in winning Shizuka's heart. The tool made available to Nobita to combat these problems is technology, in the form of Doraemon, the robot cat powered by a nuclear reactor in his chest, and the many high-tech gadgets Doraemon produces from his magic pocket.

Japan's first atomic-powered robot hero was *Tetsuwan* (or "Mighty" Atom). Atom was created by Tezuka in 1951, just six years after the atomic bombs were dropped on Hiroshima and Nagasaki,[12] and became so popular in Japan that by 1981 over 100 million copies of Mighty Atom comics had been sold.[13] With Mighty Atom's theme song (above), the popular imagery of robot as reliable friend emerged to heal postwar Japan's wounded confidence in science and technology. But how could "atom" become the name of a friend who protects mankind, in the only country in the world to experience firsthand the horrible consequences of an atomic bombing?

Czech writer Karel Capek coined the word "robot" from a Czech word, *robota*, in his 1920 play, *R.U.R.* (Rossum's Universal Robots). In post-World War I Europe, this play created a sensation, and the metal men have since starred in hundreds of novels, plays, and films. The plots are generally quite similar to the original, which Schodt summarizes as: "Men mass produce artificial slaves, or robots, to take over their work and later to wage war as well; the robots, of high intelligence, decide not to kill each other, and instead slaughter their masters, the humans."[14] *R.U.R.* was staged in Tokyo in 1924 but did not gain popularity as it did in the West. The theme "Man makes robots, robots kill man" held little appeal for Japanese and did not take root.[15] In the Japanese mind, robots with humanoid forms embodying advanced technology were not, by themselves, that interesting. What *did* interest Japanese was the relation of robots and technology to humankind. When Tezuka created the robot hero Mighty Atom, "robots" became what they still are to the Japanese: reliable friends of people, and especially of children.

In the story, a leading scientist builds Mighty Atom as a replacement for his own son who has died in a traffic accident. His creation is an incredibly strong, atomic-powered superrobot with the body of a young boy and sensitive, innocent eyes. When the father discovers that his robot son will never grow up, he sells Atom to a circus. Thus, like postwar youths in Japan, the orphaned Atom is freed of the past and of traditional familial authority. He is born of the marriage between advanced technology and dreams of the future.

Tezuka, who had read *R.U.R.* and personally witnessed the destructive effects of modern warfare—when he was a medical student after the war, most of the patients he treated were suffering from malnutrition—originally conceived Atom's character as a cynical parody of science and technology. But, as Schodt explains, "publishers, the public, and the times pushed him to a more romantic depiction of the future, and as is often the case his character took on a life of its own. 'In the days after the war,' says Tezuka, 'the publishers wanted me to stress a peaceful future, where Japanese science and technology were advanced and nuclear power was used for peaceful purposes.'"[16] Thus, contrary to his original intention, Tezuka created the image of a friendly technology which helps men, women, and children to attain a peaceful and prosperous life.

Such a view of technology struck a chord in postwar Japan. Schodt writes, whereas "the carnage wrought by technology in World War II had deepened distrust of it among many intellectuals in the West, in Japan it had a decidedly different effect."[17] The disastrous war between humans and technology had already happened in Japan with the atomic bombs, but in the West the worst had "yet to happen." What Tezuka did was create a "day-after" scenario in which scientific knowledge and technology would be trustworthy partners in rebuilding the land. *Tetsuwan Atom* begins with the destruction of the earth and is the story of subsequent human efforts to rebuild society on a new planet and of Atom's role in bringing peace to the new world. The central theme is that the awesome power of the atom can be a friend to a human with a pure heart. Robots in Tezuka's story become harmful to people only when they are controlled by men of evil intent or when they are not made with precision. These ideas are expressed in Tezuka's "Principles of Robot Law," which state: "Robots are created to serve mankind," and "Robots shall never injure or kill humans." The tricky part is that robots can only fully obey their law when they are freed from their creators, men, who are prone to make mistakes. "All robots have the right to live free and equal," reads another Principle. This was a declaration of the republic of children and robots, where the future is no longer shaped by the past, and where the image of a bright and peaceful future guides and defines the present.

In both *Tetsuwan Atom* and *Doraemon*, science and technology are intimately associated with children. Atom and Doraemon, both nuclear-powered, are symbols of the confidence and hope people place in technology as the trustee of the future of their children. Technology, which once caused total devastation, is purified by its association with and use by an innocent child, and children are conceptually empowered as those who are responsible for befriending and advancing science and technology.

Nobita has his great-great-grandson, who lives in the future world of the twenty-second century, to thank for his access to technology from Doraemon's pocket. Nobita's descendent and benefactor knows all about his great-great-grandfather's (i.e., Nobita's) childhood trials and crises, and sends—or should I say "will send?"—his own toy robot, Doraemon, to be Nobita's full-time, live-in tutor, guardian, and friend. Doraemon also understands Nobita's frustrations and pains, and endeavors to relieve them with the aid of the high-tech gadgets he pulls from his pocket. This is user-friendly technology at its finest. Most of Doraemon's gadgets are portable; have no intrinsic weight; readily expand or shrink as needed; rarely break down; and easily transcend time, space, gravity, energy, and volume. They are an impressive testimony to the standards of quality control and innovation that exist in the twenty-second century.

TV audiences and comic book readers must love these gadgets because there is now an encyclopedia dedicated to them which lists and explains over a thousand of Doraemon's devices.[18] The best-known is the *take*-copter, which, according to the encyclopedia, Nobita and his friends have used 214 times. Second in popularity is the time machine (which has appeared 97 times), and third is the anywhere door (68 times). Other frequently employed gadgets are the small light and big light, which shrink or enlarge whatever they are shined on; Momotarō brand *kibidango* (rice cakes), which when given to wild animals cause them to become tame and friendly; and the *kisekae* (dress-up) camera, which enables its holder to instantly clothe people in different outfits simply by aiming and shooting.

While these gadgets are a vital feature of the series, it is Doraemon who occupies the central position in the story. Though Doraemon is himself a high-tech product, he possesses an endearing personality that captivates young audiences. He is both a full member of Nobita's family and an intimate friend to Nobita and his companions. Portrayed in this way, Doraemon represents the optimistic view of the relationship between technology and humanity. At the same time, Nobita exemplifies man as master of technology, secure in the view that technology brings benefits to man, not fear, enslavement, or harm. Nobita, it turns out, is a vigorous experimentalist with an imaginative mind. Whenever Doraemon produces a high-tech toy to solve Nobita's latest problem, Nobita cheerfully experiments with it to find a new application not intended by its designer or by Doraemon. These experiments generally result in mishaps. The story "Human Remote Control," shown in Figure 16.1, is typical. In response to Nobita's complaints that he has too much homework, Doraemon produces from his pocket the "human remote control," and "fast-forwards" Nobita through his homework in an instant. Nobita then uses the device to his further benefit, "fast-forwarding" himself out of the path of Jaian's punches (causing Jaian to smash into a telephone pole and a wall) and "rewinding" Suneo to catch him in a lie. In the end, Nobita accidentally "pauses" himself while running to show Shizuka the new toy; as a result, he loses the chance to impress Shizuka and ends up not getting home until after dark, which earns him a one-hour scolding from his mother. Still, optimistic, good-natured Nobita never loses his curiosity, and his mettle is as much a source of the comic's charm as are its breathtakingly fresh ideas for high-tech products. Nobita's fearless and playful engagement with technology, in fact, makes the entire structure of the story persuasive, for it is this curiosity and the free and creative mind of a child that will eventually produce the fabulous high-tech products that Doraemon brings back from the future.

Television Animation, Character Merchandising, and the Image Alliance

In Japan, artistic creativity and innovation in one popular medium quickly expand to other media, thanks to a web of "image alliances" among producers of the print media, television, movies, and character merchandise. Mutually beneficial relationships among these "divisions" of Japan's cultural industries not only work to increase the size and earnings of those industries, they also provide a vehicle for the spread of Japan's popular culture to other Asian countries.

Television broadcasting began in Japan in 1956 when the public network NHK and private network TBS went on the air, followed soon after by Nihon TV (1957), Fuji TV (1959), and TV Asahi (1959). American cartoons such as *Popeye*, *Mighty Mouse*, and *Woody Woodpecker* were televised beginning in 1959, introducing Japanese audiences to animated cartoon TV shows. Japan's first animation production company, Tōei Animation, was set up in 1956 to produce animation movies for theaters. Osamu Tezuka, a big fan of Walt Disney's animated movies,[19] participated in Tōei's early productions.

In 1962, Tezuka established his own animation studio, Mushi (Beetle)

Production, and in January of the next year—when the number of television sets in Japan had reached fifteen million—*Tetsuwan Atom* was broadcast by Nihon TV as the first Japanese TV animation series. Animation is an extremely labor-intensive industry; producing a half-hour animated cartoon takes forty-five days for forty people working full time. In the early 1960s, imported American cartoons, which were sold to a worldwide market, cost only a little over ¥100,000 yen per thirty-minute program, while it cost more than ¥1,000,000 to produce thirty minutes of animation in Japan. The ¥550,000 per episode that Meiji Confectionery Company initially paid to sponsor *Tetsuwan Atom* did not even cover Mushi's production costs.[20]

At Mushi Production, Tezuka implemented several procedures to cut costs. For a half-hour program, only 3,000 to 4,300 pictures were used. Tezuka's "bank system" further simplified the process; several kinds of mouths, eyes, noses, and arms were prepared and, when possible, only these parts were exchanged instead of drawing entirely new figures. While Disney used 200 colors, Mushi made do with only 80. Tezuka wanted his products to be enjoyed by many, even if he had to sacrifice quality at the beginning.[21] Still, animation costs were high and other means to generate profit from the images were sought.

It was noticed that, after *Tetsuwan Atom* went on the air, sales of the comic books went up. This demonstrated a synergistic effect whereby exposure to televised animation entices a wider population into the printed visual narration, and vice versa. Today, the close relationship between the popularity of a TV animation and the sale of its comic books is well understood and has given rise to close cooperation between publishers and television companies.

Tezuka raised money to meet the costs of animation production by selling licenses to use his animation characters on merchandise. Four hundred merchandise contracts were signed for *Tetsuwan Atom*, putting the boy robot's image on stationary, toys, sporting goods, clothes, foods, electronic products, and many other items. Mushi Productions received ¥3,000,000 for each license.

Another piece to the image alliance fell into place in 1965 when Fujiko Fujio's manga *Obake no Q-Tarō* (Q-Tarō the Ghost), called "Oba-Q" for short, was made into an animated television series. Children were enraptured by the endearing ghost, and Oba-Q's television sponsor, Fujiya, saw its chocolate sales quickly catch up with and surpass those of its rivals, Morinaga and Meiji. This demonstrated the profound effect that a popular children's cartoon show could have on the sale of its sponsor's products. Oba-Q comic book sales also exploded after Oba-Q appeared on TV, and when the publisher built a new ten-story office building in Tokyo, it was promptly called the "Oba-Q Building."[22] Through experiences such as these, the advantage of linking televised animation, comic books, character merchandising, and product sponsorship became clear, and the "image alliance" was cemented. As Schodt explains, "the typical pattern is for a popular story first serialized in a comic magazine to be compiled into books and sold as a paperback series, then made into an animated television series, and, if still popular, finally made into an animated feature for theatrical release. . . . Animation stimulates further sales of magazines, reprints of comic paperbacks, and massive merchandising."[23] Merchandising increases the visibility of the story's characters in daily life, which in turn further boosts the TV program ratings and comic book sales.

It is also possible for merchandising to initiate the entire process. In 1986, Lotte Confectionery Company's Planning Division devised a series of illustrated cards that were to be wrapped inside the packages of a new product, "Bikkuri-Man Chocolate." Comic artists were enlisted to draw the original "Bikkuri-Man" (Flabbergasted Man) characters for the cards, but there was no story. Children were intrigued by the mysterious characters, however, and began competing to collect all the characters of the series as if to decipher a hidden story. Lotte kept adding to the number of characters and the children kept collecting them. By 1989, more than 500 Bikkuri-Man character images had been created, and annual sales of the thirty-yen chocolate reached ¥5 billion (around $40 million in U.S. dollars). Forged images were even discovered being sold to children, without the chocolates.

Lotte's Planning Division, itself showing no sign of being flabbergasted, coolly arranged for its artists to make up stories for the Bikkuri-Man characters, and in 1988 *CoroCoro Comic* began printing serialized Bikkuri-Man stories. At one point in 1988, Bikkuri-Man's popularity exceeded Doraemon's. That summer, the publisher released a "Bikkuri-Man" special issue, and its 200,000 copies sold out in just one day. Soon after, a television animation version was produced, and its rating exceeded 20 percent. Finally a Bikkuri-Man video game was developed.[24]

The beauty of the image alliance is that each partner helps promote the others. The image is the central component of the alliance, and the copyright to the image is shared by the original artist, the publisher, and the television company. As character images circulate, in print, animation, and merchandise form, demand for the products of all members of the alliance grows. This in turn enhances the value and the revenue-generating potential of the copyright. The result of all this is a larger profit pie for all participants in the alliance to share in.

Ironically, although Osamu Tezuka played a leading role in creating the image alliance and thereby making the manga and animation industries more viable, Tezuka's own company was a victim of the industry's evolution. In the early the 1970s, the oil crisis prompted a restructuring of many industries in Japan. Television stations were forced to cut costs by laying off employees, many of whom set up their own small independent program production houses. Tōei Animation followed suit, and a number of small animation companies sprouted. Mushi Productions went bankrupt in 1973, for Tezuka could not bring himself to fire his assistants.

Doraemon and the Image Alliance in Asia

It was to reduce production costs that Japan's animation industry first branched out into Asia. In 1980, animation studios were set up in Seoul and Taipei, and by the middle of the 1980s, 50 percent of all animation programs broadcast in Japan were being made overseas, where artistic talent was available at lower wages than in Japan. However, like Japan's world-famous automobile and electronics makers, the image alliance viewed other Asian countries not just as low-cost production sites but as growing, and potentially huge, markets for their products.

Television and Animation Come to Indonesia

Television got its start in Indonesia in 1962 (the same year that Osamu Tezuka set up Mushi Productions in Tokyo) when the country's national television company TVRI (Televisi Republik Indonesia) began transmission. In the mid-1970s, the Indonesian government required every village to have at least one television set and requested that villagers watch the news and cultural events; as a result, electric generators spread television to many villages ahead of electrification. In 1989, Indonesia had approximately six million registered TV sets, about one for every thirty-three persons. By 1990, TVRI's 13 regional stations, 350 transmission facilities, and 6,000 employees covered 40 percent of the nation's land and 70 percent of its population.

Indonesia's commercial television age began after a controversial deregulation in the late 1980s, and today five privately run TV stations have national broadcast licenses. Thanks to satellite dishes, many people in the archipelago have access to foreign network broadcasts as well, including CNN, ESPN, Star TV, HBO, and Discovery.

American comics such as *Superman* were introduced to Indonesia during the 1950s, and it became common for affluent parents to buy translations of Disney picture books for their children. With television deregulation, however, Japanese programming began to be shown, and it quickly took root.[25] Japanese children's animation and comics are generally regarded as suitable and educational for children; a local Muslim leader has said that he allows his children to watch only the national news and Japanese children's animation.

When I visited Indonesia in the early 1990s, *Doraemon* had been on the air for two years and the blue robot cat was already a highly popular and intimately familiar figure. One Sunday morning at 8:00 A.M., I witnessed a friend's 5-year-old son turn on the TV set precisely when *Doraemon*, dubbed into Bahasa Indonesian, started. He watched it, engrossed, for half an hour (two episodes), and as soon as it was over, he switched the set off and began to play video games. Only *Doraemon* could compete with the video games! My friend, who formerly enjoyed sleeping in on Sundays, now gets up to watch *Doraemon* with his son. He has also bought him Doraemon character toys for his birthday. An Indonesian cabinet minister confesses that he watches *Doraemon* every Sunday, and when he cannot, he asks his wife to videotape the day's episodes for him. In 1994, the first survey on children's television programs in Indonesia was conducted, and *Doraemon* ranked first in all four areas surveyed—Jakarta, Medan, Surabaya, and Semarang.

Soon after television broadcasts of *Doraemon* began, locally drawn comic booklets began appearing on the streets. Street-corner bookstands and hawkers sold these palm-size, one-episode, "pirated" editions of *Doraemon* comics at prices affordable even for children: 200-400 rupiah (10-20 cents) each. The tissue paper booklets were produced by teenage boys, and are reminiscent of the early postwar days of Japan's incipient manga industry. Japanese publishers took no direct action against the Indonesian pirated comics at the beginning. When interviewed, they explained that with Japan's domestic market so large, and the overseas pirates' businesses so minuscule, they could afford to wait and see how the situation developed. After all, narrative comics had taken root in postwar Japan in a similar fashion. Their insight proved to be correct. Thanks to the pirates' ingenuity and risk taking, handmade *Doraemon* comics spread until local publishing houses decided to join the party. They struck legal deals with Japanese publishers and began selling better-quality, copyrighted Tento-Mushi Series *Doraemon* paperbacks for 3,300 rupiah (about $1.50) through their bookstore chains. Once the market had developed to this level, the legal Indonesian publishers found it in their interest to enforce the copyright against the pirate peddlers on the streets, and the pirated editions quickly disappeared. (In fact, Indonesian publishers have asked the Japanese publishers to pay more attention to the copyright issue.)

Today in Indonesia, Elex Media Komputindo, a subsidiary of Gramedia, Indonesia's largest publishing group and bookstore chain, publishes *Doraemon* in press runs of 40,000 copies per volume. By 1996 this company had already translated and published more than 400 Japanese manga titles, and was selling Doraemon and other manga figure merchandise through its Character Merchandising Division (created in 1994). In this way, *Doraemon* has helped establish an image alliance in Indonesia similar to those in Japan. *Candy Candy*, *Sailor Moon*, *Dragon Ball,* and other popular Japanese manga and animation series have followed suit, and products adorned by their character images crowd the shelves in the first-generation shopping malls that are springing up in Indonesia's cities.

Other Asian Markets

In other Asian countries, as in Indonesia, economic growth has given birth to a consumer class living modern, urban lifestyles that increasingly resemble those portrayed in Japanese manga and animation. Many prevalent themes, including children's empowerment and technological optimism, find rich soil in Asia's developing countries as well. Children in the region are generally better educated than their parents, and they are expected to lead the national march into a prosperous future. In such a setting, manga's dream of a high-tech society built by the young generation finds strong resonance and support. Equally important, the market infrastructure which is required for an image alliance to take root and function efficiently—large-scale publishing companies, bookstore chains, television, shopping malls—is increasingly in place in Asia's growing economies.

Taiwan has already become a full member of the manga club—the term manga is commonly used in Taiwan—with its own artists, comic magazines, and paperback series. *Doraemon* has been in Taiwan since the late 1970s, when it arrived in both manga and animation form. A Taiwanese man in his early thirties recalls that *Doraemon* was quite popular from the time he was a teenager, and that a great variety of Japanese manga were already available in Taiwan at that time. *Doraemon* peaked in popularity around 1990, and today is just one of many Japanese cartoon shows broadcast daily in Taiwan, not only on the two channels devoted to Japanese programming but on other channels as well. Many of these series are backed up with comic books, videos, calendars, stationary, plastic warriors, weapons, and other toys.

Today, most *Doraemon* comics sold in Taiwan bear the marks of the companies licensed to distribute them, but clearly illegal copies of Japanese originals and some Taiwanese imitations are still found, remnants of earlier years when copyrights were not enforced. One storekeeper complained that the imposition of General Agreement on Tariffs and Trade (GATT) restrictions drove illicit manga off the market, leaving only the much higher-priced legal manga. Publisher Dong Li once produced many *Doraemon* manga, but stopped in the early 1990s when copyright became an issue. Other companies continue to publish *Doraemon*, even without copyright permissions. A manager of one of these explained that some of the drawings and stories are copied from the Japanese, while others are originals created in Taiwan.

Doraemon has played an important role in helping train aspiring manga artists in Taiwan. Before the publication rights were licensed to Taiwanese manga publishers Ching Wen and Da Ran, many local artists specialized in drawing *Doraemon*. For some, *Doraemon* was a springboard from which they went on to other projects. "No artists draw *Doraemon* now," explains a Ching Wen staff member, "they all do their own comics." Japanese publishers are themselves helping support the development of local artists. Shūeisha, publisher of Japan's top-selling manga weekly *Shōnen Jump*, has licensed two Taiwanese companies to publish *Shōnen Jump* in Taiwan with the stipulation that "more than forty percent of their pages have to be reserved for young local artists."[26] Talented artists are the most precious asset in the manga business, and for Japan's manga industry, which has a bottomless appetite for new visions and voices, Asian artists are a promising source of talent. Japanese publishing giant Kōdansha has introduced comics by overseas artists in its weekly manga, *Shūkan Morning*, and in 1990 the "Association of Southeast Asian Nations (ASEAN) Manga Artists Exhibition" was held in Tokyo.

China, Asia's largest potential market, has shown a special receptivity to Japanese comics and animation that encourage children to aspire to careers in science and technology. In 1980, the *Tetsuwan Atom* series became the first foreign animated TV series broadcast in China. Publication of the comics by Science Promotion Publisher accompanied the TV show, and *Doraemon* has followed close behind. In China, where a printing of 20,000 copies is considered average for a comic book, 900,000 copies of *Doraemon* manga were sold in a three-year period in the 1990s. The TV series has become a nationwide hit as well, and Doraemon merchandise is sold in stores, including state-run outlets, all over the country.

Difficulties in the United States

While Japanese comics and animation have captured a broad and enthusiastic market in Asia, their forays into Western markets, where they face greater cultural barriers, have produced mixed results. Western Europe has been relatively receptive. In Italy, for example, Yumiko Iigarashi's *Candy Candy* has become a favorite. Television broadcasts spawned publication of deluxe hardbound comic books, rescripted, redrawn, and colored by local artists, and when the Japanese series ended, local artists drew Italian sequels to meet continuing demand. The Italian *Candy Candy* boom has been accompanied as well by the usual heavy merchandising of stationery, toys, and recordings of the theme song. In France, which has both a thriving industry in comics for grown-ups and its own indigenous form of artistically respected comic books, the beautifully produced *bandes déssinées*, Japanese manga and animation have built a broad fan base. The existence of numerous comics and animation retailers—particularly in the Bastille area of Paris—provides a ready-made distribution system for Japanese manga and animation in France. Some are in Japanese while others are translated into French.[27]

The United States, by contrast, has proved to be less fertile ground. While a few Japanese animation series have done well in the United States—*Sailor Moon*, for example, has been extremely popular with school-age girls—and although manga and animation fan clubs are popping up by the dozens on college campuses and the Internet, the level of acceptance and the size of the market remain minuscule compared to those in Asian countries. Several reasons can be given for this. America has its own history and style of comics, and has had no Tezuka to stage a manga revolution to develop comics into the rich and diverse expressive medium it has become in Japan. There are differences between Japanese and American comic traditions in language and format conventions—left-to-right versus right-to-left reading progression, the use of sound effects and thought balloons, color versus black-and-white—which make the translation and successful marketing of Japanese manga in the United States far from easy.[28] Existing American comic distribution channels and outlets are not set up to handle thick Japanese-style comic books, and more broadly, comics in America have never achieved the place in American "image alliances" that they have in Japan. In Japan comics started the image alliance; in the United States the image alliance includes movies, animation, and character merchandising, but comics play virtually no role. Historically, there has been little need for comics to be a major medium of expression in the United States, as this role was more than adequately played by America's well-developed pop music, Hollywood movie, and television industries.

The difficulty of selling Japanese comics in the American market was demonstrated by the case of *Hadashi no Gen* (Barefoot Gen), the antiwar classic written by Keiji Nakazawa (see chapter 8). Nakazawa was a victim of the atomic bombing of Hiroshima, an event that he personally experienced and that claimed the lives of his father, brother, and sister. In the late 1970s, a nonprofit peace group in Tokyo published an English edition of Nakazawa's 1,400-page manga novel and sent copies around the world. In the United States, a San Francisco underground publisher cut the lengthy narrative into several "normal-sized" comic books, but it did not sell well. Lack of "manga literacy" and familiarity with the novel-length manga format was no doubt one reason. Another was the intervention of America's Comics Code, which was enacted in the 1950s in response to political and social pressures and which, in Schodt's words, nearly "sanitized [U.S. comics] to death."[29] The Comics Code Authority considered *Gen*'s day-after scenes "too graphically violent"; it was one thing, apparently, to drop the bomb and have children go through the experience, but another to allow an eyewitness's visual narration of the tragedy to circulate.[30] Perhaps the Authority felt that *Gen* did not present "qualities of fineness and permanence" or "experiences worth reliving," values that have been established in American literary circles for children's literature, though the strong antiwar theme of *Gen* and the integrity, bravery, and charm of its characters make such an argument seem absurd. On the other hand, American adults normally do not read "children's" accounts, which is how *Gen*'s narrative is scripted. The line between literature for adults and that for children is clearer in the United States than it is in postwar Japan, a fact noted by *Shōnen Jump* editor Kazuhiko Torishima, who has stated: "I feel sorry for U.S. children who live in a Disney-filtered world."[31]

Japanese cartoon programs have also run into problems in America. They are often categorized as "animation for small children" and censored under the Broadcasting Code, which is even more stringent than the Comics Code.[32] Ironically, animation with conspicuous violence, a relatively unpopular genre in Japan,[33] has found a smoother road into the American market because these products are categorized as "not for children." *Doraemon* has never been broadcast in the United States.

Conclusion

Postwar Japanese comics originated as a children's medium—a forum in which children could sing the themes of frustration, rebellion, optimism, and hope. They constituted a children's domain, where there was respite from the pressures of school and the concerns and rules of the adult world; in the case of *Tetsuwan Atom*, *Doraemon*, and many others, there was freedom from the laws of physics as well. As early readers have matured, manga have grown with them to become a pop culture genre for everyone, young and old. Along the way, image alliances developed to support the artistic side of the industry and to multiply and maximize the various forms of profit that manga generate either directly or indirectly. When Doraemon has gone abroad, he has been most successful where resonance with local values and lifestyles has created the "pull" of local demand, and where image alliances similar to those in Japan have formed to "push" the product. This has happened most strongly in Asia. Where resonance, demand, and industry support are weaker, as in the United States, Doraemon and other Japanese manga characters have faced a bumpier road.

Just as Hollywood films have helped disseminate the idea of the American way of life to the rest of the world, Japanese comics and TV animation are now spreading Japanese ideas about childhood, war and peace, science and technology, and the future world. Today in Asia, Disney cartoons are what parents tend to buy for their children. But

Japanese comic books, animation videos, video games, and character merchandise are what children ask their parents to buy for them, or what children buy with their own money. In doing this they are practicing and verifying the notion frequently found in manga that the children are the pioneers of the future and are capable of deciding what they want and getting it for themselves.

The popularity of Japanese manga and animation does not necessarily mean that the hegemony of American popular culture is being undermined or that the idea of the American way of life has lost its luster. Rather, a new brand has been added to the world's pop culture menu, giving the world's citizens a much expanded range of characters, stories, values, and mental universes to enjoy and learn from.

Notes

1. This chapter has been adapted, with permission, from Saya S. Shiraishi, "Japan's Soft Power: Doraemon Goes Overseas," in *Network Power: Japan and Asia*, ed. Peter J. Katzenstein and Takashi Shiraishi (Ithaca, NY: Cornell University Press, 1997), pp. 234–272. All changes to the original material are the sole responsibility of Tim Craig.

2. These figures are for the Tento-Mushi Series alone. There are other paperbacks as well, some produced by other artists, such as "study comics" in which Doraemon teaches mathematics and science. This diversity makes it impossible to count them all.

3. *Nihon Keizai Shimbun* (February 11, 1995).

4. Yojana Sharma, "If You Can't Beat 'Em . . . ," *Nation* (May 7, 1997), p. C1.

5. Joseph S. Nye Jr., *Bound to Lead: The Changing Nature of American Power* (New York: Basic Books, 1990), pp. 166–169, 188.

6. Elizabeth Long, *The American Dream and the Popular Novel* (Boston: Routledge and Kegan Paul, 1985).

7. Mark Schilling, *The Encyclopedia of Japanese Pop Culture* (New York: Weatherhill, 1997), p. 42.

8. The take-copter enables its user to fly through a combination of antigravity and the effective use of wind. The direction and speed can be controlled "as wished," that is, by brain waves. The maximum speed is 80 km per hour, and it must be recharged after eight hours of continuous use. It can be unstable in strong winds. Setagaya Doraemon Kenkyū-Kai, *Doraemon Kenkyū Kanzen Jiten* (The Complete Encyclopedia of Doraemon Studies) (Tokyo: Data House, 1994).

9. Quoted in Frederik L. Schodt, *Dreamland Japan: Writings on Modern Manga* (Berkeley, CA: Stone Bridge, 1996), pp. 219–220.

10. Schilling, *Encyclopedia*, pp. 44–45.

11. Music by Tatsuo Takai, lyrics by Shuntaro Tanikawa, translated by Frederik L. Schodt. In Frederik L. Schodt, *Inside the Robot Kingdom* (New York: Kodansha International, 1988), p. 79.

12. Ironically, Mighty Atom's name was changed to "Astro Boy" in the U.S. version, to downplay the atomic connection for American viewers.

13. Usaku Fujishima, *Sengo Manga Minzoku-shi* (Tokyo: Kawai Shuppan, 1990), p. 328.

14. Schodt, *Robot Kingdom*, pp. 29–30.

15. Ibid., p. 73.

16. Ibid., p. 76.

17. Ibid., p. 77.

18. Setagaya Doraemon Kenkyū-Kai, *Doraemon Kenkyū Kanzen.*

19. Tezuka is reported to have seen *Bambi* over eighty times and *Snow White* fifty times (Fujishima, *Sengo Manga*, p. 120).

20. For the costs of TV animation, see Fujishima, *Sengo Manga*, pp. 110–123, 224–249.

21. Today, Japan's animation industry is the world's largest, and Tōei Animation uses as many colors as it pleases. The 1994 two-hour hit animated movie *Heisei Tanuki Gassen: Ponpoko,* by Studio Ghibli, used 502 colors and 82,289 cells.

22. Frederik Schodt, *Manga! Manga! The World of Japanese Comics* (New York: Kodansha America, 1983), p. 145.

23. Ibid., p. 146.

24. For the Bikkuri-Man story, see Fujishima, *Sengo Manga*, pp. 272–277.

25. Christine T. Tjandraningsih, "Japan's *Manga* Oust Rivals from Indonesian Market," *Japan Times* (January 11, 1995).

26. *Takarajima Shōnen* (Boys' Treasure Island) and *Netsumon Shōnen TOP.*

27. Schodt, *Dreamland Japan*, p. 308.

28. For a description of the difficulties of developing a market for Japanese manga in America, see Schodt, *Dreamland Japan*, pp. 308–321.

29. Schodt, *Dreamland Japan*, p. 52.

30. On the censorship of children's books in the United States, see Paul Deane, *Mirrors of American Culture: Children's Fiction Series in the Twentieth Century* (Metuchen, NJ: Scarecrow, 1991), pp. 16–29.

31. Benjamin Fulford, "Comics in Japan Not Just Funny Business," *Nikkei Weekly* (February 17, 1997), p. 1.

32. Schodt, *Manga Manga*, p. 156.

33. Japanese in the United States are shocked to find violent made-in-Japan videos so widely available; these are harder to find in Japan.

17

Pop Idols and the Asian Identity

Hiroshi Aoyagi

開けドア、今はもう流れ出たらアジア
白のパンダをどれでも全部並べて
ピュアなハートが夜空で弾けとびそうに輝いている
火花のように

Open the door, flow out now and there's Asia
Lining up any and every white panda
Pure hearts twinkle in the night sky as if it's about
to burst
Like a spark

—Puffy[1]

The lyrics of *Asia no Junshin* (Asian Purity), the debut single of Japanese pop idol duo Puffy, speak of Japan's deepening engagement with the rest of Asia. Strong cultural ties have blossomed between Japan and other Asian countries in recent years, adding a more human dimension to relationships that in the past have been primarily military or economic. In Japan, interest in other Asian countries is booming, evidenced by a boom in ethnic foods, increased travel to Asian destinations, the popularity of studying Chinese or Korean in place of once-dominant European languages, and a growing familiarity with movies and pop music from throughout the region. In many Asian countries, Japanese television dramas and pop music stars have become as well known as

Japanese cars and electronic products. These cultural "products" of Japan offer models of a modern, urban lifestyle that students and young working people in Asia's upward-moving economies find attractive and relevant to their own changing lives.

One of the more interesting examples of cross-cultural affinity and influence in Asia is the popularity of Japanese-style "pop idols" in other Asian countries. When Puffy burst onto Japan's pop music scene in 1996, launched by the use of "Asian Purity" as the theme song in a widely shown Kirin beer television commercial, they joined a long list of idols and idol groups which have dominated Japan's popular culture since the late 1960s. Today, both Japanese idols and home-grown idols modeled on the Japanese prototype have a huge presence throughout East and Southeast Asia. Walk down any city street in Hong Kong, Shanghai, Taipei, Seoul, Manila, Singapore, or Ho Chi Min City, and you will encounter young Asian movie, TV, and pop music stars smiling coquettishly and striking appealing poses from billboards, posters, and merchandise. Despite singing and acting at a level that many would consider amateurish, these adolescent personalities headline numerous concerts, radio programs, and television shows, attracting large numbers of devoted followers. The popularity of Asian pop idols extends even beyond Asia, thanks to the expanding diaspora of Asians living abroad as well as to the countless Internet home pages devoted to these stars and their fans.

What underlies this massive and contagious celebration of Asian pop idols? What appeal do they hold for their audience, and how are they so successfully produced and marketed in Asia today? This chapter attempts to answer these questions by examining Asian pop idols and exploring some of the cross-cultural, socioeconomic, and historical roots of their popularity. Of particular interest is the way that pop idols and the industries that produce them contribute to the formation of a pan-Asian identity or consciousness among young people of diverse nationality, in an era in which the Asia-Pacific region is considered energetic and "hot," with high expectations not just for economic growth, but for growing cultural influence on the rest of the world as well.[2]

Japanese Pop Idols—Life-Sized, Cute, and Above Average

In Western societies, the possession and enhancement of high self-esteem is strongly emphasized via such notions as individualism and self-reliance. "The squeaky wheel," as the English saying goes, "gets the grease." In contrast, many Asian cultures expect their members to surrender, or at least tone down, their individual opinions and interests in deference to those of the group or the social norm, and discourage the practice of thinking too highly of oneself. "The nail that sticks out," the Japanese say, "gets hammered down," and "The truly able person," according to the Chinese, "does not reveal himself or herself so easily."

Popular celebrities embody this cross-cultural difference. In her study of Japanese pop music, musicologist Judith Herd points out that most stars in Western countries are popular because of their outstanding physical or personal attributes. Japanese idols, on the other hand, typically depict images that are "fairly standard." Their appearance and ability are above average, yet not so much so as to alienate or offend the audience—just enough to provide their fans with the sense that they too can be stars if they try hard enough.[3] Japanese refer to this characteristic as *tōshindai,* or life-sized. Sun Music Productions President Hideyoshi Aizawa explains that the life-sized image of idols helps produce feelings of solidarity and reciprocity between performers, producers, and audience:

> To be "life-sized" is to publicly confirm that idols are not living in this world on their own, but together with people who are there to support them and whom they are expected to support. I mean their customers, staff members, producers . . . adults and children . . . everyone who is interested. Human relationships are what hold idols in their place and enable idol businesses to function. Even though idols are expected to become role models of some kind, and to represent the public in certain ways, this role cannot be accomplished unless they keep pace with the people all around them. . . . To be "life-sized," that is. They cannot run ahead too fast, or lag too far behind.[4]

Playing on young people's social needs, Japan's life-sized pop idols are produced and marketed as personifiers of a typical "girl or boy next door," chosen to become "lucky stars" and to represent their generation. Sociologist Hiroshi Ogawa calls them "quasi-companions" (*gijiteki-nakama*), who provide their teenage followers with a virtual sense of intimacy. Ogawa contends that, although this companionship is understood to be artificial and impervious, and thus realized only in fantasy, the intimacy it evokes can be as strong as, or even stronger than, that shared among school friends.[5] This is due to the fact that, unlike real-life companions, with whom there is always the potential for conflict and loss of friendship, pop idols smile and appear to be friendly all the time. Unlike "real" people, idols never reject those who wish to approach them—provided, of course, that the relationship is professional in nature. In short, idols "never say no" to their customers.[6]

Activities designed to build and maintain "intimacy" between Japan's idols and their audience are carried out to a degree and uniformity that has no apparent equivalent in the American pop star scene. Japanese idol duties include "handshaking ceremonies" (*akushu-kai*), which accompany stage performances; get-togethers with fans (*fan no tsudoi*), where fans can talk and play games with their favorite idol; public photo shoots (*satsuei-kai*), where idols strike poses for amateur photographers (known as "camera kids"); and correspondence with fans by letter. When idols release CDs and promotional videos or publish photo albums or essays, autograph ceremonies *(sign-kai)* are held for buyers at retail outlets. There are also idol "hot-lines" for fans wishing to hear recorded idol messages or learn about upcoming events, as well as Web pages where one can find out about an idol's place and date of birth, blood type, hobbies, and thoughts.

Commonly accompanying "life-sized" is another fundamental idol characteristic: cuteness. The "cute style," as it is called, encompasses pretty looks, heartwarming verbal expressions, flimsy handwriting, and singing, dancing, acting, and speaking in a sweet, meek, and "adorable" way.[7] The cute style is by no means a recent Japanese invention, but has clear historical roots. The Japanese word for cute, *kawaii*, can be traced back to its classical form, *kawayushi* or *kawayurashi*, which appears in poetry and stories from the premodern era. The "cuteness" observed today in pop idols closely resembles *otome* (sweet little girl) or *yamato-nadeshiko* (girls of Japan) images found in books, magazines, advertising, and motion pictures from the late nineteenth and early twentieth centuries.[8]

To express cuteness, pop idols generally smile with bared (though often crooked) teeth and clear, sparkling eyes. Female idols strike "coy" poses, while male idols adopt a more "stylish" or "cool" appearance. Female fans generally agree that trying to appear stylish is what makes male idols cute; one female university student remarked that the earnest attempts of young and innocent-looking boys to act stylish and cool make them "somewhat pitiful, and therefore very cute." The autographs and handwritten letters of female idols often include drawings of cute animation characters such as kittens and bunnies. It was once common for female idols to dress up in "fake-child costumes" (*buri-buri ishō*) resembling European dolls. Although this practice is now considered outdated, female idols still dress in a style Japanese call the "fancy look," which imitates Western fashions. Though there is no particular outfit that typifies male idols, they also generally dress in a "dandy-ish," cosmopolitan style that, in the words of one idol costume designer, "heightens their attraction."

The combination of life-sized plus cute has the effect of engendering in idols' fans feelings of warmth and protectiveness. Tetsuko Kuroyanagi, who for years hosted the weekly pop music program "Best Ten," states that people "adore idols for their sweetness and purity, which evoke the sense that they should be protected carefully."[9] Going through a difficult period of physical and emotional development themselves, adolescent fans can easily empathize with idols who are embarking on their own growth journey: from inexperienced debutantes to experienced public figures and performers. The following excerpts from essays written by Seiko Matsuda (debut 1980), perhaps the most popular singer-idol in the history of Japanese music,[10] and Atsuhiro Satō, a member of the male idol group Hikaru Genji (active 1987–1994), exemplify this type of appeal for protection and support:

> Seiko is so happy to meet you!! As a singer and an 18-year-old girl, I feel for the first time that I can become independent. Please watch over me warmly forever!![11]

> I want to establish a personal position as a singer, actor, and all else put together! Yet, this may still be too vague to be called a dream. . . . Although I am still at a stage where I am working hard, please keep your watch over me. Let's continue spending our time together.[12]

Both Matsuda and Satō build on their status as "companions" in asking readers to empathize with their struggles and determination to mature. By sharing with fans their youthful dreams and efforts, they are in effect saying to their audience, "Let's grow up together." Statements like these, which collectivize the growing-up process and create feelings of peer solidarity, are found frequently in commentaries made by Japanese idols to their fans. It is also common for idols to give advice and encouragement to their fans through interviews and answers to letters on topics such as being loyal in friendships, working hard at school, and holding on to one's dream about a special someone.[13]

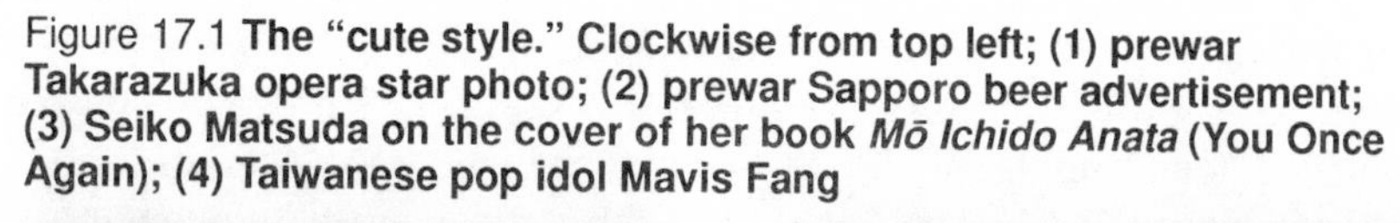

Figure 17.1 **The "cute style." Clockwise from top left; (1) prewar Takarazuka opera star photo; (2) prewar Sapporo beer advertisement; (3) Seiko Matsuda on the cover of her book *Mō Ichido Anata* (You Once Again); (4) Taiwanese pop idol Mavis Fang**

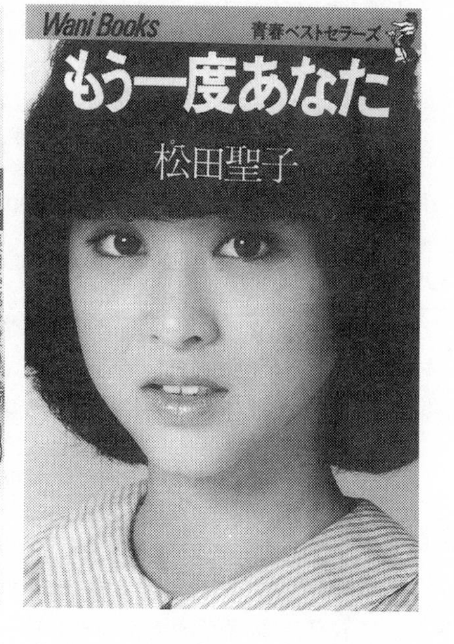

Another way in which idols communicate with their audience is through the lyrics of their songs. Idol songs are typically romantic fantasies, which dwell on the well-worn themes of being in love, hoping to win the heart of another, and physical desire.

> Oh, milky smile, I am taking a journey in your arms,
> Oh, milky smile, please hold me tight with your
> tender love.
>
> —From "Kaze wa Aki-Iro"
> (The Wind Is Autumn Color),
> sung by Seiko Matsuda[14]

> I wanna do! I wanna do! I want your shy heart.
> I wanna do! I wanna do! Isn't it okay to love you more?
> Let's dance in a party—party for the two of us.
> Why are you crying, facing the window?
> We can't understand each other if we fear the anguish
> of love.
>
> —From "Koi=Do!" (Love=Do!),
> sung by Toshihiko Tahara[15]

> Time cannot be stopped, life is a one-way ticket.
> My wings are all wet from rainfall and wind,
> And yet, my feeling of love will chase you all the way.
> I want to be with you, I want to be close to you,
> No matter how distant our future may be.
>
> —From "Ai De Xin Qing"
> (The Feeling of Love),
> sung in Chinese by Noriko Sakai[16]

> Without being caught up in the past, I want to share
> tenderness with you.
> Angels fly between us, and the sun is waiting for
> our smiles.
> I want to be in a romance with you,
> I love you 365 days a year.
>
> —From "Ai Ni Yi Nian San Bai Liu Wu Tian"
> (Loving You 365 Days a Year), sung by Dai Rao.[17]

It should be mentioned that it is not only love-struck adolescents that these singers appeal to. Many idols include among their fans people from various backgrounds and generations. Interviews I have conducted with Japanese fans show that many adult men like "cute" female idols because they see in them their idea of the ideal woman: a sweet, young girl who would make a good future wife and mother. For many young women, on the other hand, pop idols serve to lead the way in terms of contemporary fashion and lifestyle, and to help foster feelings of peer solidarity. Many older Japanese favor cute idols—female and male alike—due to their fascination with youth and because idols bring back nostalgic memories of their own younger days, when the life was "yet full of possibilities."

Pop Idols in Japanese Society, Then and Now

Pop idols emerged in Japan as a commercial genre in the general category of *kayōkyoku* (popular music) during the late 1960s and early 1970s. Unlike their musical predecessors, whose images and lyrics were more adult-oriented, the new idols and idol groups represented adolescent culture. Rough American and European equivalents would include the young Paul Anka, Frankie Avalon, and girl groups like the Shirelles and Shangri-Las in the 1960s; Shaun Cassidy and the Bay City Rollers in the 1970s; Debbie Gibson, Menudo, Candi, and New Kids on the Block in the 1980s; and the Beastie Boys, Backstreet Boys, Hanson, and Spice Girls in the 1990s.

Though ridiculed for their low talent levels by many adults, idols soon became a nationwide craze in Japan, creating a whole new domain of popular culture, built around youth and happily sponsored by the media, the entertainment industry, the advertising business, and retail corporations specializing in the creation of profit-generating teen-oriented trends, fashions, and products. Contests were held each year in which hundreds of young men and women participated, each hoping to become the next new star. Some such contests took the form of local auditions, while others, such as the television program *Star Tanjō* (Star Search), were broadcast nationally as the gateway to the "dream factory." Support groups and fan clubs sprang up to bolster the efforts of idol wannabes, the most successful of whom made it onto the record charts and into the national consciousness via appearances on television shows such as *Best Ten.* This phenomenon became known as the "idol boom."

Promotion agencies, of course, orchestrated the development and marketing of idols and idol groups. One of the most successful was and is The Johnny's, which focuses exclusively on the production of young male talent. In 1967, The Johnny's debuted their first official idol group, The Four Leaves, whose popularity lasted through the next decade. The Johnny's has dominated the male side of the Japanese idol market ever since, producing a stream of big names over the years, including individual stars such as Hiromi Go and Toshihiko Tahara as well as groups like Hikaru Genji and SMAP. On the women's side, Hori Agency and Sun Music Productions have been the dominant producers. In 1971, three female idols, Mari Amachi, Saori Minami, and Rumiko Koyanagi, banded together to form a popular trio known as *San-Nin Musume* (Three Young Girls). This was followed in 1973 by the appearance of another hit female idol trio which included Momoe Yamaguchi, Masako Mori, and Junko Sakurada, all of whom went on to establish solo careers as megastars. Countless subsequent female idols and groups have followed these pioneers into stardom, including Pink Lady in the 1970s; Seiko Matsuda, O-Nyanko Club, Noriko Sakai, and Wink during the 1980s; and Rie Miyazawa, Yumiko Takahashi, Yuki Uchida, and Ryōko Hirosue in the 1990s.

It may not be coincidental that a youth-oriented movement like the "idol boom" appeared when it did in Japan—at the height of Japan's postwar "economic miracle." This was a time when years of rapid economic growth, and the hard work and sacrifice that produced that growth, were giving birth to a new consumer culture fed by rising incomes and enjoyed by a new generation intent on differentiating themselves from their elders not just by working hard but also by enjoying the fruits of their labor. This was also a period of rapid social change, with people moving from the countryside to the cities in search of jobs and excitement, and a tradition of three generations under one roof being replaced by the nuclear family. Add to this the stress and fast pace that accompany modern, industrialized life, and you have an adjustment period not unlike the growth years of adolescence. Many Japanese people, and not just teenagers, were required to make the transition from older, established social boundaries and ways of life to an increasingly dynamic, complex, and cosmopolitan world of contemporary urban life. Pop idols, themselves struggling to find their feet on the escalator of show business, could serve as "guiding angels" for a population making a similar journey.

By the mid-1990s, however, the star of the Japanese "idol" was burning less brightly than it had at any time over the three previous decades. In October 1994 the leading daily newspaper *Asahi Shimbun* announced that "idols have been in the so-called 'winter period' for some time now,"[18] and many producers and magazine editors were declaring that idols were passé. Well-known culture columnist and idol critic Akio Nakamori attributes this to changed economic conditions.

> The times seek idols, and idols lead the times. Since idols symbolize the healthy growth of young people, and because they are personal manifestations of the shared public desire for growth, they symbolize national growth itself. The fact that idols are socially demanded implies that there is a shared national vision toward growth, and where there is such a vision, idols will continue to appear. This mutual relationship is the key. The current "idol recession" in Japan tells me that the Japanese have lost that vision. I believe the fading of idols reflects the current economic recession, in which the people have lost the energy they once had to move forward together toward social and economic growth.[19]

A competing explanation involves the increasingly blurred boundaries between different genres of performance. While Japan's first generation of idols generally stuck to singing, since the 1980s it has become common for singers to act, for actors to sing, and for both to do comedy and talk-show hosting. In the eyes of many, this has diminished both the commercial value and the level of expertise among pop idol singers, and has led to increasing demand for, and supply of, more powerful and unique performers, such as "new music" artists and rock stars, who fall into a new and emerging category: the "post-idol." Cute seems to be on the wane a bit as well, at least in pop music, as performers projecting a more mature and sensual image, such as Namie Amuro, come to the fore.

Asian Idols Outside Japan

By the mid-1980s, pop singers specifically referred to as "idols" were becoming major celebrities in places such as China, Hong Kong, Taiwan, and South Korea, coinciding with rising economic affluence in these nations. Of course, these and other Asian countries had young popular entertainers long before Japanese idols appeared on the scene. Yet the stamp of the Japanese-style idol on many of Asia's new homegrown stars is unmistakable. This is due to the popularity of Japanese

Figure 17.2 **The "mature" look: South Korean pop singer Susie Kang and Japanese "post-idol" Namie Amuro**

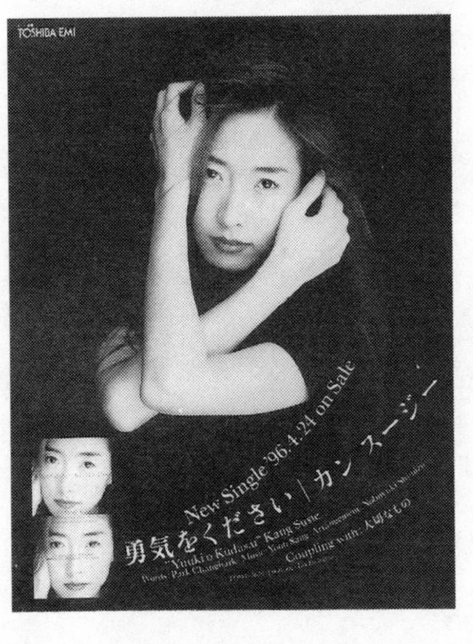

idols in other Asian countries as well as to the market-expansion efforts of Japan's promotion agencies, for whom, as for Japanese manufacturers, Asian countries represent new opportunities for business growth. Many indigenous promoters and media organizations have collaborated with Japanese idol producers and promoters, facilitating a "knowledge transfer" of Japanese-style idol production and marketing knowhow to other Asian markets. Among the home-grown big-name idols produced by indigenous entertainment industries following Japanese production and marketing methods are Dai Rao and Jie Liu of China; Soteji-Wa-Idol and Susie Kang of South Korea; Andy Lau, Vivian Chow, and Sammy Chen of Hong Kong; and Emile Chow, Vivian Hsu, and Tarsy Su of Taiwan.

In 1993, Japan's Hori Agency and the Beijing City Department of Culture held a live television broadcast audition that attracted 400,000 Chinese applicants, including the above-mentioned Dai Rao. The Hori Agency held another idol audition in cooperation with the Vietnamese government in 1995, drawing 1,800 local applicants. A continuing large-scale audition comes in the form of the television program *Asia Bagus*, based in Singapore and involving multinational corporate sponsorship which attracts applicants from all over Asia. In a 1996 collaborative

Figure 17.3 **Tokyo Performance Doll and Shanghai Performance Doll**

effort, Japan's Yoshimoto Kōgyō and Sony Music Entertainment teamed with international retailer Yaohan to recruit four young women from the Shanghai region to form Shanghai Performance Doll, a Chinese version of Japan's Tokyo Performance Doll, which debuted in 1990.[20]

Many Japanese idols have become celebrities in other Asian countries as well. A typical pattern, followed, for example, by Noriko Sakai and Mika Chiba, is for a Japanese singer to start out in Taiwan and then to move into markets such as Hong Kong, China, and Singapore using Chinese connections. Home-language magazine articles and Internet home pages, which stimulate and feed the demands of Asian fans for information about their favorite idols, abound. Even in South Korea, where Japanese television programs, magazines, music recordings, animation, and other forms of popular culture have been officially banned for historical reasons—namely Japan's annexation of Korea from 1910 to the end of World War II, which included an attempt to replace the Korean language and culture with those of Japan—many young people obtain information about idols and other forms of Japanese pop culture through underground sources.

While the marketing efforts on behalf of Japanese and Japanese-style idols throughout Asia help explain their popularity, it seems unlikely that idols would be so hugely successful were there not a receptiveness on the part of Asian young people to the culture idols represent and the messages they transmit, much as there was in Japan at the time of the idol boom there. In order to get a sense for how Asian consumers view idols and their popularity, a series of interviews was conducted with Asian students, asking for their thoughts on the significance or meaning of Japanese idols in their home countries, and whether they thought there was a relationship between pop idols and socioeconomic development in the Asia-Pacific region. The following are some representative comments from the interviews.

> People like Momoe Yamaguchi and Seiko Matsuda from Japan are extremely popular in my country. Everyone knows their songs, and many know how to sing them in places like *karaoke* bars. I think that they are famous because we admire their way of life. They show us how to make an effort, work hard, and establish oneself in contemporary society through the messages of their songs and performances.
>
> —Female, age 24, from China

> Japanese idols keep inspiring idols from Hong Kong who give us messages of love, dreams, and hopes, although whether these are valuable or

not depends on each person's evaluation. These messages can at least unite the feelings of many Asians and construct some kind of identity that is different from Americans or Europeans.

—Male, age 26, from Taiwan

There are many idols and idol magazines in Taiwan that imitate Japanese idols and magazines. Some of them adopt identical titles, or titles that are so similar that we immediately know which Japanese counterparts they have imitated. I have an impression that Japanese idols are generally like "romance dolls" that represent happiness and dreams of a developed country. I think that is why we like them so much. We also want to be "dreamful."

—Female, age 22, from Taiwan

I think that idols dramatize economic dreams and pack them into their three- or four-minute songs. They unite us, for example like we Chinese all over the world, in Chinatowns in America or Great Britain or Canada. You know, they bring us together, sort of spiritually. I think that this kind of spiritual unity is important for many people who listen to the songs of Asian idols, and that it helps support the idea of regional economic development.

—Male, age 26, from Hong Kong

If idols can contribute to the modernization of Asia, that would be because they can direct many people to one and the same economic or social issue. It is like leadership, but an entertaining one—not as serious and boring as political statements made by politicians, and not so light-hearted or ironic like comedians. I'd rather listen to idols sing than go to a political speech and hear about cross-cultural friendship or unity or development. . . .

—Female, age 26, from South Korea

Idols are simply entertainers, and I do not think they have any essential significance. But that is why I think they are necessary. People everywhere cannot live without some kind of entertainment, right? We all have to take a break and run away from the real world. That is, I think, what entertainment, including idol entertainment, is all about. The reason that idols are so popular these days in Asia is, I think, because people in Asia are working hard now and they need to take a break sometimes. Hollywood movie stars and other exotic-looking actors are okay, too, but I think as an Asian I prefer to see people who look like me, with black hair, black pupils, yellow skin. I feel like I can relax more when I see [Asian] idols. Then, I can refresh myself and get to work for Asia the next day.

—Male, age 24, from Taiwan

Two broad points emerge from the interview data. One is that Japanese idols constitute a sort of "brand," not just of pop singers or actors but of a lifestyle of urban affluence that Japanese idols represent and that Japan is viewed, accurately or inaccurately, as possessing. This recalls a 1990 survey conducted in Taiwan by Japanese columnist Takumi Hayashi, which found that Japanese idols provide their Taiwanese audience with various fictions about Japanese culture, and that the people of Taiwan use these fictions to expand their knowledge of and to construct their own ideas about other aspects of Japan: entertainment, arts, subcultures, fashion, comics, music, and so on.[21]

The second point is that idols provide a point of reference for making sense of the changing social and workplace conditions that accompany economic growth and "modernization" in Asia. While most interview respondents were skeptical about any direct impact Asian idols have on regional economic development, it was generally acknowledged that idols are symbolically significant for enhancing a developmental atmosphere in the region and helping create an Asian-Pacific identity. In a separate interview, Eric Suen, an idol singer and actor from Hong Kong, indicated that some performers are themselves very much aware of their potential role in the construction of an Asia-Pacific identity:

> It would be my greatest pleasure to be able to unify the hearts of many people all around Asia, encouraging them with my music and acting. I would like to help us cope with a variety of social problems that might occur in many parts of Asia together, and support the development of the region in any way I can.

In pursuit of this goal, Suen actively performs across Hong Kong, Taiwan, Korea, and Japan. In 1995 he released a duet and music video with Noriko Sakai, symbolizing the partnership among Hong Kong, Taiwan, and Japan, and he participated in the 1996 Asia Music Festival, held in Fukuoka, Japan. This pattern of pan-Asian performance, which more and more idols are following, is helping to transform the Asian entertainment industry from a state of separate and insulated country markets into one larger and increasingly integrated Asian market.

Some idols are also playing a conscious role in replacing historical hostilities with more open and friendly relationships between Asian neighbors. South Korean pop singer Susie Kang, who, after making it big in her home country, debuted in Japan in 1995 with an album and a

Figure 17.4 **Eric Suen and Noriko Sakai in duet**

single including Korean and Japanese in the same song, expressed a desire to become an ambassador of goodwill between Korea and Japan:

> One is prohibited to sing Japanese songs in my country, and I feel very sad about that. Through my songs, I want to communicate to the people of Japan that there exists a nation called Korea next to them, and I want my Korean fans to listen to my Japanese songs. We live so close to each other, and I wish our two nations would be more friendly to each other.[22]

Conclusion

Sociologists Eric Barnouw and Catherine Kirkland argue that pop culture personalities and performances serve not just to provide entertainment and earn money, but also to develop and offer a repertoire of themes, perspectives, characters, relationships, stories, and outcomes that can be used by the public to make sense of the world.[23] Japanese and other Asian idols indeed do this, and this relevance to the lives and new worlds of their audience is surely a key to their success. Asian idols may not be the most talented singers and actors in the world, but as long as they continue to reflect the concerns and dreams of their audience, and to offer models of attractive new lifestyles and cross-cultural friendship, theirs will be a strong, and profitable, presence in the pop culture world.

Notes

1. Lyrics translated by the author.

2. The interview and other data on which this chapter are based originated in a series of surveys conducted by the author between 1989 and 1997.

3. Judith A. Herd, "Trends and Taste in Japanese Popular Music: A Case Study of the 1982 Yamaha World Popular Music Festival," *Popular Music* 4 (1984), pp. 77–78.

4. Interview with the author, March 4, 1996.

5. Hiroshi Ogawa, *Ongaku Suru Shakai* (A Musical Society) (Tokyo: Keiso Shobo, 1988), pp. 122-123.

6. Ibid., p. 123.

7. Cuteness can be overdone, even in Japan. Young women who carry the cute style too far are known as *burikko*, a mildly derogatory term that was first used to describe Seiko Matsuda.

8. For an extensive analysis of the "cute style" in English, see Sharon Kinsella, "Cuties in Japan," in *Women, Media, and Consumption in Japan*, ed. Lise Skov and Brian Moeran (Honolulu: University of Hawaii Press, 1995), pp. 220–254. For detailed historical studies on the image of cuteness in Japan, see Eiji Otsuka, *Shōjo Minzoku-Gaku: Seikimatsu no Shinwa o Tsumugu Miko no Matsuei* (The Folklore of Girls: "Descendants of Maiden" that Spin the Wheel of Legend at the End of the Century) (Tokyo: Kōbunsha, 1989); Masami Akiyama, *Shōjo-tachi no Shōwa-Shi* (The History of Girls' Shōwa) (Tokyo: Shinchōsha, 1992); and Shun-ichi Karasawa, *Bishōjo no Gyakushū: Yomigaere!! Kokoro-Kiyoki, Yogore-naki, Kedakaki Shōjo-tachi yo* [The Counterattack of Girls: Revive!! Pure-Hearted, Clean, and Noble Girls]. (Tokyo: Nesuko, 1995). The young Shirley Temple provides an American example of the "cute style," except that by the time Shirley reached her teens, "cute" no longer worked for her, it being considered inappropriate above the age of 10 or 12; the difference in Japan is that "cute" is considered acceptable and attractive in older teens and young adults as well as in children.

9. Tetsuko Kuroyanagi, quoted in Herd, "Trends and Taste," pp. 77–78.

10. By 1993 Matsuda had produced sixteen number one albums, twenty-five top singles, and more than $500 million in record sales (*Japan: An Illustrated Encyclopedia* [Tokyo: Kōdansha, 1993], p. 1286).

11. Seiko Matsuda, *Ryōte de Seiko* (Seiko in Your Hands) (Tokyo: Shūeisha, 1980), cover page; translation by the author.

12. Atsuhiro Satō, *Shōnen* (Young Boy) (Tokyo: Shūeisha, 1991), p. 215; translation by the author.

13. See Merry White, "The Marketing of Adolescence in Japan: Buying and Dreaming." In *Women, Media, and Consumption in Japan*, ed. Lise Skov and Brian Moeran (Honolulu: University of Hawaii Press, 1995), p. 266.

14. CBS/Sony, 1980; translation by the author.

15. Canyon Records, 1981; translation by the author.

16. Victor Entertainment, 1994; translation by the author.

17. HoriPro, 1995; translation by the author.

18. "Geinō-Ran" (Entertainment Column), Asahi Shimbun, Evening Edition, October 17, 1994, p. 8.

19. Interview with Akio Nakamori, May 22, 1996.

20. For further details regarding the activities of Asian entertainment industries, see Hideo Kawakami, *Gekidō-suru Ajia-Ongaku-Shijō* (Upheaval in the Asian Music Market) (Tokyo: Cinema House, 1995).

21. Takumi Hayashi, "*Ajia no Otaku-Genshō: Higashi-Shina-Kai no Mukō*" (Geek Phenomena in Asia: Beyond the East China Sea). In *Warera no Jidai* (Our Era) (Tokyo: Takarajimasha, 1994), pp. 154–167.

22. Susie Kang, "Tōyō Bijo-Zukan" (The Sweet Girl of Asia), *Dolive* (June 1996), pp. 174–175.

23. Eric Barnouw and Catherine E. Kirkland, "Entertainment." In *Folklore, Cultural Performances, and Popular Entertainment,* ed. Richard Bauman (Oxford: Oxford University Press, 1992), pp. 50–52.

About the Contributors

Anne Allison is an associate professor in the Department of Cultural Anthropology at Duke University. She received her Ph.D. from the University of Chicago in 1986, and is the author of *Nightwork: Sexuality, Pleasure, and Corporate Masculinity in a Tokyo Hostess Club* (1994) and *Permitted and Prohibited Desires: Mothers, Comics, and Censorship in Japan* (1996). Her current research focuses on the globalization of Japanese children's culture.

Hiroshi Aoyagi is an anthropologist whose specialization encompasses cultural industries, symbolic anthropology, sociolinguistics, and Japanese studies. He received his Ph.D. from the University of British Columbia in 1999, and is currently a Postdoctoral Fellow at the Reischauer Institute of Japanese Studies at Harvard University.

E. Taylor Atkins received his Ph.D. in history from the University of Illinois at Urbana-Champaign in 1997. He teaches courses on modern Asia, Japanese history and popular culture, and oral history at Northern Illinois University. He is currently preparing a manuscript entitled *Blue Nippon: Authenticating Jazz in Japan*. His research on war art and jazz has appeared in *The Wittenburg Review*, *positions: east asia cultures critique*, *Japanese Studies*, and *Baker's Biographical Dictionary of Jazz Musicians*.

Jayson Chun is a graduate student of modern Japanese history at the University of Oregon. Having become an expert on Japan's 1959 Royal Wedding, Jayson got married himself (not televised) in Hawaii during the summer of 1999 before moving with his wife to Japan for two years of dissertation research on the historical relationship between television and Japanese society.

Tim Craig leads a dual existence at the University of Victoria as associate professor of International Business in the Faculty of Business and

Japan Program Director for the Centre for Asia-Pacific Initiatives. He has published articles in management journals on new product development in Japan's beer industry (the subject of his Ph.D. dissertation) and the globalization of Japanese companies and has written for popular publications on Japanese beer, baseball, and sumo. Current projects include coediting a new book on Asian popular culture and building up his personal Japanese karaoke repertoire.

Hilaria Gössmann was born in Tokyo, where she spent fifteen years of her childhood and youth. A Japan specialist with a focus on modern Japanese literature, she wrote her doctoral dissertation on autobiographical novels by female writers of the Japanese proletarian literary movement. From 1992 to 1995 she worked as a researcher at the German Institute for Japanese Studies in Tokyo, and since 1995 she has been a professor of Japanese Studies at the University of Trier in Germany.

Eri Izawa grew up in a Japanese household in the United States, and has therefore seen the good, the bad, and the ugly of both cultures. Currently working as a game designer for a computer game company, Eri also writes for the on-line anime magazine *EX*, and occasionally posts essays on her own Web site (http://www.mit.edu:8001/people/rei/Anime.html) in an effort to break down cultural misunderstandings and stereotypes between East and West.

William Lee was born in Canada and has lived off and on in Japan since 1983. He was a graduate research student at Meiji University in Tokyo and holds a Ph.D. in comparative literature from McGill University in Montreal. His current research interests, in addition to popular culture, include Japanese theater and folk performing arts and traditional Japanese architecture (including the old Japanese farmhouse he calls home in Akita, Japan).

Mark W. MacWilliams teaches East Asian religions at St. Lawrence University in Canton, New York. His research interests lie at the intersection between religion and popular culture in Japan.

Mark Schilling has been reviewing films for the *Japan Times* since 1989 and writing about Japan's film industry for *Screen International* since 1990. Since 1998 he has also been a regular reviewer for and contributor to the Japanese edition of *Premiere.* In addition to writing for many publications, both in Japan and abroad, about Japanese films and Japanese popular culture, and making occasional guest appearances as sumo commentator on NHK, he is the author of *The Encyclopedia of Japanese Popular Culture* (Weatherhill, 1997). A resident of Japan since 1975, Schilling lives in Tokyo with his wife, Yūko, and their two children.

Saya S. Shiraishi teaches in the Department of Cultural Anthropology at Kyoto Bunkyō University. She received her Ph.D. from Cornell University and has done field research in Indonesia, the United States, Japan, Hong Kong, Malaysia, and the Philippines. She is the author of *Young Heroes: The Indonesian Family in Politics* (1997) and the editor of *The Japanese in Colonial Southeast Asia* (1993). Her current work focuses on the spread of manga and anime in Asia and, more generally, on the globalization of popular culture.

James Stanlaw is an associate professor of anthropology at Illinois State University, with interests in linguistic anthropology, popular culture, and the intersection of language and culture. His latest project concerns Japanese bluegrass music, and his "biggest thrill" has been the chance to play mandolin with the "Shaggy Mountain Boys" in Kobe's Live House "Shaggy."

Maia Tsurumi is currently doing graduate work in the Department of Biology at the University of Victoria on the ecology of animal communities inhabiting deep-sea hydrothermal vents—hot springs on the ocean floor. Although she has lived in Canada most of her life, she is a citizen of Japan as well as of Canada and has lived in both countries. She grew up reading manga and persists in reading them to this day.

Christine R. Yano is an assistant professor of anthropology at the University of Hawaii at Manoa. Her book *Tears of Longing: Nostalgia and the Nation in Japanese Popular Song* is being published by Harvard University Press. She is currently researching the consumption of "cute" products from the Sanrio Company in Japan and the United States.

Credits for Photographs and Illustrations

Page 8, Figure 1.1. "The Great Wave at Kanagawa," by Hokusai.

Page 9, Figure 1.2. From *Hi no Tori* (Phoenix), vol. 1, "Reimeihen" (Dawn), © 1978 Tezuka Productions, reproduced with the permission of Tezuka Productions.

Page 10, Figure 1.3. Ukiyo-e kabuki actor, by Sharaku.

Page 11, Figure 1.4. "Lupin and Friends," © 1999 Monkey Punch (Kazuhiko Katō), reproduced with the permission of Monkey Punch.

Page 15, Figure 1.5. From *Dragon Ball*, vol. 7, © 1987 Akira Toriyama/ Bird Studio, reproduced with the permission of Shūeisha, Inc.

Page 30, Figure 2.1. Photograph by E. Taylor Atkins.

Page 53, Figure 2.2. Photograph by Shūichi Sugiura.

Page 64, Figure 3.1. Sayuri Ishikawa on the cover for the CD *Ai En Zaka,* reproduced with the permission of Big One Corporation.

Page 65, Figure 3.2. Saburō Kitajima, printed from a publicity still with the permission of Kitajima Music Publishers, Inc.

Page 67, Figure 3.3. Misora Hibari, printed from a publicity still with the permission of Columbia Music Publishing, Inc.

Page 81, Figure 4.1. Princess Princess (Kyōko, Tomoko, Kaori, Kanako, Atsuko), in a still from the magazine *Pati-Pati* (August 1992).

Page 83, Figure 4.2. Yuki of the Judy and Mary Band, photograph by Gorō Iwaoka, from the magazine *GIRLPOP* (May 1995), reproduced with the permission of *GIRLPOP* and Gorō Iwaoka.

Page 85, Figure 4.3. Miki Imai, on the cover of the CD *flow into space,* reproduced with the permission of For Life Records.

Page 89, Figure 4.4. Seiko Matsuda, on the cover of her U.S. CD *seiko,* reproduced with the permission of Sony Music, Inc.

Page 90, Figure 4.5. Yūming (Yumi Matsutōya), printed from a publicity still with the permission of Kirarasha Music Publishers.

Page 94, Figure 4.6. Dreams Come True (Masato Nakamura, Miwa Yoshida, Takahiro Nishikawa), printed from a publicity still with the permission of MS Artist Products.

Pages 112–134, Figures 6.1 –6.19. From *Budda*, © Tezuka Productions, reproduced with the permission of Tezuka Productions.

Page 113, Figure 6.2. Photograph by Sommer Baker.

Page 143, Figure 7.1. From *Galaxy Express 999*, vol. 3, © 1997 Leiji Matsumoto, reproduced with the permission of Shōgakukan, Inc.

Page 145, Figure 7.2. From *Chōjin Locke*, vol. 4, © 1980 Yuki Hijiri/Biblos, reproduced with the permission of Biblos Co., Ltd.

Page 146, Figure 7.3. From *The Rose of Versailles*, vol. 2, © 1974 Riyoko Ikeda, reproduced with the permission of Chūōkōron-Shinsha, Inc.

Page 147, Figure 7.4. From *Gunnm*, vol. 2, © 1999 Yukito Kishiro, reproduced with the permission of Shūeisha, Inc.

Page 148, Figure 7.5. From *Black Jack*, © Tezuka Productions, reproduced with the permission of Tezuka Productions.

Pages 155–170. From *Hadashi no Gen*, vol. 8, © 1983 Keiji Nakazawa, reproduced with the permission of Keiji Nakazawa. English translation by Tim Craig.

Page 175, Figure 9.1. From *Yūkan Club*, vol. 6, © 1986 Yukari Ichijō, reproduced with the permission of Shūeisha, Inc.

Page 177, Figure 9.2. From *Yūkan Club*, vol. 2, © 1983 Yukari Ichijō, reproduced with the permission of Shūeisha, Inc.

Page 179, Figure 9.3. From *Yūkan Club*, vol. 13, © 1992 Yukari Ichijō, reproduced with the permission of Shūeisha, Inc.

Page 197, Figure 10.1. From *Chibi Maruko-chan*, vol. 1, © 1987 Momoko Sakura, reproduced with the permission of Shūeisha, Inc.

Page 200, Figure 10.2. From *Crayon Shinchan*, vol. 1, © 1992 Yoshito Usui / Futabasha, reproduced with the permission of Futabasha, Inc.

Page 201, Figure 10.3. From *Crayon Shinchan*, vol. 1, © 1992 Yoshito Usui / Futabasha, reproduced with the permission of Futabasha, Inc.

Page 212, Figure 11.1. Shirō Sano and Yōko Nogiwa in a still from *Zutto Anata ga Suki Datta*, reproduced with the permission of Tokyo Hōsō, Inc., and the German Institute for Japanese Studies (Tokyo).

Page 230, Figures 12.1 and 12.2. The Crown Prince and Michiko Shōda at Azabu Lawn Tennis Club in Tokyo, reproduced with the permission of Asahi Shimbun, Inc.

Page 232, Figure 12.3. Michiko and the Crown Prince at the front entrance of the Kunaichō on the day of the wedding, reproduced with the permission of Asahi Shimbun, Inc.

Page 233, Figure 12.4. Michiko riding in the wedding procession, reproduced with the permission of Asahi Shimbun, Inc.

Page 249, Figure 13.1. Kiyoshi Atsumi, Jun Fubuki, Kumiko Gotō, and Hidetaka Yoshioka on the cover of a movie guide for *Otoko wa Tsurai Yo*, no. 45, *Torajirō no Seishun*, reproduced with the permission of Shōchiku, Inc.

Page 271, Figure 14.1. From *Bishōjo Sailor Moon*, vol. 3, © 1993 Naoko Takeuchi, reproduced with the permission of Kōdansha, Inc.

Pages 280–286. Reproduced with the permission of Yuka Kawada.

Page 291, Figure 16.1. From *Doraemon*, vol. 43, © 1992 Fujiko Production, reproduced with the permission of Shōgakukan, Inc.

Page 292, Figure 16.2. From *Daichōhen Doraemon*, vol. 3, *Nobita no Daimakyō*, © 1985 Fujiko Production, reproduced with the permission of Shōgakukan, Inc.

Page 314, Figure 17.1. (1) and (2) provided by Hiroshi Aoyagi; (3) Seiko Matsuda on the cover of her book *Mō Ichido Anata*, reproduced with the permission of Wani Books, Inc.; (4) Mavis Fang on the cover of the Taiwanese magazine *T.V. News Weekly*.

Page 319, Figure 17.2. (1) Suzie Kang in ad for new single, reproduced with the permission of TOSHIBA-EMI, Ltd.; (2) Namie Amuro photo from *SPA!* magazine (January 3-10, 1996), reproduced with the permission of Fusōsha, Inc.

Page 320, Figure 17.3. Tokyo Performance Doll and Shanghai Performance Doll CD covers, reproduced with the permission of Epic Group, Sony Music Entertainment, Inc.

Page 324, Figure 17.4. Eric Suen and Noriko Sakai, printed from a publicity still with the permission of Sun Music Production, Inc.

Credits for Song Lyrics

Page 3. “Butterfly Boy,” © Michie Nakatani (lyrics and music), reproduced with the permission of EMI Music Publishing.

Page 65. “Matsuri,” © Rei Nakanishi (lyrics) / Jōji Hara (music), reproduced with the permission of Kitajima Music Publishers, Inc.

Page 66. “Bōkyō Jonkara,” © Ryūichi Satomura (lyrics) / Keisuke Hama (music), reproduced with the permission of Japan Central Music, Ltd.

Page 69. “Namida no Sanbashi,” © Norihiko Sugi (lyrics) / Shōsuke Ichikawa (music), reproduced with the permission of HoriPro, Inc.

Page 70. “Kanashii Sake,” © Miyuki Ishimoto (lyrics) / Masao Koga (music) / 1966 Columbia Music Publishing, Inc., reproduced with the permission of Columbia Music Publishing, Inc.

Page 70. “Kinokawa,” © Takashi Taka (lyrics) / Kōji Tokuhisa (music), reproduced with the permission of Japan Central Music, Ltd.

Page 71. “Kita no Yado Kara,” © Yū Aku (lyrics) / Asei Kobayashi (music) / 1975 Columbia Music Publishing, Inc., reproduced with the permission of Columbia Music Publishing, Inc.

Page 71. “Ame Yo-zake,” © Toshio Arakawa (lyrics) / Gendai Kanō (music), reproduced with the permission of Burning Publishers Co., Ltd.

Page 71. “Midare-bana,” © Reiji Matsumoto (lyrics) / Kōhei Miyuki (music) / 1992 NICHION, INC., and Shin-Ei Music Publishers Corp., reproduced with the permission of NICHION, INC.

Page 79. “Squall,” © Yoshiko Miura (lyrics) / Yūichirō Oda (music) /

Sun Music Publishing, reproduced with the permission of Sony ATV Music Publishing, Toronto.

Page 80. "Diamonds," © Kanako Nakayama (lyrics) / Kaori Okui (music), reproduced with the permission of Shinkō Music Publishing Company, Ltd.

Page 84. "Chiisana Koro Kara," © Yuki Isoya (lyrics) / Yoshihito Onda (music), reproduced with the permission of Fuji Pacific Music, Inc.

Page 86. "The Days I Spent with You," © Yuho Iwasato (lyrics) / Tomoyasu Hotei (music) / 1992 Nippon Television Music Corporation / Toy Box Publishers / Gei-Ei Music Publishers / ROS Publishers, Inc., reproduced with the permission of Nippon Television Music Corporation.

Page 91. "Dandelion," © Yumi Matsutōya (lyrics and music), reproduced with the permission of Asuka Agency, Inc.

Page 92. "Dareka ga Anata wo Sagashite Iru," © Yumi Matsutōya (lyrics and music), reproduced with the permission of Kirara Music Publishers.

Page 95. "Winter Song," © Miwa Yoshida and Mike Pela (lyrics) / Miwa Yoshida and Masato Nakamura (music), reproduced with the permission of Stay Gold Music Publishing, Inc. / MS Artist Products.

Page 96. "Quavers," © Naoko Yamano (lyrics and music), reproduced with the permission of EMI Music Publishing.

Page 97. "Butterfly Boy," © Michie Nakatani (lyrics and music), reproduced with the permission of EMI Music Publishing.

Page 309. "Asia no Junshin," © Yosui Inoue (lyrics) / Tamio Okuda (music) / 1996 Sony Music Artists Inc. / Fire Music Publishers Inc., reproduced with the permission of Sony ATV Music Artists, Inc.

Page 315. "Koi=Do!" © Kazuko Kobayashi (lyrics) / Yūichirō Oda (music), reproduced with the permission of Johnny Company.

Page 315. "Ai De Xin Qing," © Su Yue (lyrics) / Li Xiao Qiang (music) / 1994 Kaku-Sui Publishing, Ltd., and Sun Music Publishing, Ltd., reproduced with the permission of Kaku-Sui Publishing, Ltd.

Page 315. "Ai Ni Yi Nian San Bai Liu Wu Tian," © Wan Jing Bai (lyrics) / Gao Feng (music), reproduced with the permission of HoriPro, Inc.

Index